THE LAST RAFT

By

JOHN H. CUNNINGHAM

This book is for
Lou Cardenas and Gloria Garcia,
two dear friends
who accompanied me to Cuba
to research this and other books.

"Cheese, wine and a friend must be old to be good."
Cuban Proverb

"... Mr. Gorbachev, tear down this wall!"

Ronald Reagan at the Brandenburg Gate in West Berlin, June 12, 1987

PROLOGUE

THE GLASS DOORS of the Palacio de la Revolución flew open with such force that one shattered. A bearded man dressed in starched green fatigues stormed out and took the stairs two at a time as he held a bucket out to his side. As he marched up toward the José Martí tower, the sound of his boots stomped loudly against the cobblestones of Flag Square where the cry of buzzards cawed overhead.

At the tower's peak was an interior observation area that overlooked the asphalt plaza and the sprawling gull-wing shaped palacio where Fidel Castro kept his office. As the highest observation point in Havana, the tower was normally crowded with visitors, but not this morning. A siege environment had permeated the country, and citizens and visitors alike were worried by the presence of troops now in place all over the city.

The uniformed man breathed heavily as he charged through Flag Square and onto the path that led to the circular deck around the tower. His calf-height boots shined black against his olive-green tunic. The liquid in the open bucket sloshed around, its fumes burning his eyes. Buzzards circled and cast intermittent shadows over him as he climbed the incline. His eyes remained focused on the tower.

A sentry slouched behind the tower was standing guard with his back to the palacio. The sound of pounding footsteps alerted him, and as he turned toward the sound his hand dropped to his holster. Recognition suddenly filled his eyes and the gun hand snapped up in salute.

The bearded man stormed past without so much as a nod, the bucket brushing against the sentry's leg and splashing gasoline on his pants. The bearded man marched onto the deck then continued toward the two-story sculpture of José Martí at the tower's base.

THE FIRST TOURISTS who had arrived at the tower were an elderly Canadian couple, determined not to allow the marshal law to ruin their vacation. They spied the wreaths on easels placed in the shadow of the gargantuan white marble sculpture of José Martí and shuffled over to read their ribbons before entering the tower. The old man held up his guidebook.

"It says diplomats leave wreathes of good tiding before visiting Castro."

"That must have been before the exodus," the woman said.

Two large arrangements sat like old Christmas decorations at the shrine. The first ribbon read: The Republic of Gambia. It was a modest composition of pine and broad leaves that paled in comparison with the large ornate wreath next to it. As they leaned forward to read the ribbon, the uniformed man burst out from behind the tower. Beads of sweat dripped from under his green cap, and his obsidian eyes appeared ready to burst from their sockets. Armed guards followed after the soldier.

The couple stepped back, their heads swiveled toward one another, and the old man mouthed a name to his wife's frozen stare.

"*Fidel Castro?*"

The uniformed man brushed past them and heaved the bucket toward the larger wreath. They watched in astonishment as he produced a box of wooden matches, lit four at once, and tossed them forward. A huge fireball swaddled in black smoke that caressed the white marble statue followed a sudden whoosh.

The man spun around and chopped the air with his palm. *"Estos hijos de puta no saban con quién están jugando!"*

He disappeared as quickly as he'd come. Only the flames remained as proof of the moment.

"What did he say?" the woman said.

"These sons of bitches don't know who they're messing with."

The Canadians shielded their faces from the pressing heat and glimpsed the last words on the blazing ribbon as it turned to ash.

'… STATES OF AMERICA.'

1

WITH ONE FOOT on shore and the other on the raft, Ernesto del Torres looked back to his '57 Chevy convertible hidden in the thicket of mangroves. Only the tail fins, trunk and chrome bumper were visible. He could just make out the Politburo designation on the license plate.

"*Coño*, man, let's get going," a voice said from behind him.

Ernesto nodded and took one last look, savoring the idea that the Policía would soon find the car and call his father. What would the great Ramon del Torres say then?

He turned and saw the anxious faces on the raft and let out a deep sigh.

Maria reached for his hand and smiled when he met her eyes. *I'll take care of you, baby, but the rest of these people are on their own.*

Ernesto looked past her to Juan, the hustler who had organized the journey. He then glanced at Manuel, a retired sugarcane worker, squatting in a pained heap next to Vilma, an equally vintage government secretary, and wondered how their ancient bodies would fare at sea.

"Whenever you're ready," Juan said. He stood in the water behind the raft and drummed his fingers on the deck.

Ernesto glanced down at the rusty oil drums beneath the eight-foot square platform and sighed again.

This thing looks like a deathtrap. "You sure this raft will actually float?"

"You think I'd risk my own life?" Juan said.

"It's not worth much."

Juan shrugged, flicked his cigarette into the water and tugged hard on the rope to pull the raft off the shore. Ernesto's foot slipped from the raft's edge and he awkwardly half-fell into the shallow water.

Asshole.

Ernesto splashed out after them, caught up quickly and pulled himself aboard. Maria squeezed his arm with a pleading look he well understood, and he pressed his teeth together. Juan was lucky she was on board, otherwise he'd gladly wring the smug *campesino's* neck right then and there. He turned and caught Manuel staring at him, a restrained smile on his lips.

"What are you looking at?" Ernesto said.

The ocean floor dropped off sharply just a few yards from shore, and once the water was up to his chest, Juan climbed on board the crowded deck.

"Next stop Florida." He winked at Maria, who nodded and returned his smile.

Ernesto put his arm around her and pulled her close.

The morning was calm, and with no wind to help launch the raft, the small waves pushed it steadily back toward shore, where the drums scraped against the coral and sand.

Vilma stopped humming and turned to Juan. "Are you going to get us out further, or are we going to spend the day at the beach?"

Juan's lips puckered as if he had just bitten into a sour lime. He turned to Ernesto and pointed.

"You. Pull us out."

"Me? Why not you?"

"Let's get something straight, okay? I'm the captain, and when I tell you to do something, you do it." The drums again scraped loudly. "And right now I'm telling you to get in the water and pull us out."

A shock of red appeared on Ernesto's neck. Nobody aside from his father had ever spoken to him that way. He felt Maria's hand tighten on his but he pulled away.

"Well I'm telling you to go fuck yourself, Captain."

Juan's face tightened and his eyes darted quickly at the others.

"Listen—" He stopped, his cheeks flushed, and let out a deep breath. "The problem is, I can't swim, and we're sitting ducks right here unless—"

"You're kidding me, right?" Ernesto said. "You were in the Guardia Frontera and you can't *swim*? What did you do, sweep the docks?"

"Come on, Ernesto," Maria said. "A patrol could show up any second. Please—"

"We paid this schemer to take us to Florida and he can't even swim!" Ernesto said. But he was already stripping to his swimsuit. He then slid into the water and began the difficult task of getting the raft out beyond the pull of the shore.

When the bottom fell away, he swam around behind the raft and pushed it out toward the liquid horizon. After several minutes the current pulled them outward, assisted by the outgoing tide.

"Ernesto was a champion swimmer," Maria told the group before she helped him back on board.

"Thank you, Señor del Torres." Manuel handed him a jug of water.

"Champion?" Juan said. "Of what?"

"His youth group."

"*Communist* youth, eh *muchacho*?"

Ernesto ignored him and focused instead on drying himself off.

Still shaking his head, Juan slowly turned to the others. "Stay quiet and keep watch for patrols. The Guardia's been shooting *balseros* on sight since the exodus."

"I read that four thousand bodies have been found in Cuban waters already," Maria said. "We need to be careful."

"Out of a hundred thousand who have fled. I don't know about being careful, but we could use some luck," Juan said.

"So many dead, how do you know?" Manuel asked.

"They keep track of the body count in *Granma*," Maria said. "They think it'll scare others from leaving."

"In the newspaper? Like a box score?"

Juan laughed. "Are you crippled *and* blind, old man?"

Maria cleared her throat. "Lots of people make it, and we will too," she said after a moment of awkward silence. Then her eyes lit up. "Just think, we're going to Florida." Her smile was big, and although her teeth were slightly crooked, her face had a natural beauty made warmer by the slight flaw.

Ernesto watched as Juan's eyes followed her legs to her stomach, then paused on her breasts. His tongue wetted his lips as he stared at her caramel skin, the planes of her high cheekbones, her amber eyes that sparkled in the sunlight.

"That's my fiancé you're drooling over, Juan."

Maria elbowed Ernesto in the ribs, and Juan let loose a belly laugh. "So I see."

Vilma stopped her humming. "Enough of this bickering, you two."

An uncomfortable quiet settled over the raft until Vilma asked Juan how long it would take to get to Florida.

"Six days at most, four if we're lucky. The wind's pretty calm, but we'll make good time once we get into the Gulf Stream."

The raft drifted slowly from shore at the mercy of the current, the breeze, the waves and the tide. Ernesto looked back to the gray smudges of the Pinar del Río mountains that loomed above the brown sand and green mangroves. The colors changed rapidly as the morning sun made its way higher into the sky. His eyes moved down the coast toward Mariel, where the Guardia Frontera base was located. A narrow finger of shoreline stretched out from the mainland to create a point, and as they floated beyond it, Ernesto suddenly cocked his head at the sound of a rumble in the distance.

His eyes narrowed to a squint and he carefully scanned the horizon. Nothing was visible, but the low rumble grew louder. *It sounds like a—*

"Ernesto, what is it?" Maria asked.

He held up a hand but said nothing.

"Over there." Juan pointed to a dark silhouette that emerged from behind the point.

"Is it the Guardia?" Maria asked.

"More like some kind of speedboat."

"Look at all those people," Juan said. The cigarette-shaped boat rode low in the water, and Ernesto could make out the silhouettes of over two-dozen heads crammed together like bowling pins. The boat moved slowly away from the coast, a dark shape on the azure sea, with a trail of thin lines of chalky wake trailing behind.

"Smugglers," Juan said.

"I didn't think there were any boats left after the exodus," Maria said.

"That's where we should be," Ernesto said. "They'll be in Florida in hours, not days."

The boat's rumble turned into a high-pitched buzz across the water. Ernesto watched as the bow lifted high into the air, and as the whine remained steady, so did the boat's angle toward the sky. Then the noise suddenly disappeared and the bow dropped back down.

"Your speedboat's having trouble getting up to speed," Juan said. "If they're too heavy, they're screwed."

The loud screech of an air horn suddenly ripped through the morning air.

"Oh, God." Vilma grasped the cross around her neck.

They'd been so distracted that nobody had noticed the triangular silhouette of a Guardia patrol boat steaming straight toward them. The horn sounded again.

"Everybody down," Juan said. "Lie as flat as you can."

"Can they see us?" Maria asked.

Ernesto put his arm around Maria and tried to cover her up. "I can't tell, just lay still." He pressed his body onto hers and shut his eyes tight. The buzz of the speedboat sounded again, as did the Guardia's horn, but neither could drown out Vilma's frantic prayers.

2

THE RIDE IN from Camp David on the president's helicopter was bumpy in the winter winds, but it offered a spectacular view of Washington that few ever got the chance to see. As the Sikorsky VH-60N descended upon the White House lawn, Terri Turner was reminded that the area looked more like an armed encampment lately than a place of government. Roads were closed off in all directions, concrete bollards had been erected outside the metal fence, an anti-aircraft station had been hidden on the building's roof, and armed patrols circled the grounds.

The walk into the White House was brisk, the cold air and busy schedule urging President Winslow, his wife Lucy and Chief of Staff Turner onward. Lucy paused by the elevator that led up to the business side of the West Wing, but the president was oblivious to her glance. Terri Turner caught his eye and discreetly nodded toward the First Lady.

"I'll see you later, dear." He kissed his wife goodbye and stepped into the elevator with Turner. Sally Miles, the president's personal secretary, joined them just outside the guarded bosom of the Oval Office. She gave him the daily green sheets and ran down the morning's appointment schedule, which seemed even more overbooked than usual.

The president took it all in stride. "Anything pressing?"

Sally curled her lip. "Senator Spinelli called three times this morning. He says it's urgent that he see you today."

"Urgent, huh?" Winslow's mouth curled down.

The women held each other's eyes, and the corners of Turner's lips turned slightly upward. "Thanks, Sally."

With that, Ms. Miles departed the room.

"You've got to talk to him at some point," Turner said. "I know you're upset, but that doesn't change the fact that you're going to need his help."

"After he double-crossed me? He has no interest in helping my administration."

"Maybe not, but if you ignore him, I guarantee this whole Cuba situation will only get worse."

Winslow looked up from the daily intelligence reports he'd been trying to read.

"Spinelli's part of the problem, not the solution. I trusted he and Dunleavy—against my better judgment—but they promised up and down to leverage their recognized positions as spokesmen for the Cuban American Coalition to accomplish my agenda. If they'd stuck to that none of this—" He dismissed the thought with a wave of his hand.

It had all been hashed over a dozen times before.

The intercom buzzed. "Senator Spinelli again, sir. Says he's going to call every ten minutes until you speak with him."

"Tell him not to waste the taxpayers' money," the president said.

"Have him hold for a minute, Sally," Turner said. "He's obviously not going away. I think you should talk to him."

"Are you not listening to me?"

Turner put her hands on her hips and tilted her head sideways, letting her dark brown hair touch her shoulder.

"That was always the difference between you and your father. He'd go right after his enemies, you look for ways to get even."

"You want to talk to Spinelli? Go ahead. I'm not wasting another minute on that traitor."

"Fine. Put him through, Sally."

The president walked to the window, where a distorted view of Pennsylvania Avenue could be seen through the thick bulletproof glass.

"Terri Turner here."

"Where is he, Terri?"

"The president's in conference. What can I—"

"You know damn well what you can help me with, and this *conference* of his better be about this mess down in Florida."

She glanced toward the president.

"Look," Spinelli said. "I need to see him today, and soon."

"Sorry, Senator, he's double booked. Prime Minister Blair is—"

"Spare me the smoke screen, okay? The Democrats are screaming for a witch-hunt, and I'm tired of covering for him. If he won't make some time for me today, he can read about what I have to tell him in the *Post* tomorrow."

She pursed her lips. "Wait a minute, let me check something." She pressed the hold button. "He sounds serious, George. You've *got* to see him."

"Not going to happen."

Winslow turned and walked out toward the Roosevelt room.

Great. Turner took a deep breath and stabbed at the blinking button.

"There's no way he can break away. Why don't you and I get together?"

"Can't break away? He's going to be strung up by his—whatever. Fine, meet me at the Capital Grille in one hour." He hung up before she could reply.

Turner stared into the earpiece of the phone and shook her head, regretting that the president ever tried to change America's long-standing policy toward Cuba.

A 50MM CANNON BLAST reverberated across the water. It deafened Juan for an instant.

"Son of a bitch!"

"They're shooting at us!" Maria buried her face in Ernesto's arm.

The projectile hit the water and blasted a white geyser into the air that was ear shattering. The speedboat's engine continued to whine, but its pitch increased in intensity.

"Not toward us," Juan said. "The smugglers."

Maria pulled free from Ernesto to peek toward the boat. Juan saw her jaw tremble. He turned back to the speedboat and sucked in a short breath. "They've turned right for us." *What's pretty boy going to do for you now?*

The speedboat's bow was again pointed skyward but was now aimed directly toward the raft. The patrol boat's horn called again. It sounded much closer.

"Let's swim for it!" Ernesto said.

"I can't swim!" Maria said.

"Wait," Manuel said. "It looks like he's turning back out to sea."

"The Guardia?"

Juan saw a moment of hope dilute the terror in Maria's eyes. Then another cannon blast shattered the air, followed by a fast whistling sound and an explosion. The speedboat disappeared in a wall of water, and then shot through the other side, its bow still aimed high.

"They missed."

"Let's swim for it," Ernesto said. "I'll help Maria."

Vilma looked from Ernesto to Juan, her face white with fear. "Swim?"

"None of us can swim," Juan said. "Just stay down and shut up!" The sound of the revving speedboat flattened to a steady growl and its nose finally dropped down onto a plane. "They're hauling ass now. Look, someone's lying on the bow."

The horn sounded again and the Guardia boat loomed much larger on the horizon. The speedboat was now flat on the water. It gained velocity and swerved an evasive course northward. Another cannon shot landed close behind it and a jet of water blasted out of the speedboat's wake. Another shot sounded, but it again missed.

The next projectile sailed true and hit its target with a deafening crack and an immense explosion of water. The impact was so strong that the speedboat launched out of the ocean and corkscrewed through the air, its occupants spilling out like bird droppings.

The hull smashed back into the sea on its side—the revving engines spraying water—and the boat spun around like a whirling dervish. Ghastly sounds of the propeller blades hitting solid matter caused Juan to look away. Then the sound of the engines quit altogether. The speedboat was silent. Only the steady hum of the Guardia boat's diesel engines could be heard as it steamed toward its prize.

Juan shuddered and took stock of his passengers.

"Stay down. The speedboat is on its side. People are holding on." He didn't tell them two children had just tried to climb onto the side of the boat and fallen back into the sea.

"Why did they shoot them?" Maria asked.

"Castro's orders. The Guardia will shoot anyone who tries to outrun them."

Another tremor ran through him as he watched the patrol boat cut a broad swath through the absinthe water toward the sinking speedboat.

"Poor souls," Vilma whispered.

A burst of adrenalin passed through Juan. The Guardia was focused on the smugglers, so with a little luck their raft could slip past undetected.

"Hey, Ernesto, still wish you were on the boat?" he said.

For once Ernesto let Juan have the last word.

3

THE PUNGENT AROMAS of cigars and cigarettes made it clear that the Capital Grille cared little for the political correctness in vogue in most restaurants. Dinners were for social affairs, but noon in Washington, DC is where power lunches earned their name.

Tuxedoed waiters scurried about to serve important men in dark suits that whispered over fat slabs of meat. Terri Turner was one of a few women in the room on this particular afternoon, and upon her arrival nearly every head turned to watch her navigate between the tables. Her tall, slender physique, dark hair and pencil skirt cut a chic swath through the dark pinstripe suits. She saw Spinelli eye her up and down as she approached but she had long ago grown numb to those kinds of looks from men like him.

She ordered what appeared to be the only piece of fish on the premises, a huge chunk of Copper River salmon that barely fit on the plate. She picked at it as Senator Spinelli rattled on about the situation he had inadvertently created and how he was the only one who could save the president from what had become a national crisis.

"It's not just Florida that's at risk, it's a national emergency. Fifty thousand refugees have been holed up in tents for over a month now. What the hell's Winslow doing?"

Turner's dark eyes bore into Spinelli's without retreat. Her chin-length hair framed her face, and as a relatively new commodity on the Washington political scene she was easily taken for a gracefully aging model—certainly not the chief bulldog and negotiator to the president of the United States.

"It's a complicated situation, Senator, you know that. The Migration Accords prohibit—"

"Don't start with that hogwash, Terri. We're both Republicans here."

"That didn't matter when you went on Cuban TV and disgraced Castro, did it? If you and Dunleavy had stuck to the plan, to the *Republican* agenda of our *Republican* president, we wouldn't have all those people stuck in tents, would we?"

"That was a month ago. How was I supposed to know what was going to happen? It doesn't matter now anyway."

"Of course it matters. Ever since our embassies were bombed in Nairobi and Rwanda—"

"After which I helped Clinton get the missile strikes approved against Al Qaeda in Afghanistan—"

"Afghanistan's a powder keg," she said. "Al Qaeda is on the rise, the Taliban can't be trusted, so the initiative with Cuba was intended to improve America's reputation."

Spinelli cocked his head at an angle. "So this is about popularity?"

"No, Senator, the president is concerned about terrorism closer to home—"

"Never happen—our intelligence network is too good. We'll never get attacked on our soil—at least any kind of significant attack."

Turner glanced around and leaned in closer. "It's 2001. The embargo has been in place for forty-two years and is a total failure. We want to eliminate the potential for Cuba to again invite in hostile nation states or terrorist organizations, and to disprove the international coalition's assertion that we're pushing an imperialist agenda. The stage was set. The president trusted you to stick to the script, but your grandstanding knocked the plan to weaken terrorism back on its heels."

Spinelli's bald dome began to glisten. "The coalition needs to mind its own business and stay focused on the Middle East. Winslow just wants to add another foreign policy notch to his belt. He doesn't know squat about Cuba, aside from them having good cigars."

"He's learning fast now, thanks to you and Dunleavy."

Spinelli snorted a laugh and launched a chunk of New York strip at Turner. "He can call me in fifteen years when he's spent as much time battling Castro as I have." The ruby on his pinky ring caught the light as he smoothed his palm over the few strands of long hair shellacked to his scalp.

"To get Cuba off the terrorist watch list was an important step to make the Western Hemisphere safer."

"Castro's so full of shit you can smell his ass when he breathes. We went to Havana with open minds and every intention to stick to Winslow's script, but after we saw the human rights situation, we had to speak out."

"Speak out?" Turner said. "Dunleavy's a Democrat, we might have expected him to sandbag us—but not you. The president trusted you and all he got was a knife in the back."

"I did exactly what he asked me to. Now Dunleavy, on the other hand, well, I can't speak for him. But the fact remains that Castro still has dissidents imprisoned, free speech is suppressed, and he refuses to play ball." Spinelli leaned in closer. "Frankly, I think it's because the Cubans haven't suffered enough yet."

Turner took a long sip of her iced tea. *What's your game, Spinelli? What was so urgent that you had to see the president today?*

"Our hemisphere's fine, Terri. Winslow doesn't need to bother with Cuba. Anyway, a big-shot Texas oilman like him must have plenty of supporters who lost property when Castro took our wells and refineries. They can't be happy about his wanting to soften the embargo."

"You're right, we both know lots of people who had their oil wells and plants nationalized there," she said. "But you know what? They've moved on with their lives. When will you allow the country to do the same?"

"Castro's only goal to have us there was to give his people some eye candy, make them think he was open to change. He used us as pawns, that's why we stuck it to him and called for demonstrations in support of democracy when the fool put us on TV."

"The press reports didn't spin it that way. You and Dunleavy were all but sainted for going into the lion's den and coming out unscathed. I even saw a cartoon that made you out to be a pair of modern-day gladiators."

Spinelli smiled. "I had that one framed for my office."

"Of course you did."

"Look, I understand Winslow's foreign policy plans have bogged down and he needs a win to get back on track, but this isn't the one. I've made a career out of battling for change in Cuba, and my Cuban-American constituents support our policies."

"You mean starving the Cuban people through legislation like the Cuban Democracy Act and Helms-Burton?"

"If that's what it takes to get rid of the old bastard, then yes. All we can do is continue to turn the screws until he breaks."

"The president recognizes that Castro's record on human rights is abysmal. He's an evil dictator who has used the embargo to abuse the eleven million Cuban people for four-plus decades. The president's belief is that the sooner we change what has been a failed policy, the faster it will bring about the change we want—and prevent additional abuse because it will empower the Cuban people."

Spinelli pursed his lips and shook his head. Turner balled her fists under the table and awaited what she knew would be a pedantic retort.

"When your boss has more foreign policy experience, he'll realize a concept like that is just wishful thinking."

Turner had had enough. She knew there was no benefit in arguing policy anyway.

"Why don't you just get to the point, Senator?"

"It's more of a warning, really. The president should have given me just a few—"

"Warning? "Turner said. "About what? The disastrous results of *your* latest twist of the screw on Castro? I think it's a little late for that."

Spinelli leaned across the table and dropped his voice to a low growl. "You've got a lot of nerve, missy."

"You created this problem, and now you expect the president to bail you out? Is New Jersey willing to pay its pro rata share to house, feed and attend those fifty thousand Cubans sitting in tents in Miami who heeded your call? And what about the thousands of others who died trying to get here?"

"You Texas people may have made a fortune wildcatting oil, but don't expect to roll into Washington and start wildcatting foreign policy. I've worked on this issue since Winslow's daddy was stomping around Mexico with a divining rod."

Turner felt a charge of anger flush through her veins.

"Do you have a seventy-eight percent approval rating? Are you the one who's faced with the potential for yet another Mariel boatlift if we don't honor the Migration Accords?"

"We're all in this together, Terri. And your boss should enjoy his approval rating while he can, because I'm here to tell you, it's about to drop like a rock."

"What's that supposed to mean?"

"It means that Florida's up to its neck and the situation's spinning out of control. Tensions are near the breaking point, and since the president hasn't done anything about it, Congress will."

Turner's stomach turned over. *Here it comes.*

"Care to be more specific?"

Spinelli cleared his throat, stuck a finger down his shirt collar and pulled it away from his Adam's apple.

"We've called for an emergency session to authorize federal funds and to appropriate military bases to redistribute the refugees. Forget about the Migration Accords. Those fears are hypothetical, the riots brewing in Florida are reality."

You bastards!

"We've been more than patient, but someone's got to take responsibility for what's happening—in our hemisphere," Spinelli continued. "You can tell your boss he's got three days to come to his senses. I hate to do this to a fellow Republican, but with Florida in utter disarray, you can rest assured that Dunleavy's chomping at the bit to make this a PR nightmare for you guys—and the Republican Party."

She could just imagine the headlines. The press would have a bloody field day.

Spinelli wiped his mouth with a napkin and tossed it on the table. "Now if you'll excuse me, I have the business of the great state of New Jersey to attend to."

He stood to leave but reached over and held three fingers in front of her nose. "Remember, three days." He put on his overcoat, wrapped a silk scarf around his neck then bent down for a last word.

"If your boss won't cover the cost of the lunch, send me the bill, okay? I'll make sure that New Jersey pays its pro rata share."

THE HORIZON OF the Cuban landmass had shrunk to indecipherable white blotches and long stretches of dark bands above the water. Havana's skyscrapers stood out above the gray mass of buildings in contrast to the mountains in the west. Juan stared at the diminishing skyline while he listened to Vilma sing.

> *"Sleeping in my garden*
> *Are the White lilies,*
> *Spikenards and roses.*
> *My soul so sad and sorrowful*
> *Wants to hide its bitter pain in the flowers."*

Juan was accustomed to hearing better singers in the restaurant where he worked. *But her timing's good.* She began to hum—he wished she would finish the song instead. It had reminded him of his mother.

Hours had passed since the Guardia sank the smuggler's boat, and the group had settled into the confines of the raft. Juan checked them all like a captain inspecting his cargo. Maria lay on her side and faced out to sea. Seated next to her, Ernesto ran his index finger along the curve of her cheek. She looked pale.

"You need to drink some water," he said.

"I can't."

The ocean had gone from luminescent milky green to a dark steely blue.

"You'll get used to the waves," Juan said. "Don't worry."

"Listen to the expert, honey." Ernesto said. "Our captain can't swim, but he's very knowledgeable, I'm sure."

Juan spun around and considered Ernesto with a half-lidded stare. *Look at you sitting there, you cocky bastard. Fancy clothes and that pretty-boy look fit you like a glove.*

"We can't all be Youth League champions," he said. "The rest of us were just slaves for the revolution. We don't have fathers in Castro's Politburo."

"You must have a friend somewhere. How else did you get into the Guardia if you can't swim?"

Manuel's eyebrows rose. Maria discreetly shook her head at Ernesto.

Keep it up, asshole. "I was a marksman," Juan said. "My job was to shoot people."

"*Balseros?*" Ernesto said. "Like this morning? Was that your old boat?"

Juan began to tap his fingers against the deck like it was a conga drum. He shrugged and the tempo of his taps increased.

Manuel coughed, smiled at everyone and turned to face the waves.

"Are you two going to argue the whole way to Florida?" Vilma asked.

"Ernesto, be nice," Maria said.

"Hey, old man, give me my cigarettes." Juan pointed to a brown sack tied to the back of the raft. Manuel reached inside and pulled out a sweater, a ball of twine, a tattered envelope and two packs of cigarettes. He lifted up the letter to read the address.

"What the hell's wrong with you, old man?" Juan said. "Put that down!"

Manuel replaced the letter in the sack and passed Juan one of the packs of Marlboros. Juan lit up right away, took a deep drag, and held in the smoke before he let it out slowly. Manuel's eyes narrowed. He pointed at the deck, his eyes squinting.

"I can see water," he said.

"Yeah, it's called the ocean," Ernesto said.

"No, he means through the deck." Juan said. He pulled on the line holding the deck together, and it lifted several inches above the boards. "The ropes have come loose."

"You can tighten them, can't you?" Vilma said.

Juan hesitated, wishing there were something to say other than the truth.

"Not really," he said. "The knots are underneath."

"Underneath?" Ernesto said. "You've got to be kidding me. Did they teach you that in the Guardia too?"

"Manuel, hand me that twine from the bag." The ball of string felt odd in Juan's numb hands. He fumbled it and watched it roll toward the water. Ernesto scooped it up and tossed it back at him.

19

Juan cut three segments of two meters each. He slipped the strands between the ends of the boards, pulled them tight, and tied them together with granny knots.

"Your raft is falling apart, and you tie pathetic knots like those to hold it together?" Ernesto said.

"*Our* raft," Vilma said. "Will that twine hold?"

Ernesto glared at Juan. "Get out of the way."

The raft was built in three sections, each with two drums underneath the wood decking. It was the last third of decking that had come loose. When he finished retying the knots, Ernesto looked anything but satisfied.

"This twine is crap. We'll need to keep a close watch on it."

Vilma reached down and pulled at the new rope, which stayed taut. The old rope, however, was quite loose. Ernesto tested all the lines and shook his head. "What the hell was I thinking, coming with you?" he whispered in a voice only Juan could hear.

"You could have been on that speedboat."

"What are you saying?" Maria asked.

Ernesto didn't answer, but Juan looked into her eyes. She offered him a weak smile. Juan appreciated her gesture. *What do you see in an arrogant prick like Ernesto? His father's influence doesn't mean shit out here on the water, and it won't mean a damn thing in America either.*

Time passed slowly for the group, and though pressed together like baled sugarcane, they settled in as comfortably as they could. Everyone periodically checked the twine, more out of nervousness than necessity. After nearly an hour, Vilma sat up and broke the silence.

"You know, Ernesto, I've been wondering. Why would you, of all people, leave Cuba?"

"I'd like to hear that one myself," Juan said. "The son of the great Ramon del Torres, born with a silver spoon up your ass, why the hell would you leave?"

Ernesto sighed and stared out to sea. Even on this raft his father would haunt him. Vilma was waiting. Finally he sighed and turned to face them.

"You think I'm lucky, right? Blessed to be the only son of a hero of the revolution and minister of the sugar industry? That sounds pretty good, doesn't it?" His lips curled into a sneer. "If you only knew."

"Oh, excuse me, I'm sure it's been hell living in luxury your whole life," Juan said. He looked at the others in disbelief. "What do you think, Manuel? Life on the farm like that?"

The old man closed his eyes. A distant smile came slowly.

"That's all you see, isn't it, Juan? Cars, money, houses … it all sounds great, right? It doesn't matter that my father's a hypocritical asshole, does it?" Ernesto shook his head and shrugged bitterly.

"Why didn't you just take a boat during the exodus with all the other government officials?" Vilma asked. "Why go on this raft?"

"You don't understand," Maria said. "It's my fault. We didn't know I was pregnant until after the exodus. And once that came out—"

"Pregnant?" Juan sat up straight.

Ernesto put his arm around her shoulder and kissed her cheek. "Maria …"

"Oh, *chica*, that's wonderful!" Vilma said.

Maria patted her belly and looked at Vilma hesitantly. "I'm not so sure. Señor del Torres did not take the news so well. He and Ernesto got on fine until I—"

"*We*, Maria, "Ernesto said. " *We* got pregnant." Then he turned to face the others. "I wouldn't call the relationship with my father fine, but at least I hadn't been exiled yet."

"Exiled? Is that what happens to rich people when they get their girlfriends pregnant?" Juan asked.

"My family's very poor," Maria said. "Ernesto's father didn't like that."

"It's not that simple, Maria. He never said—"

"You mean you don't even know what happened?" Vilma asked. Maria looked down at the deck, shrugged and slowly shook her head.

"He's an animal!" Ernesto said. "Our lives would have been hell if we stayed."

"Hell? What do you call this?" Juan said. "Adrift on a slab of wood hoping to make it to Florida where we'll have nothing? Nothing but a baby for you to feed, that is."

"You can't hold it in forever, Ernesto. At some point I have the right to know what your father said," Maria continued. "One minute you're going to tell him we're getting married, and the next we're afloat on this giant ocean!" She pushed his arm off her shoulder and crossed her arms.

"You're just a *campesina*, Maria," Juan said. "There's no place—"

"Shut up, Juan! Don't listen to him, Maria. My father was just, just ... *aarrggh*!"

Ernesto threw his hands up; his eyes appeared as though they would burst. "You really want to know? Fine! When I told him we were getting married he was shocked. He said it was too soon, so I told him about the baby, and that we were surprised, but excited. That's when he lost it." Ernesto hesitated. "The bastard lectured me as if I were a child, then before I knew it, he was on the phone to Dr. Escaloña."

"A doctor?"

"He's a pig, Maria. He was scheduling an abortion!"

Vilma crossed herself.

"I go to tell him my big news, and all he can do is take over, just like he has my entire life. So, I rip the phone out of his hand and he pushes me against the wall. It was all I could do not to spit in his face. But when I calmed down, I told him that I loved you and that I wanted the baby. And I reminded him that you're Catholic and would never consider an abortion, even if we weren't getting married."

Maria paled and looked back down at the deck. "Some Catholic," she whispered.

"It got worse after that." Ernesto continued. "He ranted and raved about his plans for me, and how I was throwing everything away. I told him he had controlled my life long enough and that I was through with it. That's when he snapped."

"That's it?" Juan asked.

"He tried to fight me, but it was a joke. I mean the man's nearly seventy years old. So I held his arms while he struggled, and then told me to get out." A tremble ran through Ernesto. "And then he said: 'Don't even think about coming back with that little bastard.'"

Maria shivered and tears streaked her cheeks.

"It never works, Maria. People like us don't belong with people like them," Juan said.

"Did you talk to him after that?" Vilma asked.

"That happened right when the exodus began. I haven't spoken with him since." He put his arm around Maria and scooted closer.

"What a sorry-ass story." Juan said. "It's like one of those Argentinean soap operas."

"That's enough, Juan!" Vilma said. She turned to Maria and stroked her hair. "God bless you for your courage, Ernesto and you for your strength, Maria."

Ernesto held Maria tightly. His own tears fell into her hair.

"How typical of our so-called classless society," Juan said. "The heroes of the Revolution are no better than the thugs before them. That's what makes me sick about Cuba. The Revolution's nothing but lies and broken promises."

"Stop it!" Vilma said. "The Revolution's been good to you, whether you realize it or not."

"If that's how you feel, what are you doing here?" Juan paused. "Never mind, I don't really give a shit, just calm down and shut up."

Juan crawled to the other end of the raft and sat next to Manuel, who had watched the entire conversation with his vacant smile. "The minister of sugar," Manuel whispered with a nod.

"Sugar!" Ernesto spat as he kneeled. "The heroin of our country. All it does is keep us a welfare state."

"It's not our concern anymore," Juan said. "When I get to America my only thoughts about sugar will be how much to put in my coffee."

"Speak for yourself, Juan. I'm going to be important in the American sugar industry if it's the last thing I ever do!" Ernesto said. "Someday, when the embargo ends, I want my father to have go through *me* to access the biggest market in the world."

Ernesto's eyes shone brightly. The intensity of his voice silenced the raft. Maria, still pale, put her head back on Ernesto's shoulder and closed her eyes. He pulled her close.

Ernesto and Maria are more desperate than I imagined, Juan thought.

"Tell me this," he said. "What will the Americans do if they find out you're a member of the Communist Party?"

"I'm not a communist. It's just that for twenty-five years I've done everything my father told me to do—"

"Except dump Maria."

"That included becoming a party member. I've never believed in that system, in fact, I've had a front-row seat to see just how inefficient it is."

"Yeah, you've suffered a lot."

Ernesto held up a finger. "I consider reality without labels. For example, you're a worthless hustler with a chip on your shoulder, and you're incapable of being anything but a laborer. It's imperative that you have someone like me to manage you, and the millions of others like you."

"What—"

"That's not communism, it's capitalism. Natural leaders lead, innovators create, and workers have a place to be useful so they can put bread on their tables."

Vilma crossed her arms and opened her eyes wide.

"The result would be far better for Cuba than what we have today," Ernesto said.

"You arrogant prick," Juan said.

"You think that's my idea? What do you think was behind the exodus? Do you think all those people left just because some American senators came down and embarrassed Castro on television? No! Those people were intellectuals, Politburo members, students, professors and doctors. They gave up because they knew communism was a joke!"

"*Coño*, boy, you are crazy. I think your old man did more than just *exile* you. We're leaving because our whole fucking country's a joke. So is your version of what it should be." Juan held up his palms and shook his head. "I don't care about Cuba anymore. I'll never go back, and I'd rather be shot by the Guardia than repatriated."

"Repatriated? What's that?" Manuel asked.

"If the Americans catch us before we reach land, they'll send us back."

"To Cuba? They'd do that?"

"They're supposed to—it's called wet foot, dry foot—but they haven't been doing it during the exodus. My father said that the Americans have broken some treaty on migration, and Castro's threatening to retaliate with another Mariel."

Juan laughed. "His usual bullshit drama. There's no boats left! And look what happened to those smugglers this morning."

"Well," Manuel said, "if Cuba let all those people go, and America let them all in, then maybe five more won't make a difference."

"Let's hope not," Juan and Ernesto said simultaneously.

It was the first time they had ever agreed on anything.

4

TWELVE MONTHS AFTER coming to the White House, Terri Turner still felt a sense of awe when she entered the venerable building. She had come to know the security staff stationed at the metal detectors, the armed guards beyond them and most of the Secret Service agents by name and several by their personality. She had even come to have a nodding acquaintance with most of the porters and staff who were constantly roaming the halls. Many of the staff had initially mistaken Turner's intense demeanor as a lack of warmth and humility, but it only took a couple months to realize that although she was quiet, she was shrewd and capable of pouncing on her prey like a hawk.

She made her way toward the West Wing, electing to take the stairs instead of the elevator. She spotted Sally Miles in the distance. Sally's devotion to George Winslow went back nearly as far as Turner's, all the way to back to the early days at Winslow Oil when George Jr. took over for his father after the senior Winslow died of a sudden heart attack. Sally was the first, and last, assistant he'd ever hired. Turner's own history at Winslow Oil actually preceded the president's and their relationship had started out on a very rocky footing because of it. Didn't help that she had been his father's mistress.

"Hey, Sally, everything all right?"

Sally looked up, and the harried glint in her eye caused Turner to pause.

"All right? Not by a long shot."

"What do you mean?"

"He's been on the phone nonstop. Something's happening in Congress over the Cuban refugee situation."

"So I've heard." Turner frowned and entered the Oval Office.

THE AFTERNOON SUN fought to penetrate a growing fog, and the visibility had dwindled to nothing. The Mohawk, a 270-foot medium-endurance Coast Guard cutter out of Key West, completed its tenth straight day on patrol in international waters along the Cuban territorial limit to search for refugees headed for Florida. After nearly a week of collecting bloated bodies offshore of the Florida Keys, the captain decided upon a more proactive approach to interdict the Cubans as they entered international waters in order to reduce the risk of them drowning during the treacherous crossing. The idea was well received by the division commander and the Mohawk began its journey.

Captain Scott Hawkes never imagined the magnitude of deceased humans they would encounter. "OOD, change course to three-six-zero, then all ahead three. Let's get well clear of Cuban waters for the night. We'll recommence the visual patrol at dawn," he said with a yawn. The orange light that radiated from the bridge accentuated the dark circles under his eyes.

Officer of the Deck Casey Killelea nodded, then repeated the order to the helmsman who made the adjustment. "All set, Captain,"

Hawkes drank from his mug of cold coffee, not sure whether it was his eleventh or twelfth of the day. Keeping track of numbers had lost significance to him during this trip. Normally proud and erect, his tall frame had stooped a little more each day, and he felt as if his hair was going from salt and pepper to white. He closed his eyes and rubbed them, not from fatigue, but trying to push the macabre images of bloated, rotted and shark-torn bodies out of his mind. Unfortunately, it didn't work.

The engines' change in pitch and the sudden turn to the north announced to the hundred-person crew that there was a change in orders. Enlisted men and women posted around the ship's deck awaited new instructions. Everyone was exhausted from peering through binoculars to search for remains too small to register on sonar. The day's scorecard registered a loss, and everyone aboard knew it.

More dead found than alive. Again.

The captain opened his eyes and wearily glanced around the bridge. "Sound the horn, Casey."

The first blast signaled the end of the shift, and a second signaled the end of the day's patrol. The OOD lifted a clipboard onto the counter next to the captain and ran her finger down two columns of numbers, one of which was twice as long as the other for today. She removed a ballpoint pen from her shirt pocket, drew a line at the end of each column and wrote a number underneath it, then initialed the page. She took a deep breath, turned to Captain Hawkes and handed over the clipboard without a word. They did not meet eyes.

Although his expression betrayed no outward sign of emotion, Hawkes knew his crew sensed his unease. Ten straight days of collecting bodies, now numbered in the hundreds, had taken its toll. *All right, let's see it.*

The number sickened him, but he found solace in the fact that they had also rescued a number of people who would have otherwise died from shaky rafts and floating debris.

Hawkes initialed the paper and handed the clipboard back. Another flash of sunburned, human carnage afloat in clumps like flotsam flickered through his mind, but he quashed it with a shake of his head.

"We saved eight lives today, people. Not a bad day's work."

"Aye, Captain." The OOD's tight smile matched her cold eyes.

After twenty-one years in the Coast Guard, Hawkes had not seen anything like this. The Cuban exodus was immense, and although the memories were vague, he recalled stories from the Mariel Boatlift of 1980, the year he joined the service. Accustomed to repatriating illegal refugees, the rules on "wet foot, dry foot" had changed in recent weeks, and for a man who excelled in a structured environment, Hawkes felt adrift in a sea of confusion and dead bodies.

THE PRESIDENT WAS on the phone, his face carved into an angry mask. "I'm not interested in what Spinelli promised you, I need your support on this, Henry." He paused while the other man, whom Turner assumed to be Henry McGranahan, Republican Senator from Ohio, responded to the plea.

"That's a superficial problem, Henry. The ramifications are a lot deeper than those poor bastards stuck in Miami, I—"

McGranahan cut him off, and the president shifted to face Turner, his eyes rolling as he rubbed his palm over his forehead. "Fine, you think about it, and I'll look into coming to Akron in March." He slammed the phone down.

"I guess you've heard the news?"

Winslow shot her a quick glance and started a circle around the room, a sure sign his adrenalin was flowing. "You're darn right I've heard. I've also spoken to Potts, Schneider, Logan and Custer. They're all dancing around the issue. Spinelli's convinced them all that I'm paralyzed with fear and have no intention of helping Florida with this crisis."

A buzzer sounded and Sally's voice came over the intercom. "Leslie Conde's here, sir."

"Tell her I'll need a few minutes, please. Damn." He clicked off the intercom. "I'm in no mood to discuss Health and Human Services at the moment."

Turner took a deep breath and knew she needed to calm his nerves and get focused on planning an offensive. "I had lunch with the Spinmaster. He tried to be coy at first, but he clearly thinks he's in the catbird seat."

"Thinks? I'd say he damn sure *is* in the catbird seat. He and Dunleavy created this mess, and now he wants to jam it up my ass because I'm trying to preserve the Migration Accords so Castro doesn't send even more people over."

Turner studied him for a moment and wondered if she'd ever seen him this mad. For a fleeting instant she wished they were still back in Austin, not giving a damn about foreign policy and its domestic ramifications. They both had enough money to never have to work again, but money was no longer the motivator.

"If Castro terminates the Migration Accords, we'll wind up with a boatlift worse than Mariel, and he'll Carter me."

Turner couldn't help but smile at the phrase. President Jimmy Carter's popularity had plummeted when Castro opened Cuba's jails and insane asylums and shipped every sick, indigent, or low-life criminal he could get his hands on to South Florida. Reagan had been smart to negotiate the Migration Accords to make sure it didn't happen to him.

"Castro believes that Spinelli and Dunleavy's trip was engineered to embarrass him and induce the exodus. If he retaliates and opens the floodgates, I'll be ruined."

"You could always send them back."

Winslow spun toward her, his eyebrow arched and his mouth angled in a sardonic grin. "Don't tempt me."

"It's an option."

"I've spoken to a dozen congressmen preaching the risks of sending emergency funds to Florida versus enforcing the accords and shipping them back. The consensus is that Spinelli and Dunleavy are the Cuba experts, and everyone wants to defer to them. In hindsight, I was a fool to ignore the wet foot, dry foot policy and allow the boat people rescued at sea to come to America."

"You're open-minded, George, not a policy hack kicking this tired old can further down the road. But between what the CIA's telling us and the reports out of Miami, we may have run out of time. If the emergency session is successful, you could always sit on the legislation if it passes both houses."

"If I pull a pocket veto, I'll really look like the bad guy. Forget that, the press smells blood and if we don't do something quick, we'll completely lose control of the situation."

He was right. What was originally intended as a highly visible move in the administration's overall foreign policy initiative to improve America's reputation internationally by seeking to end hostilities with Cuba had backfired because he had trusted the wrong men. It was water under the bridge now, but the question was how bad the flood would be.

Turner took a moment to ponder their options. When she looked up, she was surprised at the president's expression. "What are you smiling about?"

"I'm damned sure not going to sit back and let Spinelli make me look like an idiot or determine policy for my administration."

"What are you thinking?"

"To go on the offensive." Winslow rubbed his palms together and began to pace. "I think we can finish what we started, disarm Castro's threat of launching another boatlift, preserve the Migration Accords, digest the exodus Cubans, and ultimately beat Spinelli at his own game. But it's going to take a lot of finesse."

"We don't have much time. The emergency session's in three days."

"That might give us enough time in the context of what I have in mind. Sit down for a minute and tell me how this grabs you."

THE SHADOWED STREETS of Miami's Little Havana always livened up at dusk, especially in the past few weeks since the exodus Cubans had been rounded up into chain-link and razor wire at the impromptu tent city on Homestead Air Reserve Base. More at home in the darkness than during the day, Arturo Dias appeared from a darkened doorway and stepped into the road. "Aaarrrggghhhh!" He yawned loudly, stretched his arms to the sky and shook his head.

Last night's partying had finally worn off and it was time to check out the neighborhood to see what was on for tonight. Arturo's skin was the color of eggplant in the tungsten light that bounced off the aged buildings. The yellow rag wrapped around his head appeared to float in the darkness. His casual gait quickened when he spotted silhouettes in the shadows ahead, embers from what they were smoking rising in arcs toward low-watt light bulbs.

Arturo pulled a crumpled cigarette from behind his ear and lit it with a lighter he had pocketed from a Salvadoran convenience store on 17th Avenue while buying beer last night.

"Turo," called a husky voice from the shadows as the youth approached.

"What's up fellas?" Smoke curled around his broad nostrils and caressed his eye sockets and forehead as Arturo stopped on the edge of the darkness.

"Just you, man. What's the word, anything happening yet?"

Arturo's gold tooth flashed between drags on his cigarette. "Getting close, man. Got to stay ready. I've been checking out the stores around Dadeland, and once the shit comes down, it's gonna be the bomb."

Another figure stepped into the light and Arturo smiled. "All right, Rico. What's up?"

Rico was a short, muscular Cubano who stayed dialed-in with the local political movements for the sole purpose of exploiting their activities for personal gain. The Cohiba telegraph had been on fire over the exodus situation, and the atmosphere had rapidly moved toward a mayhem that would eclipse the disruptions that surrounded the Elián González incident last year.

"Opportunities are on the rise. Stay tight. The way things going in Homestead, the cops'll have their hands full. Big demonstration planned for either tomorrow, or the next day, and when that goes down, it's gonna be a free-for-all."

All three of them laughed. Rico pulled a bottle out from his baggy pocket. They passed it around, taking turns, and then Arturo produced a joint from behind his other ear and lit it with the remains of the cigarette.

"TVs, stereos, DVDs, it's all there. Smash and grab time, baby," Arturo said. Then he barked a phlegm-addled string of coughs in response to a deep pull on the joint.

"That's right, man," Rico said. "Christmas gonna come twice this year."

5

SENATOR ROBERT SPINELLI treasured a rare quiet moment at his office in the Hart office building, adjacent to the US Capitol. The frenetic energy that filled the air during business hours was gone by late evening. Most of his colleagues were off to official functions, schmoozing financial conduits, or in rare cases at home spending time with their families. Spinelli was not one to burn the midnight oil, but now up to his neck in the high-stakes game he had initiated through the emergency session, he was determined to hedge his bet.

Ice rattled around the bottom of his glass and he considered pouring another couple fingers of whiskey from the bottle on his desk. He looked at his watch: 9:15. *Where the hell are you, Puzzo?*

His "special aide," Vinny Puzzo, was fifteen minutes late, and were it not for the delicacy of the mission he had for him, Spinelli would rip him a new asshole when he arrived. He lifted the half-full fifth of Crown Royal off his desk and hesitated. He sighed and replaced the bottle in the desk's lower drawer.

His phone rang. It was security. "Yes, send him up."

The walk from the gate would take five minutes, and Spinelli unconsciously gnawed on his thumbnail as he ran through his plan and weighed the risks one last time. The door opened without a knock, which startled Spinelli back to reality. He jumped to his feet, and his heart skipped a beat.

"Evening, Senator."

The mass of Vinny Puzzo filled the doorway. They shook hands and Spinelli pointed to a guest chair. "Close the door. I'm glad you could make it. You drive?"

"Nah, took the train. You mentioned a trip, so I figured I'd be flying." Puzzo was dressed in a dark suit but wore a black turtleneck underneath instead of a shirt and tie.

"Good, there's a flight out of Reagan in two hours. You need to be on it."

"What's the deal?"

"You're going to Houston."

"Somebody down there?"

"No, it's a research trip." Spinelli peeled a piece of skin off the corner of his thumb and flicked it to the floor. Puzzo's eyes followed the speck of skin sail through the air, then turned back to the Senator without changing his expression.

"What kind of research?" The northern Jersey accent was thick, but Spinelli knew he was capable of disguising it when necessary.

"This is kind of a unique assignment, Vinny. Discretion must be absolute. If anybody asks you what you're doing, you're a journalist. If they ask again, get the hell out of there." Spinelli knew the journalist cover would be a stretch. Puzzo looked more like a wrestler than an intellectual.

Puzzo gave a slight nod of his pumpkin-sized head to acknowledge the need for stealth.

"There may not even be anything to find out, but I want you to try. Lord knows there's been a ton of research done already, but what I'm interested in is different than what most people have looked for. I don't care about DUIs, affairs, or idle gossip—we can leave that to the grocery store rags. I'm interested in revelations on what motivates this man."

"Who we talking about?"

Spinelli hesitated, then smiled. "President George Winslow."

A barely discernible crease bent Puzzo's lips. He glanced at his watch.

"Am I boring you?"

"No, I just don't want to miss—"

"Focus, Vinny. Don't look at your watch, don't think about your growling stomach, don't think about your wife, or your girlfriend. Just focus. This is important."

Puzzo's smile vanished.

"I want you to dig into George Winslow's past. Who were his supporters in Texas? What were his interests? How did he do business? Who did he do business with? I know he inherited Winslow Oil from his father, but the company doubled in size after that and I want to know why."

Puzzo's expression remained fixed, but he licked his lips. "How long do I have?"

"Two, three days max. Learn anything you can and call me here." Spinelli fished into his shirt pocket and handed over a piece of paper with his private cell number on it. "If I don't answer, leave a message."

Puzzo betrayed no emotion, surprise or interest in the reasons behind the assignment, which Spinelli appreciated. Their relationship went back twenty years, from Spinelli's tenure as mayor of Elizabeth, New Jersey, and Vinny had proven his worth many times during their association.

Once convinced that Puzzo understood the mission, Spinelli dismissed him and watched as he disappeared into the darkness of the hallway. Even though this was perfectly legal and even commonplace between opposing parties, it was an odd pursuit for a Republican senator to investigate a Republican president. Confident that Vinny would be diligent, Spinelli smiled to himself and felt like a spymaster overseeing his personal operative. He opened the bottom drawer and poured himself three more fingers of Crown.

"They say 'don't mess with Texas.' Well, don't fuck with New Jersey."

DARKNESS DESCENDED LIKE a curtain and a sense of isolation began to envelop Juan as he watched the last of the orange glow fade into the horizon. The moon had not yet begun to rise, and few stars were out to illuminate the ocean. Light from Havana still glowed like a distant wildfire. With little wind and mild seas, they hadn't covered much distance this first day and the group was restless.

"I'm still hungry," Maria said. "Can't we have just a little more rice?"

"We're tight on food as it is." Juan said. *And cigarettes.*

"If the wind doesn't pick up it could take us a week to get to Florida," Ernesto said. "We need to ration the food or we'll run out when we need it most."

Maria groaned and hung her head back. "I won't make it a week."

Ernesto rubbed her back.

Juan removed his box of Marlboros and pulled one out with a practiced flourish. Once lit, the smoke hung in the still air like a cloud.

"Keep that away from me, will you?" Vilma fanned her hands. "I'm sure Maria doesn't appreciate it either."

"Sorry, all right?" He blew the smoke downwind.

With nothing to do but talk, the topic of Maria and Ernesto's chance meeting at Cuba's first cybercafe came up. Manuel had never heard of the internet and was baffled by the concept—and then that Castro could somehow censor its content.

The conversation lulled as a half moon slowly rose out of the water. As it climbed, reflections of light danced off every wave from the raft to the horizon like water running over a sheet of cracked and jagged mirrors. Clouds, invisible in the dark, now appeared and provided a dramatic boundary to the endless sky.

Vilma's quiet hum blended in with the steady lap of waves, but she stopped abruptly when a dank, putridly sweet smell of rot suddenly hit them. "What the—"

"*Coño*, man, what died?" Juan pinched his nose.

They searched the black water with urgency as the stench got increasingly worse. When Maria covered her nose with her arm and turned face down on the raft, Juan feared she'd get sick again.

A dull thud sounded against one of the drums.

"What was that?" Maria said.

Ernesto held his breath and looked into the water. An immobile form bobbed in the waves.

"What is it—oh!"

"What?" Maria peered over the edge and spotted the floating mass. The curiosity on her face turned to horror. The remains of a human torso bobbed in the waves, its reddish-black ribs clicking against the drum.

Her scream startled Juan.

"Jesus Christ, Maria!"

"It's ... a body," Maria said through the hand clenched over her nose and mouth.

"A man, I think, or what's left of one," Ernesto said. "He probably drowned in the exodus."

Juan glanced at the decomposed corpse, then turned away and wiped at his watering eyes. He fumbled with the oar to push the remains away, but the body trailed in the draft of their light wake.

"Ernesto, please ..." Maria said. "The smell, it's ..."

Ernesto took the other oar and the two men paddled hard until the breeze diluted the stench and the torso faded into the darkness. Maria took her arm away from her face and sniffed the air like an animal afraid of predators.

"Is it gone?

"I don't see anything," Manuel said. "*Oye*, that was bad. It reminded me of my old cat after the wild dogs got to it."

"That wasn't a cat, old man, that was a *Cubano*," Juan said.

"Maybe your comrades in the Guardia shot him and left him for the sharks."

"Stop it, Ernesto!" Maria said.

The discovery had Juan jumpy. He knew that same fate could happen to any of them. The group settled into awkward positions where they watched the color of the clouds change with the angle of the moon—a bad omen. Juan feared that his dreams would be full of those bloodied remains left by whatever had ripped off the arms and legs.

He shivered and wondered how the rest of them felt. Manuel was hard to read, and something about that irritating smile was curious. Juan remembered that he'd managed a sugar farm for the government and figured there had to be more to him than met the eye. Paranoia was a necessity that kept Juan alive on the streets, and it caused him to think that something about Manuel didn't fit. What it was he didn't yet know.

Maria edged up on her elbows and glanced at the others. Everyone was lying shoulder to shoulder with their faces turned to the sky. All but Juan, who sat alone and stared into the shifting waters. He saw Maria studying his profile. They locked eyes, and she turned away, but Juan felt the sudden urge to talk to her.

"So why did you leave Pinar del Rió?"

Her eyes sparkled, glimmers of gold in the moonlight.

"I think I always realized there was no future for me there. I watched my older friends ... many of them went to school and really had dreams, you know? But they always ended up in the same place, picking leaves on tobacco farms for the government."

Juan nodded and glanced at Ernesto to see if he was really asleep.

"When I turned nineteen I had a vision that I'd wind up like my grandmother. It scared me to death. I left my father and brothers a note and what little money I had and snuck off in the middle of the night with a plan to reach my aunt's apartment in Centro Havana. She was one of the few relatives I had in the city, and I knew if I could get there she'd help me."

"Damn, girl. That took some *cojones* to just up and leave like that."

"Well, she was definitely surprised when I showed up, that's for sure. She introduced me to an entirely different world, and I realized that in leaving home I hadn't thought about what would come next."

"Living in the city takes some getting used to."

She looked at him with a surprisingly confident grin. "You have no idea. But before long, my aunt helped me get the job at the cybercafe. She thought it'd be a good place until I figured out what I wanted. That's when I met him." Maria paused to check Ernesto, who was on his side with his eyes closed. "There's a lot about my past Ernesto doesn't even know yet," she whispered.

The subtle smile again came over her lips, and Juan wondered what she meant. She changed the subject before he could ask.

"My father was long gone. He was in the military, and once he got home after Angola, he disappeared."

Angola. Just the name caused a tug on Juan's heart.

"My mother was in Havana too," Maria continued. "But we were never close, at least until I met Ernesto. She was thrilled about our being together, until Ernesto and his father had that awful fight. Everything happened so fast, and the next thing I knew, Ernesto was insisting we go to America. My mother was so mad she wanted to kill Señor del Torres."

"I thought you didn't know about their fight?"

Maria hesitated. "I didn't, exactly. I knew they had fought, but not about ... well, you know. But angry as my mother was, she thought I'd be better off with Ernesto in America than alone in Havana."

Juan sighed and had a sudden urge to put his hand on her shoulder, but he thought better of it.

"Let's hope she's right," he said.

Maria had turned out to face the sea.

"I MISS HAVANA already," Vilma said.

Everyone on the raft had been half asleep, but suddenly all eyes were on her.

"Not me," Juan said. "If I ever see the Malecón again, it will mean we failed."

Vilma smacked him on the arm. "Hey, I lived on the Malecón."

"Ah, you were lucky," Maria said. "Life in Havana was so much more fun than the countryside. Maybe Miami will be like that."

"I'll miss looking out over the ocean ..." Vilma stopped and looked at the sea, then laughed. "Maybe I won't miss the ocean after this voyage, but I will miss my view of the Morro Castle."

"Just be glad you won't be there when Fidel dies," Ernesto said. He rolled over to face them. "All hell will break loose, especially when some other relic of the revolution takes over. It's going to be a mess, and it won't be long from now either."

"The revolution's not about one man," Vilma said. "You of all people should know that."

"A mess?" Manuel said. "You should have seen it before the revolution."

"He's right," Vilma said. "I worked at the Hotel Nacional when Castro marched into Havana. You should have seen the rich Americans and Europeans flee. No more treating Cuba like a cheap whore they could come and grope whenever they wanted to." She shook her head defiantly. "Life may not have been easy since then, especially during the Special Period, but at least the people are treated better and we have more self-respect."

"You people are crazy," Juan said. "You're like dogs that are so used to being beaten that when the beatings stop, you think your master loves you. I grew up in the Revolution and you can have it. You're right, old man, I don't know how bad it was before, and I don't give a shit. It's crap now, and even though Castro does nothing but blame the Yanquis, everybody from my generation wants to go to America."

Vilma stuck her jaw out and leaned toward Juan.

"Men do not shape destiny. Destiny produces the man for the hour."

Juan looked at her but said nothing.

"That's one of my favorite quotes from *El Presidente*. Do you know what it means, Juan?"

He shrugged.

"See? Exactly. Instead of staying and working to bring change, you just run away, huh?"

"Damn right, old woman. We're not all revolutionaries. Why should I have to fight my own government to have a decent life? It's easier to leave, and like a million before me, that's exactly what I'm doing. The only way I'll ever go back is in style." He glared at her. "What's with you, anyway? If you're so crazy about Castro and this bullshit revolution, why did you leave?"

"Nothing's ever going to change," Ernesto said. "The Americans are too stubborn to back down, and Castro's too proud to budge."

"*El Comandante* is proud for a reason," Vilma said. "He's a great leader!"

"Who cares?" Juan asked. "Why are we even talking about this?"

"Cuba may be a small country, but *El Comandante* has given us international recognition, and he refuses to be manipulated."

"Then answer my question." Juan said. "If you're so devoted to the revolution, what the hell are you doing on this raft?"

The question silenced Vilma, but everyone stared at her to await an answer.

"I didn't want to leave." Her voice was much quieter now. "I had no choice."

"What's that supposed to mean?"

"It means that I have cancer, my breasts are riddled with tumors." She bunched her hands into fists. "And thanks to the damned embargo …"

Ay yi yi. Way to go, dumbass.

"We have an amazing medical system in Cuba—for most things—but not this. My husband died from cancer ten years ago. Waiting for treatment that never came. Things are no better today. The list is so long I'd probably die waiting too."

Maria placed an arm around her shoulder and gave her a squeeze.

Vilma said, "The only reason I'm going to America is for surgery and chemotherapy."

"Even though it's the American government that denies you treatment," Juan said.

Vilma bit her lip, but Juan could see her jaw quivering.

"I'll come home, one way or another, I'll be back." Vilma said. "I'm not interested in chasing fantasies in America like you, Juan. When I get well, I'll come back to Cuba." She swallowed hard then looked to the sky. "And then one day, hopefully many years from now, I'll be buried next to my husband."

6

THE GLASS WHIZZED by Raúl Castro's head and smashed against the wall, sending wet shards in all directions. Raúl, having ducked, looked up at his brother, surprise mixed with anger in his eyes.

"They must suffer!" Fidel hissed through gritted teeth.

Raúl sighed. Though Fidel surely regretted throwing the glass, he said nothing about it.

"For revenge or a deterrent?"

"Does it matter?" Fidel said.

"We'll be ready in a few days. If they thought the exodus was bad, wait until they see what we have in store for them."

Anger gave way to satisfaction in Fidel's eyes.

"Our sources in Miami say the city's like a shaken soda bottle ready to burst," Raúl said. "Riots are brewing because they've kept fifty thousand *balseros* living like dogs in pens, and their Congress has the audacity to condemn our human rights record."

"If fifty thousand survived, another fifty thousand must have drowned," Fidel said.

"Still, there were more Marielitos."

"Yes, but that was different. You can't count what we ourselves engineered."

Raúl smiled. "That was a masterstroke."

"And it's time for another, but we will make this even worse."

"As it should be," Raúl said. "Winslow can't be trusted. One day he talks about easing our people's suffering at the hands of their embargo, the next he sends down the conniving lapdogs of the expatriate lunatics as his emissaries."

Fidel pursed his lips and let out a sharp breath. "They've broken the Migration Accords, and for that they must pay."

"The military has been scouring the country for boats, and we can have 90,000 people massed for shipment within three days."

"Good. The jails?"

Raúl nodded. "Also the hospitals and AIDS sanitariums. The police will sweep the streets to collect the derelicts last."

"We don't want riots here as well."

"We've never wavered from fighting for our sovereignty on the world stage."

"Where our closest neighbor holds the leading role." Fidel sat back in his chair and stared at a painting of a worker cutting sugar cane.

"The pain of a hundred years of bad relations has returned like a herpes sore," Raúl said. "I have the list of the worms who fled."

"Let me see it." Fidel scanned the names in silence, the list longer than either of them expected, many they knew personally. He let it slip from his hands and fall to the floor, where he looked down and spat upon it. "Traitors, all of them."

Raúl nodded.

"What's the latest body count we've collected?"

"Nearly four thousand."

"*Ay mi madre.*" Fidel rubbed his eyes. "All these people chose death over the revolution. Fools. How can we preserve our progress and hand down our legacy when so many flee? We *must* prevent others from leaving, and we *must* mend the wounds caused by those that have."

"The Guardia Frontera are still running double patrols," Raúl said. "Youth all over the country are impatient. We'll lose some to flight just as others lose theirs to drugs. It's regretful, but inevitable."

"We've become old men, Raúlito. I hate to admit that I feel disconnected with our youth, but look at that list." Fidel pointed toward the floor. "The Americans reported that the majority of these refugees are less than thirty years old. Many were university students educated by the revolution that now go to America to seek the phantom rewards of capitalism."

Raúl dug in his ear, examined some wax, then flung it onto the floor. "For all we know, the Americans might send them back."

"We won't take them back. We'll jail them all so they won't pollute our population."

Raúl knew that in his heart his brother felt differently. *If only they would come back.*

"We can't continue at this pathetic rate of production and keep the regime viable when our people are leaving by the tens of thousands. If we increase tourism we can generate more hard currency, but in doing that we overexpose our people to western culture and expose our poverty. It will be like the fifties under Batista if we're not careful." Fidel shook his head. "That will blow up in our faces, just like it did in his."

"At least our joint ventures with foreign companies are profitable."

"On paper yes, but—" The phone rang and Fidel lowered his ear to the intercom.

"Captain Pino is here," the secretary said.

He turned to his brother. "Captain Pino?"

"Guardia Frontera."

The door opened and a youngish man in full naval dress strode in. He stepped right up to the desk and saluted the president and vice president.

"Captain Pino, sir!"

Fidel slowly stood and towered over the short but dapper man. He returned the salute and the captain eased his stance from ramrod erect to a medium starch. The brothers exchanged a covert look of amusement as Pino launched into the latest statistics.

"It's double the usual activity," Pino said as if he were personally responsible for the effort. "We're scouring the entire area out to the fifteen-kilometer limit. We destroyed a speedboat today, killing fourteen, sir!"

"That is a good thing, Captain?" Fidel asked, his eyebrows tensed.

"Why, yes, sir. There are fewer boats leaving our coast." The voice was almost human now, the man no doubt having expected praise.

Raúl sighed. *That's because there are hardly any boats left, you idiot.*

"Ignore him," he said as soon as the captain was gone. "He was only trying to impress us with his enthusiasm. No one wants to see our own people killed."

"I want the papers to drop all mention of the body count. The point's been made—and the Guardia are too enthusiastic. If they find any more bodies, have them weighted down and sunk. No more dead countrymen brought ashore."

"Good idea," Raul said.

Fidel began to pull at his beard. "Get ready to alert the Guardia of our new plans. Instead of intercepting *balseros*, they are to assist them. Instead of counting our dead, we'll proceed with our plan to ship out our criminals and terminally ill. Let America have our dregs along with the intelligentsia they've already taken from us, no?"

Raúl was comforted at his brother's resurgence of passion and anger.

"That will give the foreign press something to talk about besides speculating on what happens when I die." This wasn't something Fidel spoke of often. "That, I can tell you, is starting to bother me."

"What, that you will die?" Raúl smiled.

"Imagine if after a lifetime of devotion to the revolution—and after forty-two years of surviving the American blockade—my successor succumbs to American demands. I've never uttered these words aloud before, but since the damn exodus, thoughts like these have been rattling around in my head."

Raúl was quiet.

"One hundred years of American oppression, Raúl. The idea of my successor bungling Cuba's reconnection with the United States is my biggest concern. History will absolve me for subjecting Cuba to suffering and isolation as a worthwhile price to pay for sovereignty and independence."

"But?"

Fidel rubbed his hands downward across his cheeks and unsteadily rose to his feet, passion burning anew in his eyes.

"But ... I'd like to oversee the transition to ensure that the great strides we've made are not jeopardized." He shook his fist as he spoke. "I must make sure Cuba doesn't sell its soul to expedite growth, only to give up all we've gained. Is that too much to want?"

Raúl was not surprised. His brother's success was fueled by his insatiable need to control everything. Why would this be any different?

7

WINSLOW AND TERRI TURNER sat in the darkened Oval Office huddled over an impromptu dinner. A cheeseburger for the president, a turkey burger for Turner, potato chips, cold beer and chardonnay. It was fast and easy, and the kitchen could whip it up to order in about fifteen minutes. Van Morrison crooned from a speaker in the background, and as they often did when working through difficult situations, the two brainstormed ideas.

Turner shook her head and stared off toward the floor. Winslow recognized the body language and sensed she was holding out on him.

"What?" Seeing her frown, he braced himself.

"Persico thinks your idea's crazy."

"When I want his opinion, I'll tell him what it is. As hard as I fought to get him confirmed as attorney general, he needs to do better than that."

"Don't get me wrong—he's trying, he's trying hard. It's just that he thinks the odds are too steep."

"I'll worry about the odds. He just needs to find me enough wiggle room in Helms-Burton and the Cuban Democracy Act to pull the rug out from under Spinelli. Without that, we'll be relegated to the back seat of our own car."

"I've got meetings tomorrow about the emergency session with several illustrious congressmen," Turner said. "Each of them has some kind of legislative package up for discussion, and all of them want your help. How much latitude do I have in negotiating?"

"With who?"

"King's focused on NIH, Simon's still flogging the gun-control bill—"

"Forget him."

"Hammond on equal employment, Tower on anti-ballistic missiles and Sudarsky on diabetes and asthma research—"

"All right, I get the picture. Use your discretion. But keep in mind that the only chance we have to stop Castro from opening the floodgates is to delay Spinelli from sending aid to Florida. Money to help them will signal that we have officially broken the Migration Accords. I want to help those people, but the solution's got to be part of a bigger picture."

"Cuba's lost so many high-level politicians, academicians and intellectuals—you know Castro is furious," she said.

Winslow nodded. "I can't imagine what that would be like to face such a mess. Well, I can. It would be chaos."

"But from chaos can come opportunity."

"That is the morsel of hope I'm counting on," Winslow said.

"But can we rally support?"

"Hell, I don't think there's a congressman out there who doesn't know Spinelli's loyalties to the Cuban American Coalition are his top priority."

"They're his largest financial supporter, by far. Without the CAC, Spinelli would be up the creek without a canoe, much less a paddle."

"Letting Spinelli speak for me in Cuba was the dumbest thing I've done since taking office."

"I tried to warn you—"

He held up his palm. "The House's recent vote in favor of ending the travel ban proves we can count on some support there—"

"There will be major opposition to ending the embargo in order to salvage the accords and solve the exodus mess, George."

"I have no choice but to try. I mean, hell, how could we send those people back? Morally speaking. We build up their hopes by announcing our interest in ending the embargo, and then the glimmer twins double-cross Castro and criticize his human rights record and demand democracy. Hell, if I were Cuban I'd have given up too."

Turner spun her dark hair around her index finger. "Spinelli thinks we can starve Castro out."

"Same old story."

She hesitated, then shook her head. "With as much diplomatic energy as we're focusing in the Middle East, do we really want to fight the Cuba issue now?"

"What choice do we have? The exodus isn't going away, and the law says we're supposed to send them back. Unless, of course, you and Persico find me some room to maneuver."

She grunted and looked around the room, her gaze stopping on a twenty-year-old picture of them next to Winslow Oil Company's first gusher after George Sr. passed away. Their arms were around each other, and they were entirely covered with thick black oil. Neither of them was recognizable, with the exception of their huge smiles.

Winslow followed her glance, and out of the corner of her eye she noticed him subtly shake his head.

"Those were the days, huh?"

She smiled warmly at him. "Sure were."

"You know the biggest irony of this whole mess? Winslow Oil actually once owned a bunch of oil fields and what's left of an old refinery right outside of Havana."

The color drained from Turner's face.

"Oh God, you're right. I forgot all about that. They came with the Southern Oil acquisition, what, a dozen or so years ago?" Her eyes became wider. "That's not—"

"It was '87, I think, but there's nothing to worry about there. It was the Houston refinery and Mexican leases we wanted. The Cuban assets were worthless."

She looked up at the microphones in the ceiling and stood up.

"Maybe we *should* let the exodus Cubans stay and leave the embargo alone."

"You know I'd love to, but what about the next bunch? Send them back under the old Migration Accords when we let the first ones stay?"

"It's a fine line, George. No matter what we do, it could backfire."

"That's why we have to act quickly. Dropping the embargo altogether will help us keep the coalition going, and I'm convinced it will work to change Cuba's politics. The signals we got out of Havana were great before Spinelli and Dunleavy upset the applecart."

"This isn't like digging blindly for oil, George, you know that."

"Maybe so. But my gut tells me Castro's ready to deal. And if he does pull the plug on the Accords, they won't need boats anymore."

She cocked her head. "What do you mean by that?"

"Thousands dead already, Terri. Things keep up at that rate and you'll be able to walk from Havana to Key West using corpses as stepping-stones."

A SEA OF PEOPLE filled the horizon like an invasion force. Vikings, bare-chested rafters, children, uniformed men, tall ships, cruise ships, canoes, sailboats, speedboats, swimmers, and giant icebergs appearing from nowhere, dotting the sea. And then there were the bodies: floating infants; grandmothers; naked women; sailors; friends from Texas; teenagers; Senator Spinelli and Fidel Castro all washing atop the waves; some with eyes open and hair streaming in the water, others looking perfectly alert, but dead just the same.

The apocalyptic dream swirled in George Winslow's mind like an electrical fire in a phone booth, and whenever the scene shifted, he twisted in the bedding. After what seemed like hours, he got up, pulled on his robe and stepped into his slippers. With the light on in the bathroom, he checked himself in the mirror. His hair was a mess, but it was his eyes that made him groan. Red, bloodshot and baggy, they were always the best harbinger to his state of mind.

"You look like crap," he informed the mirror.

It had been hard enough getting to sleep to begin with, and now this dream. He couldn't stop thinking about how much was on the line, and how quickly his credibility had been jeopardized. What infuriated him most was that there was so much to gain by normalizing relations with Cuba. There was a huge political, social and humanitarian triumph within his administration's reach, he was sure of that. The only question was how to get there.

He kissed his sleeping wife on the cheek and retreated to the small office next to their bedroom. An idea had emerged from the fog of his nightmare, and he couldn't wait until morning to pursue it. He thought for a moment before picking up the telephone. Ten digits later, he heard the familiar message of Senator Roy Perkins.

"George Winslow, Roy. It's late, well, early Tuesday morning really. I need to see you as soon as possible. Please give me a call when you get this, it's urgent."

Roy Perkins and George Winslow had both come to Washington after the same election, one a former governor, the other a former state senator, and both from Texas. Perkins was a dyed-in-the-wool Democrat but honest as the day was long, and one of the few people Winslow felt he could really trust outside his own party.

With a big yawn, two Tums in his stomach, and renewed confidence from his idea, the president returned to bed. He was asleep before his head hit the pillow.

8

"I'LL HAVE A BIG car, a house with a swimming pool, a view of the ocean, and food, lots of food," Juan said.

"Food …" Maria whispered.

"That's it? That's all you care about?" Vilma asked.

"Oh yeah, I forgot about women. Lots of women too: *Latinas*, blonds, redheads, brown sugar, Americans, Europeans and Canadians, all of them."

"Hoarding is against the law," Vilma said.

Juan laughed.

Manuel stared into the waves. *I just want to see my family again.*

"It's morning, Juan. You can wake up from your dream," Ernesto said. "Are you relying on your charm and good looks to make these wishes come true?"

"You had those things in Cuba and left it all behind. Now you're going to criticize me for wanting the same thing? We're just poor *campesinos* who had nothing but a day-to-day struggle."

"That's not true, Juan. Not all of us were always poor," Vilma said.

"You were a rich heiress or something?"

She shook her head and nodded toward Manuel.

"You?" Juan asked.

"His family owned a huge farm in Birán, just down the road from Ángel Castro's plantation," she said.

Manuel, sunburned and unshaven, slowly turned to face the others, and everyone except Vilma scrutinized him in disbelief.

"Actually," he said, "Ángel Castro's twenty-six thousand acres was leased from United Fruit Company's two hundred forty thousand. Ours was only six thousand acres, but my family owned it."

Juan and Ernesto's jaws dropped. Vilma winked at him.

"Six thousand? You've got to be kidding me?" Juan said. "A sugar plantation? Yours?"

Manuel shrugged. "My father's. When the Revolution succeeded I was in the middle of my first cut as the farm manager. He wanted to focus on selling our sugar, and I was to run the field operation, but ..."

"So what the hell happened?" Juan said.

"The Revolution happened. Our lives were turned upside down."

"Damn ..." Juan winced. The government had taken his farm.

With a wave of his wrist, Manuel dismissed the growing atmosphere of pity.

"It was a lifetime ago," he said. "That was supposed to be the most important year of my life. I remember thinking it was the beginning of such a glorious future and wondering how large I could grow the farm for my boys. But then ... well, that was not to be the case, at least for me."

"All the farms were taken," Vilma said.

Manuel said, "The Revolution was supposed to be temporary, with elections soon to follow. My family had supported the Revolution. Fidel and Raúl were like us—neighbors, friends, patriots. Then their henchmen came and kicked us out."

"You lived near Ángel Castro?" Maria asked. "Fidel and Raúl's father?"

"Ángel's farm was down the road, but I never knew Fidel and Raúl. They were off at boarding school from the time they were young."

"What happened to their farm?"

"Gone like the rest. Everything was taken under the guise of agrarian reform."

With his knees pulled to his chest, his chin resting on top of them, Ernesto had remained quiet throughout Manuel's revelation. He was undoubtedly accustomed to hearing history from his father's side—the revolutionary account.

"What about your father, Ernesto?" Juan said. "Where was the 'hero' during all of this?"

"He fought alongside Che Guevara," Ernesto said.

"Señor del Torres saved Che in battle," Maria said. "That's why Ernesto is named after him. Ernesto Che Guevara."

Ernesto shot her a glance. He looked embarrassed.

Juan, who had started to tap the conga beat against the deck again, suddenly stopped.

"And what did the hero do when the fighting was over?"

"Leave it alone, Juan," Ernesto said.

"Why? What's to hide?"

Ernesto crossed his arms. "What do you think? He was in Havana helping establish the new government."

"So that's when he became the big shot?"

"Why don't you do something useful, like catch a fish, or check the ropes," Ernesto said.

"I guess you don't want to answer the question—"

"He became minister of sugar when the nationalization process started, all right? Now drop it, Juan. I'm done with my father, I'm not going to discuss him, and I'm done with being needled by a street urchin!"

Juan, of course, wasn't done. "So if your father took the foreign companies' land, did he steal from his countrymen too? Like Manuel's family?"

Ernesto balled his hands into fists. "I warned you!"

Juan coiled his body to strike, but Maria grabbed his arm just as he was about to spring. He whipped his head toward her, and it must have been the desperate look on her face that stopped him cold. Ernesto saw only that he stopped.

Manuel sat forward. "Let me tell you, our farm was lost to the Revolution, and whether Ernesto's father was involved or not, it doesn't matter. It's all history now. If I had held on to the bitterness for the last forty years it would have killed me long ago, if not physically, then emotionally."

"That's right, Manuel. You see?" Vilma said.

"When the land takings first happened, there was panic. My father wanted to fight to get our property back, but we sent our family out of the country instead. He decided we should get them settled temporarily in Florida. I stayed behind and met with other landowners that clumsily tried to plan a revolt. Most were shot, so I disappeared into the fields to await an uprising. It never came."

"Our government for the people," Juan said.

"Listen," Manuel said. "Our country had no control over its industries. We were a slave colony with the foreign sugar companies as our masters. It took me years, tens of years, but one day I realized that my loss didn't matter. Cuba finally had control over its own destiny."

The old man sighed and surveyed the endless water and sky. The horizon was clear now. Clouds had formed to the north, and the water was a calm bottle green.

"My father lived thirty more years and died at ninety, just ten years ago," Manuel continued. "My sons and daughter are grown, married and have children of their own…And my wife's still alive."

"Why did you stay in Cuba so long?" Maria asked.

"We thought one day my family would reclaim our farm. Years go by quickly when others control your life. And then it was too hard to leave."

"You could have left during Mariel," Juan said.

"Like you, I can't swim. And rafts? Well, they scare me—including this one though not so much now that I'm used to it. The State let me manage the cuts on the land that had belonged to my family, and I grew accustomed to my life. Birán hasn't changed much, and I just *couldn't* leave. The stars kept me company."

"And your family's been in Florida all this time," Juan said. "So close…"

"My father was a strong man, neither geography nor politics could defeat him. Once he settled in America he leased some land in western Florida and slowly built up another farm. As my sons grew, they worked the land. Now they have a big business."

Ernesto had been brooding since arguing with Juan, but he now perked up. "I plan to start a sugar company in America, or at least work for an American firm," he said. "I could be in an excellent position to help the company when the embargo is over, provided my father survives as the Minister of Sugar."

He was looking at Manuel, who seemed to be suppressing a smile.

"Perhaps I'll introduce you to my sons, Ernesto."

Juan's arms dropped from his lap, his knuckles knocked against the deck.

"I'm going to puke. If that's not the luck of the rich. Even when they're down and out, shit falls out of the sky."

Vilma laughed. "Ernesto, did you ever imagine this is how your life would go?"

"No way. If someone would have told me I'd leave Cuba, and on a raft? I'd have thought it as unlikely as God reaching down and plucking us off the water right now."

Vilma suddenly crossed herself. "Be careful, *compadre*, it's not wise to suggest such things to God."

"ROY BOY, HOW the hell are you?"

"Great, George, I mean, *Mr.* President."

"We go back too far for that. Let's just keep it at George, all right?"

Senator Roy Perkins nodded and sat down in one of the brown leather chairs in front of the Teddy Roosevelt desk in the Oval Office.

"Where's Terri this morning? She's usually here to watch your ass, isn't she?"

"Meeting with the Attorney General."

A slow smile spread over Perkins' face. "That's one fine woman there, George. Hell, my wife would never let me travel with a gal that good looking."

The president laughed. "Terri? Yeah, she's a looker, but she's also smarter than hell, Roy. My daddy knew how to pick his women, I'll give him that."

"Right," Perkins said. "I forgot they were, ah, an item."

"That's not what I meant. Daddy liked to hire women who would distract you with their looks, then kick your teeth in with their brains. Terri was the best—is the best."

"Sorry I missed her. Anyway, what's so important that you called me at 3:00 in the morning?"

"Hell, Roy, I just had a little insomnia. Those damn cheeseburgers, you know?"

"They'll do it." Perkins nodded, and the president had an uneasy feeling about what he saw in his guest's eyes.

"Hey, I wanted to thank you again for your support on the tax cut. We couldn't have got that done without it being a bipartisan effort, and you were a big help in rallying Democratic support," The president said with a Texas-sized smile.

"No problem. But you know I'm counting on your help with this welfare-reform bill. I'm getting stonewalled from the Republican side, and a couple kind words from you would go a long way."

The president nodded sharply and cleared his throat. The bill had been porked-up beyond recognition, but a deal was a deal. "Fair enough. But tell me, what's your opinion on this emergency session scheduled for Thursday?"

"You really want to know?"

"Give it to me straight, just like old times."

"The truth is, I think that you've…that Florida's been hung out to dry. Shoot, George, you haven't sent a dime to Miami, and you know as well as I do that the whole town's primed to go up like a dried-out mesquite bush in a lightning storm."

Crap.

"Think of what Florida's National Guard has been up against. Then you've got the police and the Dade County Task Force scrambling to meet demands they just don't have the resources for. Seems to me we've got to do something to help, and if an emergency session of congress is what it takes…"

Winslow held up his hand, palm forward.

"Do you understand my side? What I'm faced with—hell, what we'll all be faced with if we fold on the Migration Accords instead of cutting a deal with Castro?"

"Castro's threats don't change the situation in Florida. We can't just sit back and leave those people in tents and expect the Sunshine State to foot the bill. Dammit, George, it's been a month."

"I realize that, but the way I see it, there has to be a larger plan here, which means we have to negotiate a broader deal with Castro."

"Why should we deal with Castro?"

Winslow stood and walked over to his desk. He opened a drawer and retrieved a thick envelope with the CIA emblem on its cover.

"That's why," he said.

Perkins' eyebrows arched.

"This is eyes-only, Roy. I'll save you some time. The executive summary pretty much says it all."

He gave him a moment to read and watched his face carefully until Roy's eyebrows rose even more sharply, then continued.

"Spinelli and Dunleavy humiliated Castro and he wants to get even—in spades, as you can see by that report. If word gets out on this, there'll be pandemonium in Florida."

"Damn, I see your point. You have something in mind, I take it."

"I can't exactly say just yet, but I'm working on a plan that'll involve a much broader solution. One that will not only diffuse the mess our colleagues created but also bring about the change in Cuban politics we've always wanted. What I need is time."

"You plan to share this with Congress?"

"I can't without compromising our sources. At least not yet."

"Then unless Castro unleashes his hordes before the emergency session, you've got the better part of three days left to figure something out. Is that going to be enough?"

"Not much choice is there. And what do you mean three days left? I thought the session was scheduled for Thursday."

"Friday. It's scheduled for Friday."

"But Spinelli told Terri three days."

"When he and Dunleavy called for the session, they said they were going to give you three days' notice. If you didn't do anything by close of business Thursday, then we'd have the session on Friday. Now, I don't have any horses in this race, but it seems to me you're in a fix. If you don't share that intelligence report with Spinelli and Dunleavy, then the emergency session's going happen, and based on what I'm hearing, the consensus will be to send immediate aid to Florida."

"That's exactly what Castro wants. It'll give him the perfect excuse to launch his human salvo. You can help prevent that, Roy. You can persuade some of your colleagues to either delay the vote, or to vote against sending aid just yet."

Roy Perkins sat solidly in his chair while the president paced the room.

"What are the other Democrats saying?"

"They're focused on the obvious, that Florida needs the money. It's a done deal."

"Done deal?"

Perkins nodded solemnly.

The president took a deep breath, exhaled it slowly.

"Roy, that's why I need your help. This is a hell of a lot more important than anything we ever worked on back in Texas. You help me now, I'll owe you big time."

In the silence that followed Perkins didn't move in his chair, but Winslow knew he was fighting the invisible demons that would be warning him not to go against the grain on what was supposed to be a slam-dunk in Congress.

Finally, Perkins sagged in his chair. "You can always veto it, right?"

"And look like an even bigger jerk? That would be political suicide," Winslow said.

"All right, I'll do what I can. But I can't make any promises."

"Great, that's great. I knew you'd understand." Winslow's big grin was back.

"You should talk to Dunleavy," Perkins said.

"Are you kidding?"

"It might sound crazy, but the rest of Florida's so upset about this mess, he might have to repatriate the Exodus Cubans if the emergency session fails. That's not playing too well with the Cuban-Americans, and the CAC's threatened to kill his funding. So the way I see it, Dunleavy's well on his way to becoming a pariah in his own state, too."

The news tickled the president in a way nothing had in a long time. Could this be a chink in the glimmer twins' armor? Time to divide and conquer.

9

TERRI TURNER BRISTLED at the gaping stares she received from congressional staffers as she walked the halls of the Hart building. They weren't the kind of stares she was accustomed to, more like they were accompanied by snickers behind her back.

I wore a bra. She checked her skirt. *My zipper's up. What's the deal?* And then it hit her. *They know why I'm here. The fix must be in.*

She swallowed hard and sped up her pace to Senator Bell's office. After a ten-minute wait, Bell's assistant said that the Senator would see her.

"Ms. Turner." Bell stepped forward, offered his wrinkled hand, and apologized for the wait. He motioned toward the round conference table in the corner of his office, and she sighed at the cut-glass donkey placed in its center.

After exchanging pleasantries, Turner clasped her damp palms together and placed her elbows on the table. "We're getting a lot of dangerous signals out of Cuba, Senator."

In a flash of conscience she remembered how she used to entice the State Senators in Texas with the same pose, the difference being that when she was in her thirties she would wear low-cut blouses to expedite cooperation.

Senator Bell stared her straight in the eye.

"I'm sharing this with you because of your position on the Foreign Relations Committee, but it has to stay confidential." She paused to let the fact that the White House was letting him in on classified information register, then sailed on.

"We have new intelligence that Castro is planning to unleash another and much more damaging boatlift because he thinks we've broken the Migration Accords."

"Is the president suggesting we incarcerate the refugees indefinitely?" His southern accent was thick, very South Carolina.

"Of course not—"

"Because they've suffered enough. The president ignored the wet foot dry foot rule and allowed them to come to Florida rather than sending them back." She held her breath. "But we cannot let some tin-pot dictator like Castro terrorize us and determine our policies, especially when it comes to human rights."

Turner had to look around the glass donkey to meet Bell's eyes.

"You're absolutely..." She stopped, thrust her arm out and slid the donkey aside. "Senator, the Exodus Cubans have created a difficult dilemma, and the president needs your help to flesh out a solution to the bigger problem."

"Dilemma? How do you consider this a dilemma?"

"Based on the existing constraints, we're damned if we do and damned if we don't."

Bell glanced at his cut-glass donkey and sat back. "I'm sorry, Ms. Turner, you'll have to excuse me. I'm just a simple country boy. Would you mind explaining that a little further?"

"That's what I was doing, Senator, let me continue. If we let the Cubans stay, Castro creates a bigger mess for Florida by sending thousands more people our way. If we send them back, we're human rights hypocrites. The president wants to do something more profound by changing our policy and engaging Cuba instead of continuing to make their people suffer. That will take the wind out of Castro's sails a lot faster than the game of brinkmanship we've pursued for so long."

Bell's forehead became a series of deep wrinkles, and a contrived air of surprise filled his eyes.

"The president wants to *embrace* Castro?"

Not being a career politician, Turner had little patience for feigned ignorance and games. As a businesswoman, she had negotiated multi-billion dollar oil deals with men who were a lot shrewder than Senator Bell, and at times like these Turner had to remind herself that she was here to help the man who had made her wealthy beyond her dreams.

"We've done nothing but try to smother and destroy Castro for 40-plus years, using the most aggressive policies imaginable. We've intentionally starved their people, and when the Soviet Union crumbled, and we had the chance to be the white knight and come to Cuba's rescue, we just kicked them harder with the Cuban Democracy Act and Helms-Burton. The bottom line is that none of that has worked."

"So he *does* want to embrace Castro?"

Turner bit her lip. "Don't be ridiculous. He realizes we'll never get rid of Castro, or whoever his handpicked successors might be, if we continue the same failed course. The president wants to establish better relations with Cuba as a means to bring about democracy there. Unfortunately, Senators Spinelli and Dunleavy deviated from that plan, and we got the Exodus instead. Now Senator Spinelli has exacerbated the problem by calling for this emergency session, which will end in disaster."

"You need a glass of water, or something?"

"What we need is your help."

A laugh surprised the chief of staff. "You know," he said, "I've been on the Foreign Relations Committee for fourteen years. I was first elected to the House of Representatives in 1972, and then came to the Senate in 1982. I'm very familiar with Cuban-American relations, and I agree that at some point things need to change, preferably when Castro is dead and gone. But right now, we have fifty thousand people who risked their lives for freedom, and they're being treated like cattle in Florida. I'm sorry, Ms. Turner, this can't wait. We'll have to count on the Coast Guard and the Navy to repel those hordes you're referring to, if in fact Fidel Castro does what you say."

Thousands of additional people would die, and Florida's infrastructure would burst if more refugees got through. There was just no sense in pointing that out—at least not with Senator Bell. She stood to leave.

"Thank you for seeing me, Senator. Do what you think will be best for those people, the State of Florida and the thousands of additional Cubans who will soon be on your doorstep."

Turner checked her watch as she stormed past the assistant, already late for her next meeting. *Next time, I'm digging out one of my old blouses.*

TOCORORO BIRDS FLUTTERED UNDER the mid-day sun, their brilliant blue, white and red plumage sparkling against the dark green canopy where they darted after bugs, suckled pools of dew from the troughs of flowers and chattered incessantly to one another. Oblivious to the walls that surrounded the small compound, they were the only ones who could pass over the rusted chain link at will. Palm trees and thicker swaths of pine coated with strangler figs dotted the area between the squat concrete buildings inside the compound where patients languished in anonymity.

A military jeep kicked dirt and gravel onto the clinic's porch as it sped away, up the unpaved road leading to the highway. Doctor Emilio Cárdenas didn't notice the sound as pebbles ricocheted off the metal door of the cramped three-room clinic. The shock of Captain Roque's sudden visit and astonishing news had left the doctor with but one thought. All his work would soon be irrelevant.

When the Jeep's sound dissipated, the familiar cackle of the birds slowly returned but were lost on him. Dr. Cárdenas sat still, feeling smothered by the dead air. He abruptly stood, knocking his chair over backwards, and lost his balance. Reaching to steady himself, his hand slid on loose papers, flipping him sideways onto the floor.

"Are you all right, Doctor?"

He raised his eyes and focused on Able Lopez, who helped him up.

"What's the matter?" Able asked.

Dr. Cárdenas wanted to speak—but when his lips moved no sound followed.

"I'm going to get Norris, Doc. He's napping in our room."

"They can't do it." The doctor's voice was a whisper.

"Who can't do what?" Abel said.

The doctor tried to speak but began to cough and gag. He caught his breath, and a desperate, defeated look came over his face.

"The Government, they can't do it. They—" He started coughing again.

Able's eyes narrowed. Doctor Cárdenas knew that any mention of the Government made the patients nervous, and if they were threatening to do something that caused him such distress it would be beyond alarming to Able and the others.

He reached down, put his hand on Doctor Cárdenas's shoulder. "The Government can't do what?"

Able's hand on the doctor's shoulder was as light as a rag, but his voice had become shrill.

"They can't do *what*?"

"They're closing the sanitarium," the doctor said. "All of the sanitariums."

Able's eyes grew wide. "And the patients?"

"Everyone is being rounded up and shipped to America tomorrow," Doctor Cárdenas said.

"FRANK. WE'RE SERIOUSLY OUTNUMBERED," Turner said. "We're not having much luck with the Democrats, and the president— our country—is on a crash-course for disaster."

Senator Frank Hammond exhaled a heavy sigh. "It's a pretty tough sell. Help Florida and the fifty thousand people in tents or do nothing so Castro doesn't make things worse."

"You're missing the point. Nobody's saying 'do nothing'. The pres—"

"Both sides are too paranoid."

"Castro's the one who is paranoid. Who could blame him after the most powerful nation in the world has tried to topple his government for the past four decades."

Hammond took a bite from his sandwich. They were meeting in his office over a quick lunch. She knew he had been working feverishly to get a major bill on Equal Employment ready for ratification once the next session started, and the emergency session had left him strapped for time.

"Terri, I'm sensitive to the president's concerns, and Lord knows I'm interested in Cuba too, but at the moment I'm anxious to get my bill finished, get the emergency session over with and get back to Boston for Spring Break."

"What's your interest in Cuba, aside from this?"

Hammond smiled. "The Bank of Boston financed several sugar mills there in the '30's and '40's, and when Castro nationalized everything we lost millions." The statement was made matter-of-factly, probably because Hammond was too young to have been affected by the issue.

"Frankly, I'm on the fence," he said. "I'd like the embargo to end so we can work something out for our mills there, but it's hard to ignore their human rights policies. Plus Florida's a mess, Castro's a nut, and Spinelli's a shark. Not a good combination to risk my reputation on."

Turner sighed. "I couldn't summarize it any better, Frank, but the president needs your help. We need full Republican support to prevent Spinelli from making things worse, and then to take action to end this stalemate."

Hammond nodded his understanding, but Turner knew he was still undecided.

"If Castro dies, Frank, then another hard-liner will take over, probably Raúl Castro. And worse, with Cuba lacking any major foreign benefactor, they're open to countries hostile to the U.S. to establish trade, or even terrorist camps. Our future would be better served if we had an open relationship with the Cuban people instead of a hostile one."

Again, there was no response, though Turner sensed she had scored some points.

Frank Hammond had all the right credentials: he was quick on his feet, sharp as a razor and honest to a fault, but she could understand why he was, as he'd put it, "on the fence."

"Part of me thinks our history with Cuba is a typical Greek trage-dy," he said. "I know first-hand that the embargo was founded more on economics than ideology. All Castro did was change masters by trading the greedy yet capable Americans for the inept but opportunistic Russians."

"It's a tragedy all right, but we can still change the ending," Turner said.

"It's easy for us to sit back and be critical of history, but Eisenhower obviously never realized that he was playing chicken with a guy who ran cock-fights on his father's farm when he was a kid," Hammond said.

"True but—"

"Sorry, Terri, I've got to run. I hear what you're saying, and natural-ly I want to support the president. But I'll have to think about it."

Turner was back to wandering the halls of the Hart office building looking for the next senator on her list.

10

JUAN FOUGHT TO wrap the line back around his yo-yo and was finally rewarded when an aquamarine flash slashed through the moss-green water. When it broke the surface, the gold and blue shimmered brilliantly in the sun. Everyone was excited at the prospect of fresh food.

"Dorado!" Juan said.

Ernesto bent down to help him pull it on board, but at the last moment Juan tried to jerk it up on deck and the hook pulled free.

"Ay shit!"

"Why'd you do that? I was just about to grab him!"

"I'll handle the fishing. I'm an urchin and you're a big shot, remember?"

"We need food," Vilma said, "and you two need to cut it out. El Jefé says, 'If we work together, perseverance will give us victory.'"

"Will you quit quoting the Beard," Juan said.

She lifted her chin and crossed her arms.

"At least we know we can hook them," Maria said. "We'll catch the next one, right?"

Juan lit a cigarette instead of dropping his line in again.

Ernesto was pleased to see that Juan's last pack was almost gone. He turned to Maria, who pointed at the back of the raft.

"Something doesn't look right," she said. "That corner is lower than the rest."

All eyes turned to the back corner of the raft.

"Are the ropes loose again?" Manuel asked.

"I don't think so." Ernesto tugged at the twine. "Looks like one of the drums is taking on water. Where did you get them, Juan?"

"At the Marina Hemingway. They were empty oil drums."

"How did you attach them to the deck?"

"A friend of mine from the Guardia welded some metal rings to them. That's where we tied the ropes."

"We're in big trouble if one's not watertight."

Ernesto reached into the water and tried to tap on the back right drum. It was completely submerged except for where the loops connected it to the raft. *Not good.* Then he looked at the left drum. It bobbed buoyantly in the waves. A hollow metallic sound could be heard as he rapped his knuckles against it.

"Sounds a lot different, doesn't it? All right, Juan, here's your opportunity for heroism. You built this beauty, now jump in and check the—"

"I told you, I can't swim." He flicked his cigarette past Ernesto's head and into the water. "You check the fucking drum."

"Oh, how could I forget?" He paused. "By the way, I'm curious. What kind of ship did you serve on?"

"Get in the water and check the damn drum!"

"Seriously, what kind of—"

"A patrol boat, all right?" Juan reached for another cigarette.

"So this patrol boat, how many tons was it?" Ernesto said.

"How the hell would I know? You think I weighed it or something?" Juan looked at the others, then back at Ernesto. "You want to talk shit, or figure out what's wrong with the drum?"

Ernesto slowly stood up and removed his shirt and pants, lowered himself into the without a splash—and began to shiver.

"What do you think?" Manuel asked.

"I think the water's freezing. Hold on, I'm going under the platform." Ernesto inhaled and exhaled a few deep breaths, then sucked one in and disappeared.

Ernesto pulled himself under and groped around, finding an air space between the drums where he could breath. It was dark, but filtered sunlight trickled through the boards on the platform. He reached up to the exposed area on the submerged drum and tapped the tips of his fingers against it. There was a dull thud.

He stared at the drum and studied how it was attached to the raft, then watched as the water washed over the top and caressed the rings. He put his ear against the rusty drum and heard water sloshing around inside.

Damn.

Back on board, he wrapped his clothes around his shoulders and shivered in the breeze.

"It's full of water," he said. "Bubbles are coming out from the weld on one of the rings." Now more or less dried off, Ernesto pulled his clothes back on and turned to Juan. "Did you fill them with water to make sure they didn't leak?"

Juan started to speak but froze with his mouth open.

"I didn't think so. That's great, Juan. We've got six drums to float us across the ocean, and now one's full of water. How about the others? What if they leak too? Then what?"

Vilma said, "You told us you and your friend from the Guardia checked everything."

"Juan was never in the Guardia Frontera!" Ernesto said. "That was a lie to take our money."

"Shut up, Ernesto!"

"Quit bullshitting us, it's pointless now, we can't go back! You never spent one minute in the Guardia. I guarantee if you had, you'd remember the tonnage of your ship."

"That's not true," Vilma said. "Is it, Juan? You were in the Guardia, right?"

"Yeah, Captain, the Guardia Frontera. Where you learned to swim and tie knots.

"That's it!" Juan jumped to his feet, his eyes wild.

Ernesto was on his feet a half-second later, and they dove at each other like a pair of ten-point bucks during the rut. The raft dipped hard with the sudden weight change, the low end just below the surface as they wrestled. Water surged onto the deck. Manuel scuttled to the dry side, Maria struggled to her knees, and Vilma yelled at the top of her voice.

"Juan! Ernesto! Stop it! You'll sink us!"

The two men were locked in a death clutch, each trying to force the other down. They lost their balance and careened into Maria—knocked her to the deck. Ernesto had one of Juan's arms and was twisting it. Juan had hold of Ernesto's head and was pushing it down.

"Stop it!"

They were deaf to the others. Their swinging arms and twisted legs suddenly veered into Vilma and nearly knocked her off the edge. Her eyes turned as wild as theirs. Her scream was so loud it stopped both men cold, and everyone turned to face her. Vilma had ripped her shirt open, revealing her bare breasts.

"Look! Look at these!" she howled as she squeezed one of her breasts. "They're filled with cancer! My own breasts! If I don't get to America, they'll kill me! I won't let you do it first when I've given up everything for this!"

With every sentence her voice had become louder. Now she was out of breath and panted on the brink of hyperventilation. Juan, also breathing heavily, turned away. Ernesto saw Maria sobbing hysterically and bent down to hug her, unaware that they had nearly knocked her into the water. Manuel picked up Vilma's shirt, got up unsteadily and draped it over her. She began to wail, sending her pain across the water.

"I can't stand to be out here!" Juan suddenly shouted, then slapped his palm against the deck. "I hate this damn raft!"

He tried to step over Maria just as she shifted in Ernesto's arms—Juan's toe caught her shoulder and spun him sideways toward the water. A barely audible wail of terror accompanied him as he fell, and then vanished into a black wave.

Everyone sat frozen with their eyes wide—except for Ernesto, who let go of Maria and leapt into the water where Juan had fallen in. As he disappeared below the surface, Maria let go a stomach-curdling shriek.

Seconds went by, then a minute, with no sign of either man.

Suddenly they burst through the surface without warning, twenty feet away. Ernesto held fast to Juan, who seemed to be fighting to climb up Ernesto's chest.

Vilma and Maria watched in terror. Manuel grabbed one of the empty water bottles tied to a rope and threw it out toward them.

Ernesto wrenched free Juan's hand clutching his neck and got behind him. With one arm around Juan's chest he started dragging him back to the raft as he kicked and flailed his arms and squealed like a pig on the way to slaughter—then sucked in water and started to choke. Ernesto used his free arm to paddle to the floating water bottle, and the moment he had it Manuel pulled it as hard as he could.

Close to the raft, Juan's body went slack. No choking, no struggling.

Manuel and Vilma took his arms and with Ernesto pushing, pulled Juan's inert body onto the deck. Ernesto crawled on and without missing a beat turned the rubbery body onto its back. He angled Juan's head, bent down, and began to blow into his mouth.

Between breaths, Ernesto pumped Juan's chest and counted to five. He repeated the process again and again while the others watched, none of them saying a word.

11

"THE NUMBERS ARE getting closer, but you're still ahead," Dan Eagan said.

Spinelli glanced from the spreadsheet to his pollster, then back down again.

"I don't like the trend."

"Of the 46 Republicans, 21 support you, 5 are undecided and 20 are opposed."

"It's the Democrats that surprise me. Out of 54, only 35 want to send help."

"There were 40 yesterday," Eagen said. "There are still 9 undecided, and now 10 opposed."

Spinelli dropped the paper onto his desk and did the math in his head. It was only a cushion of 6 votes, with 14 still undecided. *Shit.*

"What's happening? Why are they going the other way?"

Eagen looked up from the informal poll, which had been derived from speaking with his counterparts in the Senate.

"The president has Terri Turner lobbying hard for votes against, or a delay of the session, and—"

"Wonder why she hasn't called me?" Spinelli snorted.

"Roy Perkins has been making the rounds on the Democrats' side."

"Perkins? What, he and Winslow have a little 'Lone Star' good ole boy deal working, do they?" The grin was now a sneer. "No junior West Texas hillbilly is going to stop this steam roller."

Eagen kept his eyes on the figures.

"Get me a list of all those still undecided and those who have switched sides," Spinelli said. "If Winslow wants to lobby, I'll show him how it's done."

Confidence radiated from his face, but his stomach was churning. Spinelli considered his tactics. Who could he turn his way? What bills were close to a vote? Who was losing popularity at home? Which seats were up for a vote next year? Who was recently embarrassed? Who needed help?

He sat down and looked at the phone.

Come on Puzzo, find something!

SURROUNDED BY A SEA OF CONCRETE, Dadeland was an oasis of air-conditioned retail amongst a sea of strip centers, apartments and low-end housing. Traffic at the mall on a Wednesday would normally be light, but with the post-holiday sales, the parking lot was full, traffic was snarled and tempers on edge. The decreased activity after the holiday season came with reduced police patrols, and with the phenomenon of the Cuban Exodus hitting the greater Miami area like a hurricane, nervous residents screamed for additional police patrols, and got them. These same residents were blissfully unaware that many of the enhanced forces were rookies fresh out of the academy who had been injected onto the street—months ahead of schedule.

Robert "Buzz" Luffer was one of 30 rookies in exactly that position. While he walked his beat around the perimeter of the mall, he considered each car with suspicion, looked at every pedestrian as if they had criminal intent, and kept his hand near his sheathed night stick ready for action. Buzz walked tall in his starched uniform, happy to be done with his studies and out in the real world, especially at a time when there was such heightened tension brewing. He adjusted the nightstick, ratcheted up the volume on his two-way radio and wished his buddies from up north could see him now.

Buzz had moved to Miami from Apalachicola for the sole purpose of becoming a Miami-Dade Police officer. Tired of life on what was referred to as the Redneck Riviera, he had decided that if he was going to follow in his father's footsteps and become a cop, he was going to go where the *real* action was, not just under-age drinkers, spousal abusers, and skinny-dippers. Once his old man had finally consented to what he called a foolhardy idea, he had been able to pull some strings and get Buzz into the Academy, where just two weeks ago his son graduated in the bottom fifth of his class.

Buzz had to frequently hitch-up his size 30 pants on his size 28 waist as he walked. He had been ribbed mercilessly at the Academy over his physique, which he finally squelched, at least in his own mind, when he took off his shirt one day after a three-mile run and flexed his washboard abdominal muscles. Between them and his protruding ribs, Buzz was a series of ridges and valleys that looked like the ripples on a beach after the tide recedes. He walked along with his arms cocked, and although he was attentive to every visual stimulus possible, he kept his head tilted toward the microphone and speaker Velcro'd to his epaulet.

A pair of caramel colored women in skimpy mini-skirts dashed out of one of the public exits from the Mall. He squinted at them, his hand poised above his nightstick, certain that they had just stolen something. He started to jog in their direction, glancing from the women back to the door, wondering when Mall Security would arrive in pursuit.

A Mercedes pulled up and an elderly Latin woman waved at the girls, who hurried in her direction. Buzz saw that they were not carrying any bags or parcels. Their big German car drove past him as he stood on the curb and saw the old woman scolding the girls.

Teenagers. He took a breath, shook his head and continued his route.

No little chicitas better steal shit and cross my path.

The blend of nationalities, languages, skin colors, and types of people that comprised the patrons of the Dadeland complex kept Buzz nervous and on his toes. The plethora of coded violations that streamed over his radio speaker was a constant distraction. His captain had instructed Buzz to pay attention to the numerical codes that indicated what infraction was being announced. If he didn't know what the code meant, he was to immediately review the list.

There was an informal competition among the rookies on who could make the most arrests, and 4 of the 30 had already been involved in felony apprehensions—3 of which required them to produce their weapon—and that was just in the first two weeks! Buzz was sorely disappointed that he had only handled misdemeanors, so far. But the rising tensions amongst the Cuban populace had spread throughout the area, so Buzz knew his time would come.

The radio clicked and the dispatcher's voice breathed in his ear: a 10-50 was occurring on the 1100 block of Cutler Boulevard, with instructions for patrol car 112 to respond. Buzz smiled. *Car wreck.*

A moment later he heard the click again, this time it was a Code 30 on the 800 block of La Jeune Road. *Armed robbery.* Each time this happened, Buzz considered the distance to the reported infraction and estimated the time it would take him to get there if back up was needed. Since he was on foot, the only things he could help with would need to be close by.

I'll run my ass off if I have to.

Over the first two weeks of his patrol, Buzz had kept track of the number of times he had to look up the numerical code or signal being announced, and he was concerned that it had averaged once every eight calls. He studied the codes and signals every night, but there were 189 of them. The one number that he repeated to himself like a mantra in case he got in trouble, or one of his colleague's needed help, was Signal 25, which meant *officer needs assistance.*

He prayed that he would not have to make the request for assistance himself. But with these Cubans all hopped up, he knew he needed to be ready.

WITH ONLY ENOUGH time for a quick update, the president and Terri Turner stole a few minutes in the Oval Office. Turner had been up late the night before with the Attorney General working their way through the bureaucratic minefield of anti-Cuban legislation, and then she spent a futile day on the Hill to lobby against the emergency session. Winslow thought she looked haggard, and he saw a haze of vulnerability in her eyes.

A sudden flashback hit him, as it did occasionally when concerned about Terri. They had been on an emotional roller coaster after his father suddenly died. It was two weeks before George's wedding to Lucy, and Terri's five-year involvement with the elder Winslow had cooled a few months before. They were equally devastated by his death.

Winslow had not approved of her relationship with his father, and because of that there had always been friction between them. Over time, though, he and Terri learned a mutual respect that later matured into a deep friendship.

But that night was different.

They had left the funeral home after finishing the arrangements, bent on a mission to drown their sorrows. Hours later, it was clear that Terri had too many martinis to drive, and even though he was in no better condition, Winslow offered to take her to the condominium she kept in downtown Houston.

After leaving the restaurant they had held each other out of a sense of loss, but when he suddenly kissed her, everything changed. Their shared pain, ragged emotions, and fear of the future launched them into a passionate embrace. Once in the car, they kissed again, and before they knew it they were in front of her building.

"I'll drop you off here," he remembered saying, intending to park the car then come up. But he hadn't said so, and after holding his eyes for a long moment, she opened the door.

"Goodbye, George."

Her door had slammed shut, and through his disappointment, George Winslow wasn't sure if she'd misunderstood him or had a last minute attack of conscience and nipped the situation in the bud.

They never spoke of that evening again, and Winslow convinced himself that it happened for the best. But from time to time he still wondered what might have been.

Today they sat in the yellow armchairs in the center of the Oval Office. Turner removed some notes from her briefcase.

"Before you start," the president said, "I had a call from Danny Besing today."

"He's not supposed to call you on Winslow Oil business."

"He called to tell me that some investigative reporter was digging around Houston asking a lot of questions."

"There's nothing to find, it shouldn't be any concern."

The president shook his head. "He was digging in places that had not been covered before."

"Like where?"

"Mergers and acquisitions."

A long silence spread out between them, and Winslow pointed to his ear, reminding Turner that all Oval Office discussions were recorded.

"Who is this guy? Who does he work for?"

"All Danny said was that the guy's name was Puzzo, and that he's an independent out of New York. Anyway, we don't have much time, so before we talk about your meetings on the Hill, tell me what you and the Attorney General came up with last night."

"Not a heck of a lot. The AG has some good ideas but no ironclad guarantees. Between CDA and Helms-Burton, only Congress can end the embargo. Bottom line is there's little room to maneuver, and you'll be sticking your neck out."

"How far?"

"Far enough for Spinelli to chop your head off."

"Lovely." The president checked his watch. "Give me the highlights."

Turner yawned and poured herself a glass of water.

"Am I keeping you up?"

"You did last night."

The comment caught him off guard, but then he smiled. "I couldn't sleep either. No more cheeseburgers."

"We obviously don't have the time to create a decent strategy, and I'm afraid if we make any more mistakes the administration will be mortally wounded." She handed Winslow a copy of her notes. "Here's what we've got."

He took the single sheet of paper, read, and shook it.

"Not much, Terri."

"Both CDA and Helms-Burton require an interim government to be in-place with democratic elections scheduled in order to terminate the embargo. And even if you submit such a determination to Congress, they could overrule it."

"So how are we going to do anything in the next two days? Congress holds all the cards and Spinelli's dealing from the bottom of the deck."

"Your hands are tied, technically, but the AG and I think the ropes may be loose enough for you to wiggle around."

"Or hang myself?"

"That's a distinct possibility," she said.

"What choice do I have? Spinelli has forced the issue, and with all those people stuck in tents, it's hard to refute his argument."

"Frankly, George, it's a very risky proposition."

"Why is it so clear to me and nobody else? Between the Exodus and Castro's threats, preserving the Migration Accords is critical. The only way I can think to accomplish that is to change our strategy toward Cuba once and for all."

"Based on the existing legislation, and the response I got on the Hill today, I don't see how we can change anything in two days."

Winslow jumped to his feet. He paced the yellow chairs like a shark that smells blood in the water—could it be his own? He spoke as he walked, his conviction filling him with adrenalin.

"The answer is so simple, I *know* that it would work." He continued to circle, letting the words form in his mind. "Normalizing relations with Cuba would cause a bloodless, peaceful revolution of freedom and ideas that would wash over that island like a tidal wave. Even if they tried to fight it, the Cuban government wouldn't be able to turn the tide back. It would get rid of Castro and his thugs once and for all."

Turner looked doubtful.

"How do you think Reagan and Bush toppled the Soviet Union and Eastern bloc? Through people-to-people exchanges. Reagan let backpack-toting college kids explore through Eastern Europe, Nixon did it with China, and their human rights record is a lot worse than Cuba's. Hell, Carter even lifted the travel ban from Vietnam just two years after the war ended."

She listened intently though she knew where he was headed.

"If Castro suddenly dies and there's a fight for succession, violence could erupt 90 miles off our shore. The way it is now, we're leaving the door open for some undesirable country, or terrorist organization, to step into the vacuum—again. If we could establish a strong relationship with the Cuban people now, we'd be in a lot better shape to help facilitate and determine the post-Castro future."

"If we had time to build some consensus and get a public relations campaign going," she said, "I think the voters might support you. But we've only got two days before Spinelli pulls his finger out of the dike."

The president had never shrunk from a challenge in the past, and he wasn't about to now.

"If it's going to take a miracle to stop this mess, we're going to have to produce one ourselves."

"Based on the response I got on the Hill today, I'd say that's right."

"Then let's force destiny to take its course. If the United States is to be the guiding light against oppression, it needs to be through example, not coercion, or we're no better than those we condemn."

"Are you willing to risk your presidency over this?"

Winslow didn't answer her question.

She stood up, and Winslow watched her pace around the room.

"The AG and I came up with a crazy idea, and there's an infinitesimal chance we could ever pull it off, much less in two days...But it's the only chance of creating the room you need to maneuver."

"Ah yes, the rope."

Turner's face remained serious. "Indeed."

12

ERNESTO STRUGGLED UNDERNEATH the raft with the bad drum.

Eight pounds a gallon times 50-gallons, this bastard must weigh over 400 pounds...

In the darkness below the deck he untied all but one wrap of the bad drum's rope while being sloshed around in the waves.

"Juan, you got it?"

"Got it."

Before Ernesto was even in the water, Juan had wrapped another rope around his own waist and asked Manuel to hold the end. Since Ernesto resuscitated him after he had nearly drowned this morning, he was taking every precaution not to fall back in.

"There's no way to drain the water," Ernesto said. "We'd have to get it on board, and it's way too heavy."

"Forget it, man," Juan said. "Can you untie it and move the good one to the center? This pig's so heavy I can hardly hold it."

"I'll salvage the rope before we drop the barrel," Ernesto said. "Lower it slowly."

A moment later the rope started to come through the deck. Ernesto was startled when he heard Juan fall to his knees. Ernesto hung onto the rope and tried to leverage himself against the good drum, but his own body weight kept pulling him under. He held fast to the bad drum and tried to prevent it from sinking before he could untie the twenty feet of rope to salvage.

"Here's the end," Juan said.

As soon as the rope passed through the boards, Ernesto felt an immediate pull from below. The weight became incredible. He fought against the force—held on to the raft with one hand, had the rope from the sinking drum wrapped around his other hand.

"Come on, baby."

The weight threatened to rip his arms apart. He sensed a stall to the descent and quickly spun his arm to wrap more rope around his wrist. The sudden movement caused him to lose his balance, and his elbow slipped off the good drum. His body was instantly jerked below the surface. He tried to hang onto the raft, but the pull from the drum as it sank was relentless, and with his arm wrapped tightly to it, he was pulled down into the depths.

Now untethered, the drum's descent accelerated as it dragged him down with it. He fought against the dead weight by trying to swim toward the surface, but the effort quickly exhausted his oxygen.

Ernesto tried desperately to get his arm free while the drum sank, but the rope was taut since he instinctively swam upward. His ears filled with sharp pain and his lungs burned painfully.

With what strength he had left, he spun his body around like a diver performing a twist until his wrist broke free. His chest was on fire and his head pounded, but he kicked toward the rising bubbles, toward the brightness of the sunlight, then toward the square patch of darkness that was the raft—all the while fighting the urge to suck in air knowing it would be water instead that would fill his lungs.

He exploded through the surface just as his vision began to blur.

"Ernesto!"

The sound of Maria calling his name penetrated his fog. He waved a hand and saw Juan smile. He paddled in exhaustion, and once there he hung onto the raft long enough to catch his breath.

"Ernesto, you nearly drowned!" Maria reached down and touched his head. "Let me help you up."

"I can't, not yet." His breathing was ragged. "I still need to move the other drum."

"Untie the knot," Juan said. "I'll slide the ropes from here."

The back section now leaned at an angle with only one drum, and the raft bobbed unsteadily in the rise and fall of long waves. Ernesto blew his nose into his hand to expel the water from his sinuses.

Breathing normally at last, he slipped under the raft to finish the job. Seaweed and saragasso grass clung to him from a long line of yellowish-green floating weeds.

"OK, I've got the knots." He broke each one free.

"It's loose, can you move it yet?" Juan asked.

Ernesto pushed his shoulder against the rusted drum, then he and Juan slowly slid the drum toward the center of the platform. Again exhausted, Ernesto dove under repeatedly to check every rope and every connection between the drums and the platform.

Finally, his teeth chattering and his body shaking from cold and exertion, Ernesto grabbed at the edge of the deck. Juan pulled him on then handed him one of the water jugs, and Ernesto took a long draw.

"Good job, *compadre,*" Juan said.

"Indeed," Manuel said. "How do the drums look, Ernesto?"

"The rest are fine. I tried to save the rope on the leaky one but couldn't." Ernesto stole a glance at Maria, then he caught Juan's eye. He could tell Juan knew how close he'd come to dying.

Thanks for keeping your mouth shut, compadre.

WHAT DETERMINES WHETHER you win or lose is how you play the game, Spinelli thought as he walked down the main hall of the Hart office building. Having already met with three senators from his 'undecided' list this afternoon, his confidence was again on the rise. Only Percy Witherspoon, a democrat from Rhode Island, specifically said that he would vote with Spinelli, which only took supporting Witherspoon's request for a federally funded Maritime Museum in Portsmouth, but he also felt confident in the republicans from Colorado and Louisiana.

With three more scheduled meetings before the day was out, Spinelli hoped for a few impromptu ones as well. A glance at his watch caused him to pick up his pace to a near jog. He was already fifteen minutes late for his meeting with Senator Hatch, and the republican from Utah was a stickler for punctuality.

The moment Spinelli stepped out of the elevator on the 3rd floor he felt a vibration against his waist. Without missing a stride he pulled the cell phone off his hip and flipped it open.

"Spinelli."

"It's me." The voice was gravelly.

Spinelli was surprised but kept up his pace. "I haven't heard a word from you."

"It's been a good trip."

"I'm glad you enjoyed yourself. What have you accomplished?"

"There's no doubt that the subject was aggressive—and at times maybe even reckless...."

"But?"

"But he pretty much operated within what would be considered reasonable business practices."

The news was not what Spinelli wanted to hear, but he sensed something else in Puzzo's voice. He increased his pace as he rounded a corner and spotted Hatch's office at the end of the hall.

"That's supposed to be good news?"

"There *is* one thing that I think you'll like."

"What's that?"

After Puzzo gave him the news, Spinelli didn't even notice the phone drop from his hand until it crashed against the floor. His eyes bulged wide and a slow smile spread across his lips. Then he actually jumped into the air.

With what looked like a bow, he scooped his hand down, swept up his phone and took off running in the opposite direction from Senator Hatch's office.

"I'LL BET THIS weed line's a good place to catch some fish." Juan had no sooner finished the sentence than a half-dozen flying fish broke the surface and skimmed across the water before they disappeared into a wave. *Hell, I'd even eat one of those.*

"We used to troll along weed lines for dorado," Ernesto said.

Juan unwrapped a yo-yo and baited it with bread.

"Good, then you should be able to catch one with this."

Ernesto laughed. "We had our mates bait and hook the fish, we just reeled them in."

"Those days are over, *compadre*. Out here we're all mates."

Juan had a vision of his father carrying a fishing rod in one hand and a brown paper bag in the other. He was only a small child then and he begged his father to take him too, but his older brother pushed Juan down then laughed as they left. Juan ran after them and grabbed at his father's arm. The brown bag flew into the air, followed by a loud crack of glass when it hit the street. As Juan stared at the chunks of glass and amber rum, his father's hand slapped him across the face. The memory made him shudder. With the exception of the fish they had lost earlier, they'd seen none.

"I don't think we're going to catch anything with this bread," Ernesto said. Then, scanning the weed line directly out from the boat, he said, "Hey, what's that?"

Juan followed Ernesto's finger. "Looks like a dead fish." He looked at the balled up bread in his hand and tossed it in the water.

Using one of the oars, Juan paddled toward the dead fish but could not keep a straight course. Ernesto took the other oar and tried to help. Together they closed the distance quickly.

"You boys do well together," Manuel said.

Juan bent down and grabbed the fish, and a strong smell of rot burned his nose.

"Gotcha you stinky bastard."

"Wooh, that's awful." Maria pinched her nose. "I'll stick to the rice and beans, I'm not eating that."

"We're not going to eat it, we're going to use it for bait," Ernesto said.

The strips of meat Juan cut from the dead fish proved much more effective bait. Juan and Ernesto both caught small Dorado. Vilma cut them into squares and wrapped them together with the lime slices to marinate in their one piece of plastic.

"Tonight we'll feast on ceviche," she said. "That'll help keep our strength up."

Juan knew they'd need it but didn't say so.

"DO THE MIAMI CUBANS REALLY THINK that when Castro dies they'll return and take over?" Vilma said.

"We'll find out what they think soon enough," Manuel said. *Politics, at my age who cares? I've had enough politics.*

"What are those people thinking?"

"*Coño*, Vilma, *you'll* be a Miami-Cuban pretty soon," Juan said. "Then see how you feel. I bet they just miss their homeland."

"Huh!" She waved her wrist at him. "I'll never be like them. I'm proud of what El Commandante has accomplished."

Vilma was a fighter, even at 60 years old. Juan admired that.

"Unfortunately," Ernesto said, "you're going to the one country that hates his guts."

Juan took a strong pull on his cigarette. "For once, my having nothing is a benefit. I'm leaving nothing behind, and yesterdays are over my shoulder."

"Vilma, I feel so sorry that you have to give up your home to get medical attention," Maria said. "We had no choice, thanks to Señor del Torres."

"Don't be sorry for me, be sorry for Cuba," Vilma said. "If it weren't for the embargo, I wouldn't have to give up my life to try and save it."

"If you didn't get pregnant, we wouldn't be on this raft," Ernesto said.

"Oh, so it's my fault? You had nothing to do with it?"

Ernesto grabbed her and planted a big kiss on her lips. She pushed him away with a grunt and crossed her arms. He whispered what Juan assumed to be an apology in her ear, and her expression softened a fraction. Then he looked up and rolled his eyes.

A large bird drifted in the sky above them. Manuel watched as it meandered a slow course.

"One of the ironies of the embargo?" Ernesto said. "Castro blames America for all Cuba's problems but he benefits from all the expatriates. My father calls them worms."

"I don't feel like a worm," Juan said.

"When they started to send money back, Castro said the worms had turned to butterflies. To me, the joke proved that money outweighed ideology," Ernesto said.

"Do you feel like a worm, Maria?" Juan said. "No, you're a butterfly, even with no money to send back," Everyone laughed. Maria reached up and pulled the ribbon from her hair, which spilled over her shoulders. It was as if an artist discovered the one detail that could change a portrait to a masterpiece.

She lay her head in Ernesto's lap. He whispered to her and traced the contours of her face with his finger. Manuel watched them and recalled fuzzy memories of his wife. The recollection pierced his heart like an errant arrow from Cupid's ghost.

Beneath his arrogant demeanor, Ernesto seemed like a good young man. Growing up in the shadow of a hero would cause most men to cover their self-doubt with defiance.

Yes, Ernesto, I'll deliver you to my sons, they'll see the wisdom of employing the son of Cuba's Minister of Sugar. You'll be my legacy.

The irony caused Manuel to smile. He hoped his father would find it a just retribution.

The image of Ramon del Torres barging into his home in September 1959, accompanied by a small army of thugs, played in Manuel's mind like a silent movie. He remembered when Juan mentioned Ernesto's name for the first time. Until then, leaving on a raft was something Manuel had never been willing to consider, but upon hearing "del Torres," his decision to go was instantly sealed. Even though he had no idea how being with Ernesto would make a difference.

13

"MY DAD SAYS PARAMUS is a dump," Emery Dunn said.

Senator Spinelli glared at his aide. *If your father wasn't one of my biggest donors, you wouldn't be sitting here.*

"So, you're saying he hasn't developed any buildings here?"

"No way," Emery said. "He only does the top markets."

Spinelli shrugged and shook his head. "Well, it's plenty important to me."

"Who are these guys and what are the Cubans doing here anyway?"

The senator closed his eyes and ignored the question. What with the unpredictable outcome of the emergency session scheduled two days from now, the Spinmaster was skittish, and he had come to New Jersey to calm his benefactor's nerves. The ultra-conservative Cuban American Council might be based in Miami, but their next most active chapter was in Paramus, right in the middle of Spinelli's state.

"Hector Ramon San Martin is CAC's executive vice president in New Jersey, and José Mas Fina, the president, is up from Miami for the meeting."

If you had more than half a brain, Emery, I'd tell you that as the great grandson of Radon Grau San Martin, who was the president of Cuba from 1944 to 1948, Hector felt an unalienable right to assume the throne upon Castro's demise, which he had attempted to hasten a number of times over the years. And that José Mas Fina had risen to success in the Miami Cuban community as an aggressive general contractor who'd managed to convert his financial prowess into political clout. But that would all be lost on you, kid.

"The funny thing is, both Hector and José think they're the rightful successor to Castro."

Emery's eyes narrowed. "They both can't be, can they? I mean, that's not—"

"No, they both can't be the president of Cuba," Spinelli said. "It has never even entered their minds that the Cuban people wouldn't want them."

"So—"

"It's my job to make them think they'll get the chance."

Confusion slowly changed to a fragile grip of the obvious, and Emery returned his boss's smile, though they were smiling for different reasons.

"But with Hector being sixty years old and Mas Fina fifty-eight," Spinelli said, "time's not on their side. And even though they're anxious to get rid of Castro, they're sensitive to how it's done."

"Why is CNP—"

"CAC. Cuban American Council, Emery, let's get that right."

"Right. What's their deal? Why do we care so much about them?"

Spinelli's eyebrows rose, he took in a deep breath and let it out slowly, reminding himself that Kenneth Dunn, Emery's esteemed father, was a substantial campaign contributor.

"They spread a lot of money around on Capitol Hill."

"I see," Emery said.

"At the moment they're juggling the hot potato of what to do about the Exodus refugees, which is especially delicate because of the public relations nightmare of their over-zealous efforts to keep Elian Gonzalez in Miami."

"They kept him, right?"

Spinelli bit his knuckle. "No, Emery, they were in the thankless position of supporting the boy's Miami relatives who had laid claim to him after he was rescued on a raft last year. Elian going home was a major-league black eye for the CAC."

Emery looked back out the window.

"Hector and Mas Fina are terrified that Winslow's going to stick to the Migration Accords and send all of the refugees back."

With the emergency session in his pocket, Spinelli felt confident that the return of the Exodus Cubans was unlikely, especially with Puzzo's discovery yesterday. He had learned long ago that there was no better time to visit large political donors than when you had their issues sewn up tight.

The huge backlash brewing outside the Cuban-American community over Florida footing the bill to house and feed the fifty thousand immigrants was a perfect backdrop to the emergency session of Congress. Spinelli would appease the CAC and the non-Cuban-Americans in one *coup de grace*.

Two birds with one stone.

Florida's Governor Cox was stuck pandering to his non-Cuban-American constituents, assuring them that if the emergency session didn't produce some quick financial aid he would demand that the Exodus Cubans be repatriated, so the pressure was on. Even Dunleavy had mealy-mouthed about sending the émigrés back if Congress failed to produce funds, which was just fine with Spinelli as it left the CAC entirely to him.

The limousine pulled up to a squat, four-story building with antiquated gold reflective glass.

"This is it?" Emery said.

You're an imbecile and *a real estate snob?*

"Don't judge the book by the cover." Spinelli paused. "Wait in the lobby, this is sensitive."

CAC's offices filled an entire floor, its walls decorated with Latin art and photographs of Hector San Martin with high profile politicians and celebrities.

Cigar smoke filled the air as Spinelli's hosts marched in, the ancient smoke-eater laboring fruitlessly in the conference room ceiling. Spinelli wasn't sure whether the noisy machine really did suck out smoke or was just insurance against listening devices.

"I trust you were happy with my negotiations in Havana," he said.

"Humiliating the Beard is always useful," José Mas Fina said. He adjusted his large girth in the small leather chair.

"You did exactly as we hoped," Hector said. "The result was an exodus of intelligentsia unlike any before, leaving Castro naked in the spotlight. It was brilliant. Were it not for the controversy over the boatlift, and the current political dilemma, we'd be exuberant."

"Winslow is stalling because he's afraid of what Castro might do," Spinelli said. "Even though he resents it, the emergency session will protect him against Castro claiming that he abandoned the Accords since he ignored wet foot, dry foot. Winslow doesn't want to deport anybody."

"So what's the problem?" Mas Fina asked. "The law says if they set foot on American soil then they can stay, but if they were intercepted at sea they'd be repatriated."

"A lot of them *were* rescued at sea, and when the numbers got too big the president told the Coast Guard to let them through. Cox and Dunleavy are hammering him over that decision, and to release Federal support. It's just politics, boys."

Mas Fina grunted. "Sounds like a bunch of ass-covering to me."

"This issue has caused a huge rift between me and the Administration. The president is furious. He thinks we betrayed him in Havana—and as you know, gentlemen, he's right."

"Your political games are costing us credibility," Mas Fina said. "If the refugees go back, the CAC is finished, and I don't need to tell you what that means for our supporting certain political campaigns."

Hector winced, and Spinelli steeled himself with a gulp of rum.

"You did right to double-cross President Winslow in Havana," Hector said. "The United States can't end the embargo or Castro's policies will never change. Now that Castro's been weakened by the Exodus, embarrassed through your negotiations, and faces the prediction for another flat sugar harvest, the people will finally rise up and demand his removal."

"The reports I'm hearing out of Havana are a little different," Spinelli said.

"What do you mean?"

I'm about to twist your expectations to suit my needs.

"Castro's sounded his usual rallying cry," Spinelli said, "blaming the United States for inducing the Exodus and breaking the Migration Accords to undermine the Revolution. But the real news is that he's planning a foreign trade exposition to showcase the progress they've made in attracting international trading partners."

"What foreign trade?" Mas Fina shouted. "The deals they've done don't provide any money for the people, it's a sham!"

"It's not a sham. There's been huge growth in foreign investment in the last couple years. Canada's very active there, as are most European countries, Argentina, South Korea, Japan, Mexico, Brazil, even Russia."

Mas Fina scowled and rocked forward toward Spinelli.

"Exactly! Nobody's paying attention to your Helms-Burton Act. Why make these laws if you can't enforce them?"

His cigar breath made Spinelli cringe. "You can only push your friends so far when they don't support your policies. We've been—"

"The pressure *must* be maintained," Hector said. "Castro must fail before he dies, otherwise his death will create an ideological vacuum, and succession will be a bloody mess. That would be bad for the CAC, America, and Cuba. I will not, or I should say *we* will not be denied our right to return to Cuba to rescue them from poverty and isolationism."

"The good news is that Castro won't be entertaining any other American good will ambassadors any time soon for fear of opening himself up to additional embarrassment," Spinelli said.

"Unless he can manipulate them for his own benefit," Mas Fina said.

Spinelli raised his chin. "Winslow's doing his best to rally a consensus against the emergency session, but he doesn't have a chance. When we kill this deportation issue on Friday, the CAC will be bullet proof. The embargo's been in place for 42 years, and it won't end on my watch."

"It better not," Mas Fina said. "I've invested too much to be denied my destiny in the future of Cuba. Straighten Dunleavy out and turn the heat up on Castro."

"Is there any chance the president could succeed in rallying a consensus?" Hector asked.

The senator offered a smug smile. "Suffice it to say that I have an ace-in-the-hole that will prevent Winslow from pressing too hard. If he doesn't heel when his leash is pulled, he could be destroyed altogether. So, gentlemen, when I tell you not to worry, trust me. All right?"

"That's the same thing you said about Elian Gonzalez. Don't tell us about what you *say* you can do, just do it!"

Spinelli resented Mas Fina's tone but kept his face neutral.

The president of the CAC took a strong draw on his cigar, narrowed his eyes and blew smoke at Spinelli.

"And start enforcing the damn Helms-Burton Act while you're at it."

14

THE SALMON SKY faded to purple, and Juan watched the darkness erase the detail from the world. The glow from his cigarette provided the only light.

Our second night begins.

A half-moon gradually rose illuminating a dissipated jet contrail into a silver slash across the sky. The line extended from the southwest across to the northeast, the same direction the raft was heading. Juan stared at the fading water vapor and thought of it as a railroad track leading them toward their destination. Never having flown on a plane he imagined what it would be like. The thought reminded him of being at José Martí airport as a child, seeing the line of coffins that had been unloaded from a military aircraft. He pushed the coffins back into the depths of his memory.

"If we were on a plane, we'd be there in minutes."

"I'm going to fly with my wife to New York to see the Statue of Liberty," Manuel said.

The wind remained out of the south, but its velocity had increased. Intermittent white caps now broke on the crests of waves, lit by the moon like puffs of smoke. The raft sloshed around with growing instability, but not so much that Juan was concerned. Nobody had discussed his nearly drowning since it happened, but it gnawed at him as the day wore on.

They've all had to be wondering if what Ernesto said was true. My starting the fight made it obvious. His heart began to race in his chest. *Fuck it.*

"I need to apologize." He blurted the words out in the darkness. "Ernesto is right, I was never in the Guardia."

His confession was greeted by silence. Juan wished clouds would cover the moon so he wouldn't have to see them averting his eyes. After a lifetime of lies to survive, admitting to one now was a new sensation for him. Even in the silence, it felt strangely liberating.

"There were no boats left anyway, and I don't have the money to pay a smuggler," Vilma said. "You were my only choice, so forget about it. Between you and Ernesto, we'll be fine." Her hand on his shoulder left a lingering sense of warmth.

Manuel nodded.

Maria nudged Ernesto.

He kept his eyes toward the stars. "Yeah, well, I came on board thinking I was something special. You can thank my father for that. He raised me to think that way. And based on the life I led, it wasn't hard."

It would stink to be a hero's son. Juan would not forget that Ernesto had saved his life.

"But being here with you people?" Ernesto said. "Seeing what we have seen, and surviving on a moment to moment basis, I realized that I'm no different from you, or anyone else."

Maria put her arm across Ernesto's chest and squeezed him.

"It took me getting away from my father and his ruling class comrades to finally see the reality of the so-called Revolution…. There are a lot more important things than being a hero's son."

"We're your family now." Maria placed Ernesto's hand on her abdomen.

Juan felt a sting of loneliness. *You're a lucky shit, Ernesto.*

"It may sound crazy, but the problems we've faced out here have made me feel like I was able to make a difference," Ernesto said. "Having our survival on the line has opened my eyes for the first time in my life."

Maria took his cheeks in both hands and turned his head to face her. There was a tear on his cheek. She brushed it away, then kissed his closed eyelids.

His admission surprised Juan. "*Coño, compadre,* sounds like we've both learned a few things out here." He chuckled. "I do have one piece of bad news." He flicked his spent cigarette into the sea. "That was my last cigarette."

"Maybe you could eat some more of that raw fish," Maria said with a laugh. "That killed my appetite for wanting anything."

"You didn't like my ceviche?" Vilma said.

"I think I'll stick with the beans and rice."

"We've only got about three days' worth left," Manuel said.

Juan was watching the whitecaps. "If this wind starts to blow harder, we might make it to Florida in three days."

Vilma buttoned her red sweater and wrapped one of the ropes around her waist.

With a sense of embarrassment still eating at him, Juan checked the ropes on the raft and filled the smaller water jugs from the 20-gallon container on the bow. Moving around had become more difficult in the choppier seas, and it was especially noticeable on the back where there was now just one drum.

"Maybe if we move this monster to the back it will work like ballast," Ernesto said. He slapped his palm on top of the large water container.

"Let's try it," Juan said. He and Ernesto slid the container to where Manuel had been seated.

"I wish we had done that earlier," Manuel said. "That deck has been jostling around so much it made me nauseous. This is better."

"Go ahead and stay there. I'll take tonight's watch from here," Ernesto said.

"You sure, man?" Juan asked.

"You did it last night, it's my turn."

Juan felt exhausted and guessed that Ernesto must too, but he didn't want to second guess his volunteering and seem uncooperative. Together they helped secure everyone to the deck with ropes. Since Ernesto was on the back, above the single drum, there was no rope left to tie around his waist. It had sunk with the leaky drum.

"How are you going to tie yourself down?" Maria asked.

Ernesto looked around. He untied the rope that connected the large water container to the back of the platform, tied it around his waist and then back to the container.

As the quiet settled in, Vilma stopped humming and turned to Juan.

"Maybe you should have joined the Guardia, it might have been good for you."

Juan reached for a cigarette forgetting there were none left.

"Yeah, right. I've seen what that shit can do to you. My older brother was in Grenada, and before that, my father was in Angola. He wrote my mother these God-awful letters about that shit hole. Nothing but sickness, disease, and starvation. No thanks. Cuba may be poor, but it's a paradise compared to Angola."

"He must have been happy to come home," Maria said.

The image of the airport again popped into Juan's mind. He took a deep breath.

"Maybe if it wasn't in a pine box, he would have been. The rotten food there gave him heartworms and killed him."

"So, your father was a hero too," Ernesto said.

"Yeah, sure, so we've got that in common. I'd have rather had him around."

"The Revolution has required many sacrifices," Vilma said.

Juan was still thinking about his father, the only artifact of their relationship was a photo his mother had given him. Then it struck him that this was the longest amount of time he had spent with a group of people in as many years as he could remember. He looked from face to face. The old man, nice but pitiful, wasting his life waiting for someone to change it for him, Vilma reminded him of his mother, but she was hell-bent on the Revolution. Maria, so fine, found herself a rich man, but his father disapproved of her.

And then there's Ernesto. He's lost the most, but through that he's also learned the most. *What a bunch we are.*

Surrounded by liquid blackness, claustrophobia overcame Juan as he stared into the night sky. He could hear Vilma humming again, and then Manuel mumbling to the stars, just like last night. *Crazy, old man.*

Ernesto was still awake. He lay on his back and faced the sky. Juan bit his lip.

"Ernesto?"

"Yeah?"

"I never said anything about what happened today, about what you did."

"Forget it, you'd do the same for me." He shrugged and let out a short laugh. "The funny thing is? We're a lot alike. Our worlds may have been different, but neither of us likes to be told what to do."

Juan was quiet for a moment. "Yeah, maybe, but at least your father loved you enough to *exile* you. I hardly even knew my old man."

"Some men just like to have a dog by their side, and my father expected me to bark, fetch, and roll over at his whim. But I'm no dog, you know what I mean?"

Juan turned back to the sky.

"I'll never forgive him for that, for trying to control every single thing I did. I hope losing me has hurt him like leaving Cuba in shame hurt me. I know it must sound pathetic, but that will be my goal until the day I die, to make sure he feels that same sense of loss."

"To lose your only son has got to hurt, hero or not."

"Nothing hurts Ramon del Torres." Ernesto tightened the rope that connected him to the water container.

A cresting wave jolted them, and the raft dropped into its trough. The sudden fall startled Juan. He looked back at Ernesto staring into the sky and thought he saw stars reflected in his eyes.

15

THE PRIVACY OF AN unmarked Chevy Suburban offered a discreet location for the political opponents to meet. After making a public appearance at a charity dinner at the Ronald Reagan building, disappearing through the kitchen, then shuttling from one unmarked car to another, President Winslow was confident that his whereabouts were secret, as was his destination. He checked his watch. *Right on time.*

Agent Scott, the head of the president's Secret Service detail, guided the Suburban through light traffic on Pennsylvania Avenue then turned up 1st Street toward the illuminated Capitol rotunda. The dome shone bright against the night sky, and the snow-covered lawn reflected onto the building's façade.

They arrived at the designated location a couple minutes early and circled around the block to kill time. On the next pass, a man stepped out of the shadows. Agent Scott braked to a stop, the door opened, and the man got in.

"Evening, Mr. President."

"Senator Dunleavy."

They merged into traffic and wound their way around to Union Station, which stood out brightly in the darkness. Two other Secret Service agents watched closely from behind a clear soundproof panel, neither looked happy with the circumstances.

"Thanks for meeting me on short notice."

"Your call was too intriguing to pass up," Dunleavy said.

"I don't have much time, so I'll get right to the point," Winslow said. "We have fresh intelligence that Castro's massing a significant boatlift to launch on Florida, Mariel-style."

Winslow read Dunleavy's expression and the ensuing silence to mean he was surprised but understood the implications.

"When?" he said finally.

"Soon, maybe too soon to stop. Our best chance to head it off is to control the factors he'll claim caused it. That's why I needed to see you. I need your help to delay the emergency session."

"How's that going to help? We're already—"

"I understand the urgency of the situation, but the Exodus refugees are a drop in the bucket of what's to come, both quantitatively and qualitatively. I intend to send you help within a couple weeks, at most, and I have people working around the clock on a strategy that will reduce the mounting pressure in Cuba—but I need a little more time."

"You've got to tell me the strategy. I can't back off the emergency session without something to tell my constituents, they'll crucify me."

The president was fully aware that the situation had put Dunleavy at odds with his non-Cuban-American citizens and the CAC. He also knew he was taking a huge risk—his instincts had better be right.

"I can't tell you what we're doing," he said, "and frankly, it's better that you don't know, but I've got to preserve the Migration Accords and salvage the situation before all hell breaks loose."

"You expect me to voluntarily delay the aid my state needs, and you won't even tell me what you're doing? How…I mean, what do you think—"

"I'm asking you to trust me. I give you my word that I'll send help to Florida as soon as possible." Winslow hoped the reports of Dunleavy being desperate were not exaggerated. He waited.

"I'm sorry, Mr. President, but the best thing I can do for Florida right now is support the emergency session. We need help."

"You *will* get help, but if Castro goes on the offensive, Florida will be forced into martial law."

"You think delaying the session will keep him from launching his attack because the Migration Accords will still be intact?"

Winslow nodded. "Basically, that's right. Without a public decision on the fate of the Exodus Cubans, Castro won't have his excuse to dump their least desirable citizens on Florida."

Dunleavy grunted. "You're not giving me anything. What am I supposed to tell the press, or Congress?"

"Say that I promised you I'll come to Florida soon—next week"

"What else?"

"That I've briefed you on a plan to prevent the situation from getting worse—"

"That's a stretch."

"Look, I'll issue a statement that I made these assurances to you personally. We can't make the intelligence out of Cuba public, or you'll have pandemonium. My statement will put me on the hook—and buy us both some time."

Agent Scott had pointed the Suburban back toward the Capitol. The brief window the president had covertly carved out of his charity dinner was rapidly closing. They needed to drop the senator and get back to the Reagan building.

"How good is your source in Cuba?" Dunleavy said when the Capitol dome filled the windshield.

"Multiple sources, and all well placed," Winslow said.

The Suburban pulled to a stop.

Dunleavy shook his head and heaved a deep sigh, then turned to face the president.

"All right, I'll play, provided you issue a statement tomorrow that we met, and you assured me that you were coming to inspect the refugee camp next week."

Dunleavy extended his hand, and the president grabbed it, his smile bright in the dark interior.

"Deal."

After they dropped Dunleavy, the president closed his eyes and considered himself lucky. But he knew the sentiment would be short lived. *When Dunleavy finds out the trip to Florida was already part of my plan, he won't be happy.*

16

RAMON DEL TORRES sat in his chair on the beach at Varadero, tossing a ball to his son and daughter. Military bodyguards stood in the shade of the trees. Their beach home served as a backdrop, its tan stucco walls and red tiled roof standing majestically in the bright sunlight. Ernesto glanced up into the sun as his mother appeared on the balcony and waved to him. He tried to wave back but couldn't, his arms frozen. Turning to his father, who was now dressed in his best suit, Ernesto felt the anxiety that always consumed him when he received that impatient nod and quick wave of his hand....

Ernesto ran up the tarmac by the moveable stairway to stand next to his father as a man with two bodyguards disembarked from the long white plane with the strange letters painted on its side. He looked around and saw many of his friends standing with their fathers, some smiling and waving, others like Ernesto looking bored and resentful. His mother had told him the man in the plane was Gorbechev, the Premiere of the Soviet Socialist's Republic. He—

Darkness interrupted the images, and Ernesto was back in their house in Miramar sitting on the edge of the bed in his parents' room. Home alone, he had been listening to music on his parent's record player when he saw the closet door move. The music stopped and Ernesto tried to stand but couldn't—some invisible force pushed against him. He tried to scream but couldn't do that either, and he fought against the smothering feeling that enveloped him.

THE NIGHT SKY over the Florida Straits was clear, but the wind had continued to build. Everyone was asleep, exhausted from anxiety, hunger, dehydration, and the relentless sun. Ernesto, who was responsible for the night's watch, had also succumbed to sleep, spent from the struggle to save Juan in the water and then nearly drowning himself while he worked on the drums. He knew volunteering for the watch had been a mistake, but he couldn't let Juan do it again. Consumed with dreams and a kaleidoscope of childhood memories and fears, he was oblivious to the mounting seas.

FIDEL CASTRO APPEARED in the doorway and Ernesto froze. Here was the man from his father's stories, the radio and television and the paintings on the buildings. He was the Revolution. He smiled at Ernesto and mussed his hair as he walked past him and into his father's study. Ernesto saw his father smile broadly as El Presidenté hugged him. His father's expression turned to grief, seated alone at his desk in a darkened room, and Ernesto knew the sugar harvest must have been another failure. His father spotted Ernesto spying on him and screamed, but there was no sound. Ernesto ran, certain that he was behind him, counting the steps until his father would catch him and lash his bare bottom with a bootstrap.

Running turned to swimming, and Ernesto battled frailty and a youthful lack of coordination as he struggled in the deeper water of their family pool to learn the overhand stroke his father wanted him to master. Ramon del Torres ran the length of the pool alongside Ernesto, shouting instructions and encouragement.

WAVES LIFTED THE raft, and set it down gently, and lifted it again in a hypnotic rhythm. A dolphin surfaced next to them, circled once around and disappeared into a wave. The moon lit the spray off the whitecaps. Huddled on the tight deck, the group was in a deep sleep, the waves rocking them like babies in a cradle. Occasionally a large wave would lift them higher and the raft would come down hard but still they slept. Provisions bounced and limbs might become airborne for an instant, but it was not enough to penetrate their exhaustion.

LYING WITH MARIA on a hilltop in the Pinar del Río, they looked down on the farm where her family harvested tobacco. Ernesto traced his finger along her cheek and studied the curves of her body. They were naked on a blanket, a small picnic lay spent around them. He marveled at her beauty, even more at the incredible emotions he'd never before experienced until now. Ernesto knew that he had fallen in love with this peasant girl, but he was afraid of the ramifications. A hawk flew over them and landed nearby atop a dead tree. Was it watching them? Did it approve? How could it not? Look at her beauty, her tenderness! The hawk just stared at them. Ernesto stood, clothed now, and shook his fists at its tree, but the hawk would not leave. Instead it looked away, now bored with them.

SEATED ON THE platform, Ernesto's head slumped to the side, and his body leaned heavily against the nearly full water container. The sound of muffled sloshing inside it further relaxed his tired mind.

Whitecaps splashed upon crests in the darkness, and wind blew the spray over to the next rise. Waves splashed and lifted the raft as if it was being offered up on the ocean's altar, but the occupants slept on. A large wave moved toward the raft, larger than any they had yet encountered, and it came at them head-on.

RAGE FILLED HIS father's eyes. Ernesto had continued with Maria after he demanded they break up, and now she was pregnant. And worse, she refused to have an abortion.

"I am a man now, father, I will make my own decisions." The words had been spoken, but Ernesto's lips had not moved.

Then his father's lips had moved, but Ernesto could only hear the sound of a dog growling. His father lurched toward him, his arm raised to strike—Ernesto easily blocked the blow, and then another, and his father's eyes bulged in rage. The words became more biting, the growl more violent. Ernesto spun wildly as he tried to get away from his father's yoke, his father's anger.

NO WHITECAP DRESSED the larger wave as it lifted the raft at a sharp angle. The rise lasted twice as long as anything previous, the bow of the raft pointed high into the night. Ernesto's weight pressed hard against the large water container, and as the raft crested the wave and dropped, the momentum toppled the water container over the back edge of the raft and dragged Ernesto with it. The container cut silently into the black water and sank fast. The rope that was tied around Ernesto's waist, connected to the container on one end and the raft on the other, jerked him into the ocean while dreams still swirled in his head.

The shock of the frigid water cut off the images of his father's wrath, and his eyes burst open. With little air in his lungs, he screamed—but was already under water—the sound was garbled in bubbles.

The container, tied off like an anchor, hung from the bottom of the raft with Ernesto suspended and his oxygen spent. After a brief struggle in the blackness, he gagged once on the seawater that had filled his lungs—partially purged them, only to fill them again.

Neither the large wave that had shaken the raft with great force nor Ernesto and the container plummeting into the sea had awakened the others.

17

THE MACEO BARRACKS in the center of Old Havana had minimal frontage on Calle Empedrado behind the Plaza de la Catedral, but since all the patrolmen traveled on foot, the central location was a necessity. Behind the fifteen-foot tall wooden gate was a cobblestone courtyard where the fifty-five PNR—Police National de la Revolución—forces that were stationed there had assembled. They had been summoned together even though many were off duty, and the loud hum of their speculation could be heard by pedestrians who ambled along Calle Empedrado outside the gate. Tourists paid little attention, but residents of the area hurried past, nervous at the anomaly.

The streets in the district were devoid of the PNR's who were normally posted on every other corner to provide tourists with a sense of ease while they wandered through the impoverished neighborhoods.

"Are they all here?" Captain Pinera asked.

"Yes, everyone's assembled," Lieutenant Cepero said.

The captain read the directive one last time. *Unbelievable.* He folded the paper and placed it in his breast pocket.

"Get my hat."

Lieutenant Cepero retrieved it from the back of the office door and held it while the captain examined himself in the mirror. Once finished smoothing his moustache and his eyebrows, he donned the cap, checked the mirror again and left the room. They took the steps from the third floor to the second and walked down a poorly lit hallway to a pair of French doors. Captain Pinera dramatically swung them open and stepped onto the small balcony that overlooked the courtyard.

Within seconds there was complete silence below. The captain's temper was not one to be tested. He leaned on the metal railing, gripping it tightly with both hands. The distance down to the courtyard masked his anguish, but Captain Pinero's stomach turned as he searched for the words his troops waited to hear.

"I have called you here tonight at the direct request of El Commandante himself. Our government has prepared a response to the American-induced Exodus that took so many of our people last month, and each of you will play an important role in the execution of this plan." He paused to let the words sink in.

"Starting at 9:00 tomorrow night, we are to collect as many of the jobless derelicts, malcontents, known dissidents, and criminals as possible and bring them to the Sierra Maestra Terminal to be processed."

The captain clenched the railing tightly and scanned the collection of stunned faces below. He couldn't hear their words, but a collective group of whispers floated up to his ears. After allowing them to digest the information, he held his palms up.

"El Commandante is relying on each of you for your commitment and diligence. Our goal is to assemble 3,000 people here in *Havana Viejo*. This operation is to remain secret until you receive your final orders tomorrow night. Any indiscretions will be severely punished." He paused again, searching shadowed faces for insolence.

"Although I am not permitted to tell you what the second phase of the processing will be, I assure you these people will not be harmed. Return to your posts, or to your homes, and do not tell anyone of this operation."

With that, the captain turned around abruptly, entered the building, and closed the doors behind him. He exhaled deeply and imagined thousands of people being ushered onto boats of all sizes at the Terminal. He closed his eyes then rubbed them.

I hope you know what you are doing, El Commandante.

REMINDERS OF CUBA'S STRUGGLE for autonomy and self-rule surrounded the Palacio de la Revolución. The huge black mural of Che Guevara on the Ministry of the Interior diligently observed visitors in the Plaza, and his words, "Always toward Victory," were sprawled underneath the mural, which forced even the most aggressive dissidents to think twice about challenging the State.

A fresh wreath lay at the base of the José Martí tower, placed there moments before by the Canadian Ambassador, who then walked through the Plaza named after the Revolution and down across Flag Square to the Palacio.

President Castro was hosting a late evening dinner at the Palacio for the Canadian delegation, inclusive of the ambassador and the president of St. Lawrence Air & Sea Ltd., a large company that had recently completed the renovation and expansion of the José Martí Airport, south of Havana.

The dinner had been arranged after repeated requests from the Canadian Ambassador to thank President Castro and Foreign Minister Ricardo Allasandre, who was also the former Cuban Ambassador to the United Nations, for what had been a lucrative and successful project to modernize Havana's airport.

During dinner it was obvious that both Ambassador Magill and Henri Micheaux from St. Lawrence Air & Sea had more on their minds than celebrating the finished project. They proposed new opportunities and suggested immediate action to keep pace with Cuba's skyrocketing influx of European, Asian, and Canadian tourists.

"With the exception of some minor improvements to the Sierra Maestra Terminal, Havana's harbor has not been modernized for anything beyond naval vessels and cargo ships," Micheaux said. "And with international cruise lines now considering Havana as a future major destination, the same rationale that applied to the airport should be used to further augment the harbor."

Although Castro was happy to have foreign companies improve Cuba's infrastructure, he had his own agenda for the evening. *If the Canadians knew what was planned for the Terminal tomorrow, they would be horrified.*

Micheaux continued, "When things open up, Cuba needs to be positioned for—"

"Let's talk about medical and pharmaceutical supplies," Castro said. He leaned into them and wagged his wrinkled index finger. Gone from his eyes was the jovial glint that had accompanied the light conversation over dinner, and the dark circles under them now looked ominous. Dessert was finished, and it was time for business.

"We have one of the best health care programs in the world, but we need to improve the flow of American and foreign pharmaceuticals into the country to supply our doctors with the latest medical advancements. What can Canada offer us in *this* area?"

The Ambassador squirmed in his chair. Regardless of the Cuban leader's shrunken physical stature, a fire still blazed in his eyes.

"Canadian pharmaceutical companies are at the leading edge of research and development," he said. "But…"

"You were saying, Mr. Ambassador?" Allasandre said after too long a pause.

Embarrassment reddened the diplomat's face. "There are problems…ah, complications shall I say, with American products of this nature."

"Problems? What problems?" Allasandre asked.

Do you think I will let you off the hook easily on this? Think again.

The Ambassador glanced at Micheaux, but his associate was studying his fingernails. As Magill was about to speak, there was a knock at the door.

Fidel furrowed his brow and glared at Allasandre. Although he was the Foreign Minister and not used to hopping to attention when there were knocks on doors, he stood to see who had disobeyed the president's instructions.

Castro pressed forward. "Canada is one of our largest trading partners, and in choosing foreign partners to invest with us in these important industries, we also expect them to participate in other critical areas of comparable magnitude."

"Yes, but—"

"Our own research and development has produced several ground breaking discoveries in the medical field, but we're not interested in replicating existing drugs that are patented worldwide. We must rely on our global trading partners to work with us to reciprocate our good faith."

Henri Micheaux looked upon Ambassador Magill with pity as Castro turned up the heat, but Allasandre's return from answering the door interrupted them. He bent down, his lips nearly brushing Castro's ear.

"You have an important call, sir."

Castro looked up as if Allasandre was insane, but the Foreign Minister raised an eyebrow and nodded once. Ambassador Magill and Henri Micheaux exchanged looks—relief, then curiosity.

The president's visible rage was so intense Allasandre looked toward the floor. He stood abruptly and without excusing himself marched from the room, his fury obviously mounting with every step.

ARTIFICAL LIGHT BATHED the sea of concrete, which provided an ethereal atmosphere that was lost on Arturo Dias. The vast open space between North Kendall Drive and the mountain of concrete known as Dadeland was filled with lonely light-posts that stood at attention like a platoon of soldiers. Arturo avoided the light and scurried between the few cars left at the Mall that had closed two hours earlier.

As he followed serpentine shadows toward the illuminated beacon atop the building, Arturo stopped below it and touched the concrete, then looked up to pay homage. Burdines Department Store was his equivalent to Mecca, and Arturo's rewards would come soon. He held a bottle of wine wrapped in a brown paper bag aloft toward the sign, tilted his head back and took a long pull. He wiped his mouth with his sleeve and dropped the empty bottle on the small patch of grass next to the building.

Arturo gazed around the empty lot and smiled. There was serenity to the quiet Mall, but then he imagined how it would look when his army of thugs stormed forward under the lights. *With me leading the way.*

He walked the perimeter of the large store and checked occasionally for the security patrols that sporadically drove the parking lots around the Mall. He scoffed at them, more worried about how he could control his accomplices. Arturo had a dual mission: to wreak havoc by leading a throng of looters through one of South Miami's largest shopping areas, and to grab as much booty for himself as possible.

After he had meandered around several corners, he found himself on the 72nd Avenue entrance, which was surrounded by huge glass display cases. Light from the windows pressed into the darkness, and the contents inside sparkled in lonely solitude. Arturo forgot entirely about caution as he leaned against the glass and pressed his nose as close as he could to the gleaming electronics on the other side.

Stereo equipment, DVD's, boom boxes, hand-held gadgets, VCR's, video games, computers, flat-screen TV's!

"Oh yeah, baby, tomorrow night you gonna be mine."

"HOW DARE YOU interrupt me! Do you have any idea how bad your timing is?"

"I'm terribly sorry, *El Máximo*, but you have a phone call. It's—"

"Phone call? You interrupt me for a *phone call*? Who could possibly be on the line that is more important than our largest trading partner? The President of the United States?"

"Close, sir."

"*What*? What's that you say?"

"It is the Chief of Staff to the President of the United States."

Fidel Castro's eyes tightened to slits, his hand lifted to pull at his ragged beard, and his nostrils flared as he inhaled—then exhaled with tremendous force.

"I will leave you now, *El Máximo*."

"Water. Bring me water," Fidel whispered.

He sat heavily at his desk, the Canadians a distant memory.

Why would Terri Turner be calling me, especially at this hour?

His heart pumped rapidly and his fingertips were numb from the nervous energy coursing through his body. He could count on one hand the number of times he had received phone calls directly from the White House over the past 42 years. Something was up. His paranoia and deep-seated mistrust of the United States were redlined.

Sources in America had informed their handlers in MININT that Congress had called an emergency session to decide how to handle the groundswell brewing to force the refugees back to Cuba by demanding federal assistance instead. That and the civil unrest percolating in Miami must have the Americans nervous.

He looked at the phone and saw the blinking light. For a split second he longed for a forbidden cigar, but sucked in a deep breath, smiled and punched the button with the force of a lifetime of conviction.

"Yes?"

"Hello? This is Terri Turner, chief of staff to the president of the United States. I'm holding for President Castro."

Fidel smiled and found the moment funny for reasons only he could understand.

"Hello, Miss Turner, what do you want?" he said in perfect if heavily accented English.

"Good evening, Mr. President, I hope I haven't caught you at a bad time."

"I'm in the middle of dinner with the Canadian Ambassador," Fidel said. His smile grew wider, always happy for a chance to irritate the White House. Her chuckle surprised him.

"Then I apologize for the intrusion, sir, and I promise to be brief."

Fidel detected little if any nervousness on the other end and his curiosity was further piqued.

"I'm calling you at the request of President Winslow." Her voice was faintly garbled and Fidel recognized the distortion common to satellite phones.

Why would she be calling me on a satellite phone?

"He's asked me to have a confidential discussion with you about the embargo."

Her voice sounded persuasive, even seductive. Fidel smelled a rat. The wound of his recent humiliation caused by the last American ambassadors wanting to improve relations was still raw.

"What about it? You want to discuss that here and now on your satellite phone, Miss Turner?"

"No sir, of course not. The president has asked me to meet with you for a confidential talk, just the two of us."

Fidel again pulled on his beard. His aide reappeared with a glass of water then vanished.

"What do you mean confidential?"

"He doesn't want Congress or the media to know about the meeting. He hoped you would appreciate the discretion."

"And when do you propose we have this confidential meeting, just you and me?"

"Tomorrow, if you're available."

"Tomorrow!" Fidel rocked forward in his chair.

"Yes, sir. I have a jet ready to take me down first thing in the morning."

His mind quickly calculated moves the United States might be making on the chessboard of their two country's' long and embattled past. None of them fit.

"I can't meet you tomorrow morning."

"How about tomorrow afternoon?"

He surprised himself. "Fine, that would work."

"Wonderful. If you'll alert your air traffic control, I'll arrive in Havana at one o'clock."

"No, not Havana. If this is to be confidential, then fly to Varadero. I'll have a car meet you at the airport at 1:00."

"My plane will be coming through the Bahamas."

"You're not defecting are you, Miss Turner?"

"No sir, but nobody aside from President Winslow and Attorney General Persico know that I'm coming."

They exchanged goodbyes, then Fidel sat stiffly in thought. An image from CNN of Terri Turner in an evening gown at some official function popped into his head, and he remembered thinking her attractive.

Unbelievable.

He had not been as surprised about a phone call since Nikita Khrushchev called in 1960 offering Soviet assistance to buy the sugar that the Americans had cancelled.

The door opened and Ricardo Allasandre peeked in. Fidel was sitting back in his chair, and Allasandre held his hands up in question.

"What about the Canadians?"

Fidel sat up straight. "Get rid of them."

"What? You're kidding? What about the medical supplies? It's critical that—"

"I said get rid of them! Call Raúl and Sanchez. Tell them to get here immediately. And put tomorrow's operation on hold. What is it the Americans say? We have bigger fish to fry!"

Allasandre stared wide-eyed, then turned and disappeared behind the door.

Fidel Castro's booming laugh followed him down the hall.

18

A LARGE WAVE shook the raft, and Maria awoke from her deep sleep. Nauseous from the motion, her pregnancy, or both, she stared into the star filled sky and tried to let her eyes focus. A brilliant shooting star slashing through the darkness startled her. She reached for Ernesto but felt nothing. She lurched up and looked toward the back of the raft where he had been.

He was gone.

She hurriedly checked each sleeping person, but none were Ernesto. "Am I dreaming?" she whispered. All of a sudden her chest collapsed and she could not breathe. Maria searched frantically as if she might have missed him somewhere on the tiny platform, but he was not there.

"ERNESTO!" She screamed at the top of her lungs.

CAPTAIN SCOTT HAWKES FOLDED the flash communiqué with the change in orders and placed it in his breast pocket. He let the news sink in, then allowed himself a slight smile.

"What's the news, Captain?" Ensign Hildebrand asked.

"Back to reality, Hilly." He paused and looked around the Combat Information Center, then out to the black sky. "We're being joined by the Intrepid."

"Why do we need another medium-endurance class cutter here now, sir?"

"Apparently, Fidel's up to his old tricks again."

The lieutenant scratched his head.

Hawkes knew he was too young to understand. "The spooks think another massive boatlift could be coming out of Cuba. The difference is this one's being organized by the government."

"But sir…"

"Don't ask me, son, I stopped trying to make sense of these things a long time ago. The Mohawk's orders have changed, though. From here on, we're back to repatriating the 'illegals.' No more gathering them up and bringing them to Florida, they're going back to Guantanamo."

A big smile came across the lieutenant's face. "Now *that* I understand, sir."

"Captain?" the radar operator said. "Looks like we have company, sir."

Hawkes looked over the man's shoulder and bent down toward the circular screen. A large anomaly appeared and it was heading north.

"What the hell's that?"

"Can't be sure, sir. She's not responding to radio contact. It's got size, and it's coming out of Cuban waters."

Shit. With no helos or fixed-wings in the region there was no way for a quick identification of the contact.

"Could be a Cuban Navy vessel or a ship filled with illegals," Hawkes said. "Either way, we need to find out. Distance and coordinates?"

The petty officer moved a mouse, clicked, and coordinates appeared on the screen.

"Eight miles, one-five-five, sir."

Captain Hawkes repeated the coordinates over the microphone to the OOD on the bridge, then turned to Lieutenant Hildebrand.

"Condition 1, Lieutenant. Announce it on the 1MC. We're changing course to intercept the contact. Keep trying to raise her on the radio."

When the announcement was made over the ship's intercom, the Mohawk turned sharply to the southeast. Word traveled through the ship that the Cubans were preparing to launch a human flotilla and that the orders were to consider it an offensive strike against the country. Even after the twelve-day cruise, where more dead bodies had been found than live, and even though it was the middle of the night, everyone on board was roused to battle stations to match the ship's official state of readiness.

Helmets were donned and armed crew scattered about the deck to observation stations. The Mohawk would proudly sail into the eye of the coming storm, and Captain Hawkes would fight off fatigue to intercept any vessel that was illegally pointed toward the United States.

"WHAT THE HELL?" Juan yelled. It was too dark to be awake.

"Ernesto! He's gone!"

To Juan's amazement, he was. Vilma crossed herself and wrapped her arms around Maria, who was sobbing uncontrollably.

What the hell?

Manuel searched the water, lifting his head and mumbling incoherently—then suddenly stopped his search and pointed to something dragging behind the raft.

"The rope!" he called out.

Juan crawled around the others and took hold of the rope. It weighed a ton and was angled straight down. He tried to pull it up, but it was too heavy.

"Give me a hand."

Maria watched their every move as tears streamed down her cheeks.

"What is it?"

"The rope to the water container," Manuel said. "Ernesto had it around his waist,"

"How—"

A large wave cut Juan off and soaked all of them then passed under the raft, which fell at a steep angle into its trough. The large water container surfaced behind them in the swell, attached to it a dark, lifeless form in a yellow jacket.

Maria shrieked, her body buckled, and she would have fallen overboard had Vilma not grabbed her just in time.

"Oh my God," Juan said. "Grab his arms."

Juan couldn't control his shaking hands as they pulled Ernesto onto the deck. Vilma held tight to Maria, whose sobs had become heartrending wails.

Ernesto's skin was chalky, his eyes open and opaque. Manuel gently pressed his eyelids shut as Maria fell onto his corpse, wailing and shaking violently. Juan untied Ernesto from between the water container and the raft, then retied the container to the deck.

"What happened?" Manuel asked. "How could I have lost him?"

Juan looked sharply at Manuel. *You lost him?*

Maria's wailing settled into a steady cry. Vilma, holding her in a bear hug, began to hum.

Juan knew nothing would console Maria. He saw the slight swell of her abdomen. *Coño, man, the baby.*

"Why did this happen? Why Ernesto?" Maria said.

Juan had no idea what time it was, but based on the position of the moon he guessed they were closer to dawn than dusk. Maria dropped her head in Vilma's lap, and the humming continued while Vilma stroked her hair.

Manuel lay back down and turned his attention to the sea. Juan followed his gaze—and gasped. A light was ahead of them, a searchlight scanning the waves!

"Manuel! Vilma!"

They didn't need to ask what he saw. The searchlight tore through the night.

"A patrol boat!" Juan said.

"How do you know?" Manuel said.

"Who else would be searching out here in the middle of the night?" Juan looked around the raft. "Cover everything up." He looked down at Ernesto's yellow jacket, then pulled his own sweater over his head and covered Ernesto's torso.

"Stay down. Don't move, don't talk." The patrol boat was less than a half-kilometer away. He looked at Maria, calmer now, and hoped she would stay that way. If he could just get images of the Guardia chasing and shooting the smuggler's boat out of his mind—

He couldn't, because Maria was looking at the patrol boat and starting to cry louder than ever.

"You *have to be quiet*, Maria," Vilma said.

"I don't care, I don't—"

"Stop it!" Juan said. "I *told* you Castro's ordered the Guardia to shoot all *balseros* on sight. They won't repatriate us, they'll kill us!"

"I don't care, they can—" Now came a wail.

Manuel put his arm over his face and lay down.

Juan poked Vilma and leaned down so his mouth was close to Maria's ear.

"Ernesto wouldn't want his baby killed by the Cuban Navy," he said.

"You know that," Vilma said. "We *must* be quiet."

Maria buried her face in her hands, continued to shudder but had stopped wailing.

Juan studied the patrol boat. *Maybe they're checking the perimeter of Cuban waters, and we've reached the Gulf Stream.*

The ship moved on a line from left to right and traveled slowly past them, the beam of light pointed ahead of its path. Diesel engines rumbled above the waves, the pungent smell of burnt fuel carried on the breeze. As the boat continued past, it suddenly changed heading and turned directly toward them.

"They're coming at us!" Manuel whispered loudly.

"Stay quiet and keep down," Juan said.

The patrol boat was moving in fast on a 45-degree angle—Juan estimated that it would pass within 100 yards of the raft. The searchlight began a 180-degree scan from left to right, which would include their position if the patrol boat maintained its course.

Did they pick us up on radar? Are they searching for us?

The silhouettes of people walking on deck were visible in front of the lights aboard the ship, and the beam was getting closer, only a hundred yards away now. The others had their heads buried in their arms and were silent, except for Manuel, who Juan heard praying. A gust of wind blew over the waves and Juan's sweater fell off Ernesto. The searchlight swung back toward them, and Juan fumbled with the sweater to cover the yellow jacket back up, getting it done just as a faint wash of light spread over them.

He held his breath. *Come on, baby, go past us, just keep fucking going.*

Then Juan spotted another light on the horizon.

The patrol boat's engines suddenly revved and the boat slowly continued, parallel to the raft, its searchlight now swinging in a painfully diligent circuit. The raft had picked up speed and moved more quickly now. Through his fear, Juan hoped they were in international waters. The beam of light had an incredible reach and slowly came straight at them.

"Oh God, please—" Vilma said.

"Ssshh," Juan said. It was too late. The beam of light was upon them, blinding him as he stared back at the patrol boat like a raccoon caught in a trashcan.

A horn pierced the darkness, and the beam remained fixed on the raft.

"Freeze." Juan ducked. "Hide your faces—play dead!"

Vilma elbowed Juan in the side as Maria shrieked.

Y, coño. How stupid am I?

The horn sounded again.

19

THE AMPHORA CAFÉ in Herndon, Virginia was a discreet little diner a half-mile off the Dulles Toll Road and a half-hour outside the nation's capitol. Nestled behind a Texaco station and an office building named after President Ford, the squat silver building was hard to see unless you knew it was there. Fortunately for the owners, plenty of people did.

Two customers who frequented one of the back booths for clandestine meetings were always surprised that nobody recognized them so few miles outside of Washington. Dressed casually, they blended with the low-key dot-commers and mothers who had just dropped their kids at school.

"Everything's set for tomorrow," Spinelli said. He licked the remnants of frosting off his finger from the Danish he'd devoured in three bites.

"That's why I needed to see you," Dunleavy said in a low voice.

His tone triggered alarm bells in Spinelli's mind. *You should be kissing my ass right now.*

"I didn't want to blind-side you tomorrow," Dunleavy said.

"What the hell are you talking about?"

"I met with Winslow last night," he whispered. "He called at the last minute, we drove around and discussed the situation."

Spinelli's features twisted more with every word Senator Dunleavy spoke.

"The CIA's dug up some fresh intelligence. They say the shit's going to hit the fan."

"Meaning—"

"Castro is going to launch another exodus. They think it'll be as big as Mariel, or worse." Dunleavy's eyes narrowed. "Do you know what that would do to me? To Florida?"

"What the hell are you saying?"

"Winslow asked me to stall or vote against the emergency session. He thinks Castro plans to use that as his excuse to light the fuse."

"*What?*"

"He said he has a plan, just needs a couple weeks."

"Weeks!" Spinelli said. "And you agreed to this? Christ, Bob, your state's on the brink of anarchy!" And then it dawned on him.

Winslow is hanging me out to dry. Time to improvise.

"I know all about Castro's plans," Spinelli said. "I met with Hector and Mas Fina last night and they've got their own snitches in Havana. They're pretty upset with you, I might add."

"Listen, I'm desperate. You should see Miami, it's a powder keg."

"Winslow is trying to scare you. The Coast Guard is on alert and you can be damn sure they'll be ready this time. Don't you see? He's driving a wedge between us to stall for time so he's not humiliated by the emergency session. He's using you, Bob."

"That's not the impression I got. At all."

A waiter came and refilled their coffees. When he was gone, Spinelli edged forward on his bench seat.

"I've got something that'll blow your mind." He smiled. "If you support Winslow after this, you'll get implicated in the scandal."

"What scandal?"

"The one you're going to break this afternoon. It's going to make Whitewater look like a parking ticket." His smile widened. "Winslow Oil owns a dozen oil wells and a refinery in Cuba."

"What? Are you—can you substantiate it?"

"You bet your ass I can. I've got it all in black and white. Winslow is trying to kill the embargo for personal gain. If he cuts a deal with Castro and gets his wells and refinery back, his company makes a windfall."

"Holy shit!"

Spinelli glanced around the room. Nobody was looking their way.

"Now, me being a Republican and having this information presents a dilemma. If all I cared about was myself, I'd call for an investigation or demand a meeting with the president and present him with the evidence and demand he back off."

"That puts you in a bad position," Dunleavy said.

"Exactly. But you see why you can't trust him? Or why you can't let him string you along? We'll have the emergency session tomorrow, and we'll release federal aid to help your state avoid further catastrophe."

Dunleavy nodded his head slowly.

"I'll let Hector and Mas Fina know you've seen the light. They'll be happy to have you back in the fold." *Schmuck*. But, having Dunleavy's assistance now was worth sharing CAC's money, at least for the short term.

"What are you going to do?"

Spinelli smiled. "Here's what *we're* going to do…"

20

BREAKFAST AT THE WHITE HOUSE was standard practice for the president's closest cabinet members and advisors. Invitations depended on the topic, but the sessions were always effective sounding boards to share opinions and decide on action. This morning's session was both standard operating procedure and highly irregular because of its content.

Gathered in the Treaty Room, adjacent to the Oval Office, the group passed around trays of bagels, egg sandwiches, and croissants. The aroma of fresh coffee filled the air and its caffeine further heightened the frayed nerves in the room.

"I can't believe this is happening," Attorney General Persico said.

"It's happening all right," Winslow said. "So quit with the butterflies and let's finish prepping Terri."

"I'm just glad it's not me," Persico said. "You've got brass... ah, guts, Terri."

Secretary of State Edward Abramson still looked disappointed that he was not the one going to meet Castro, but the president's rationale made sense. Secrecy was important in case Cuba refused the initiative or the press found out about the trip. It could hardly be maintained if the secretary of state went on such a controversial mission when the real purpose of the meeting was a down and dirty negotiation. It was a stretch and they all knew it.

"What about the reports of Castro's frailty? I mean, how did he sound?" Abramson asked.

"Cagey," Turner said.

"There's a surprise."

"But he also sounded intrigued that we were keeping the trip a secret."

"Remember how he paraded Spinelli and Dunleavy around? He won't risk another bite in the ass," Winslow said.

"I'm surprised he was willing to meet at all," Abramson said.

"I made it clear it was to discuss the embargo," Turner said.

"The embargo?" Abramson said. "You told me it was for the Migration Accords?"

"Both, really," Winslow said. "We can't afford another massive Exodus, and since Castro is claiming that we abandoned the Accords—"

"He's planning to Carter us," Turner said.

"I can't let Congress make this matter unsalvageable," Winslow said. "We've got excellent sources telling us that if the emergency session goes through, Castro will open a port, just like he did with Mariel, and we'll be inundated with thousands more refugees."

"Cartered?"

Winslow ignored him. "The Accords *are* paramount, but I told Terri to start with the bigger picture. Why not?"

"Because Helms-Burton says you can't?"

"Well, that—"

Persico cut Winslow off. "The President can suspend the embargo if certain things happen. He would have to submit it to Congress and prove that sufficient change has happened to warrant the move, but there is room there."

Abramson snorted. "Good luck. Shoot, Terri, forget my earlier envy, you can have this one." Then he turned to the president. "You didn't listen to my advice against Spinelli and Dunleavy speaking for you last time. Do you really think Terri can pull this off?"

"Based on trying a new approach, I think we have a shot," Winslow said.

"What new approach?"

"Let's just say that for 42 years we've beat our heads against the wall with nothing to show for it. I believe the American people will support letting democracy go *mano-a-mano* against Castro's brand of socialism, and I think we'll change their politics through embracing their people faster than we have by starving them."

"How can you overlook the human rights situation? Castro won't allow any independent monitoring of prison conditions. What do you think the Cuban-American voters are going to say?" Abramson said.

"It's only the old-timers like Mas Fina who still want to starve Cuba away from communism," Winslow said. "Not one dissident leader in Cuba supports the embargo, and lots of the younger Cuban-Americans are breaking with tradition and are willing to try a more dynamic approach. Plus we can't afford to divert our foreign policy to appease small groups of hard-liners anymore—important voting bloc or not."

"You'll get crucified if Congress finds out. What about their emergency session tomorrow?"

A smile came to the president's lips. "That's been taken care of."

"What's that supposed to mean?"

"I met with Senator Dunleavy and presented the evidence on Castro's intentions. Based on that he agreed to delay the emergency session, or vote against it if need be."

"I see. That *is* a nice wild card, but can he be trusted?" Abramson said.

"It should give us a few days, and plenty of time for Terri to convince Castro to keep the Migration Accords intact, if nothing else."

"Good luck. After what happened last month, he'll relish the chance to maul you." Abramson's face changed from concern to amusement. "Oh, I get it, Cartered. Like when Castro disemboweled Carter with Mariel."

The president waved the comment off. "Forget about Carter, forget about Mariel, and forget about Castro wanting to get even. Terri will work it out, she has to."

All eyes turned to her.

"Sure she will," the secretary of state said. "Castro's never done anything we've asked him to, Florida's in a crisis mode, and Congress is poised to sweep in and save the day."

"And make the Administration look paralyzed," Turner said.

"Congress is the only one who can end the embargo, " Persico said. "You've made your position clear about fearing a greater exodus, and the emergency session will protect you from taking the blame."

"I will *not* sit back and watch this happen, just so I could say 'I told you so,'" Winslow said.

"It's awfully risky, George. A hell of a long shot."

"Well, Terri is leaving in an hour. I guess if all else fails, then we'll kowtow to Congress and send funds to Florida." He suddenly felt very tired. "But we'll be in big trouble. Castro will have the last laugh, again, and Cubans will be washing up on the Florida coast like dead fish on a red tide."

"No pun intended," Persico said.

"Let's not give up so fast, gentlemen," Turner said. "I hear what you're saying, Edward, and you may be right. But sometimes it's the unexpected that works best. Spinelli's as confident as the day is long, thinking he's in the driver's seat and that once again he'll end up the hero. He's completely indifferent to the ramifications of the emergency session because his donors will be happy. Dunleavy won't ask for a delay until the session starts, so we've got between now and then to make something happen. It's not much, but nothing ventured..."

"You're right about one thing, Spinelli *is* in the driver's seat," Abramson said.

As the only person in the room with a long resume on foreign affairs, his opinion worried the president.

"What choice do we have?" Turner said. "If I fail, there will be a new crisis in Florida, thousands of Cubans will die, and our country's ill-fated course against Cuba will continue indefinitely."

"Terri's right," Winslow said.

"We have so much at stake trying to hold the international coalition against terrorism together," Abramson said. "I'd hate to see it all ruined because of Cuba. I can't talk you out of this, George?"

"It's your job to hold that together while Terri rectifies the Cuban mess."

"You're walking on eggshells."

"Our only chance is to take the offensive, and it's got to happen fast. We'll reconvene tonight after Terri reports in." Winslow took a deep breath. "I've got a few surprises up my sleeve for Spinelli and Congress I'll announce later. Then, depending on what happens in Havana—"

"Varadero," Turner said.

"Whatever. Depending on what happens with Castro, tomorrow should be one hell of a day."

Secretary Abramson again shook his head, then looked from one set of eyes to the next.

"All of you remember, I'm on the record against this adventure."

21

PORTUGESE MEN-OF-WAR littered the waves like wildflowers on a mountain pasture. The rising sun illuminated their purple rosebud-shaped bladders, and their poisonous tentacles extended deeply into the black sea. With dawn came the reality that last night's tragedy was not just a bad dream. The sun's first rays picked out Ernesto's lifeless body lying across the back of the raft made that perfectly clear.

Maria awoke early and Juan saw her turn half-asleep to check Ernesto, but in the split second it took her to turn back her face became a mask of grief. Her pain pulled at his heart. Experienced in losing loved ones, Juan couldn't fathom how it would feel to carry your dead lover's baby. The thought turned his stomach.

With her face in her hands Maria cried the tears of love stolen away. But then the tears stopped, and something not unlike a smile curved her lips. Juan saw that she was touching her belly—where through her baby, Ernesto's blood was still alive inside her.

Juan had slept little during the night. He wondered about the patrol boat that had shined its light on the raft and sounded its horn yet had not approached them. Either the Guardia thought they were dead and not worth bothering with, or the raft had crossed into international waters and they honored the line. Whatever the reason, Juan should feel lucky to be alive.

But he didn't. The reality that he would have drowned yesterday had he not been saved by Ernesto, who now lay dead in front of him, left him feeling scared and forlorn. He knew better than to question the justice of their circumstances, having never known anything beyond the raw end of life himself. But when he looked at the others he knew none of them would be much help during the remainder of their journey, and fear spread through his veins like a dye injected to root out tumors.

Maria shuddered and he put his hand on her shoulder. *I'll try to take care of her for you, man. If we make it, I promise to help your girl, I don't know how but I'll figure something out.*

If only I had a cigarette.

Vilma opened her eyes with a start, shivered and looked out to sea.

"I dreamt I was home...." Her happy voice caught in her throat when she turned to Ernesto. Reality hit her as it had everyone this morning.

As hours wore on, Juan exchanged glances with Vilma and Manuel, the unspoken message clear. They had to do something about Ernesto. His color had turned to a dull gray, his fingernails were white, one of his eyelids was frozen halfway open, and his skin had marbled.

Juan pictured the bloody rack of ribs they found afloat two days before. *I hope you don't end up like that, amigo.*

The blue ocean provided Maria with an endless panorama to stare at without a thing to focus on. Now seated, she held her knees and faced away from Ernesto. Her breathing was now under control. The tears had dried on her cheeks, but her complexion remained chalky. She drank from one of the bottles and turned her head sideways toward Juan.

"We need to let him go," she said.

Let him go? He looked to Vilma, who nodded.

"It's best...." Maria shuddered but wasn't crying.

"Would you say something, Vilma?" Juan said.

"Of course."

With heads bowed and their hands clutched in a circle, they made a ring of arms around Ernesto's body. Vilma started with the Lord's Prayer, then asked for Ernesto's soul to be taken into heaven.

Juan struggled to hide the tremble of his hands as he turned Ernesto onto his side. Manuel helped him roll the body to the edge.

Juan hesitated a moment in case Maria wanted to touch Ernesto one last time, but she turned her back to them. They rolled him over the edge.

The others looked away, not toward each other, not at Ernesto's body as it spun slowly in the waves, and not at Maria. But her grief enveloped them like a cocoon. Juan thought of Ernesto's saying last night that he'd make his father suffer if it was the last thing he did. With that, Juan knew that Ernesto had accomplished his wish.

22

WITH TURNER GONE, and everything in motion to at least provide a fighting chance on the Cuban situation, the president forced himself to focus on other business. The morning flew by, working with Cindy Francis, his favorite speechwriter, to prepare a state of the union address and to outline some thoughts on his anticipated comments regarding the situation in Miami. Next came a photo-session and a brief chat with the new President of Argentina, and finally, a luncheon with the New York Yankees to commemorate their recent World Series win.

The remainder of the day was heavily booked, with Congressmen seeking help on a variety of porked-up legislation, meetings with cabinet members, including the director of the Immigration and Naturalization Service to discuss the latest intelligence on the next potential boatlift. And all through the day Winslow waited anxiously for news from Terri Turner.

He was startled when the door to the Oval Office burst open and his press secretary, rushed in with Sally Miles in hot pursuit.

"What's going on?"

"I tried to stop him," Sally said, "but—"

Teitlebaum threw open the panel that hid an in-wall television and searched frantically for the remote control.

"Harvey! What the hell's going on?"

The press secretary spun to face him, a wild look in his eyes.

"We've got to get C-SPAN on. Bob Dunleavy's called for a Press Conference, and it's supposed to be bad, I mean *really* bad."

When Winslow turned on the television with the remote control from his desk drawer, he immediately recognized the scene as a conference room in the Hart office building. The few journalists present suddenly jumped to their feet and started shouting questions when someone entered the room.

"Is he announcing the delay of the emergency session?" He turned the volume up and walked around to stand with Teitlebaum. *Dunleavy didn't say anything about a Press Conference last night.*

"...I am before you today to present some very alarming information about the President of the United States," Senator Dunleavy said.

"What?" Winslow bent over to grip the top of the chair in front of him.

"...These documents were copied from official records in the Office of the City Secretary in Houston, Texas, and they clearly demonstrate that the president's company, Winslow Oil, owns several oil fields and a substantial oil refinery in Cuba." Dunleavy held aloft a binder with the Winslow Oil Company logo on the front.

The color drained from Winslow's face, and he was vaguely aware of Harvey Teitlebaum's eyes drilling into him. The phone started to ring, but he ignored it, totally focused on the screen. *How could this be? Dunleavy?*

"...In the Southern Oil acquisition that his company completed nearly fifteen years ago, one of many acquisitions that fueled their rapid growth during the 80's, these fields and the plant came into their possession. Southern Oil operated in Cuba from the 1940's through the time that Castro nationalized all American interests there in 1960...."

"Mr. President," Sally said. "Mr. President?" She touched him on the shoulder. "The Vice President's on the phone, says it's urgent."

"I can't..." Winslow sat heavily into the chair, still looking at the screen.

"...I strongly recommend that the Attorney General appoint a special prosecutor to look into this matter immediately. Based on the president's interest to terminate the embargo against Cuba, it is likely that he intended to personally profit through these assets...."

Sally tugged at his arm again. "Sir, the Attorney General is on the phone."

"…These issues will be discussed at the emergency session of Congress tomorrow.…"

When Dunleavy finished his statement and began to field questions, Teitlebaum turned the television off. "Where's Terri? She needs to start on damage control immediately,"

The president—sagged in the yellow armchair—then sat up straight.

"She's—ah…" *Oh my God.* "I'll speak with her. Harvey, those wells and refinery are worthless. All of it, junk! They were nothing more than a footnote in the Southern deal. I just met with Dunleavy last night, he didn't even hint at this. I can't believe he's that conniving."

"He *is* a Democrat, sir."

"He didn't say a Goddamn word! *And*, he agreed to stonewall the emergency session. The double-crossing son-of-a—"

The phone rang and Winslow jumped. It was line three, his private line used for emergencies. He took a deep breath and bit down hard, scooping the phone up.

"What?"

"This is a problem." It was the Attorney General.

"You think?"

"Is anybody there with you?"

The president glanced at Harvey and hesitated. He lowered the phone. "That'll be all for now, Harvey." His eyes followed Teitlebaum, and once the door was closed he lifted the phone back to his ear. "Listen, Steve, I never even thought about this crap. It's purely coincidental. Total bullshit."

"Bullshit?"

"Well, not really bullshit, it's true, there were Cuban assets that came with the Southern Oil deal, but, hell, those wells are as dry as Dunleavy's wife, and the refinery was shut down in the 1950s. It's garbage! It had no bearing on the decision to buy Southern Oil, and certainly not on my desire to change our policy vis-à-vis Cuba." He suddenly realized what Clinton must have felt like sitting here when Whitewater broke.

"Don't say any more, George. You need private counsel on this—you and I cannot discuss it any further. You know the Democrats will rally around it."

Winslow started to respond, but the words stuck in his throat. Steve Persico could not advise him on this mess. *Terri, I need you back here.*

"Off the record?" Persico said. "If you can document what you're saying, then I'd recommend you immediately appoint a Special Prosecutor to investigate the allegations and drop your drawers. If the country finds out what you were planning to do with Castro and that Turner's there now…."

"I can't back down now. If Castro launches another—"

"Don't be foolish—going through with that now would be suicide. You have no choice but to drop it. Don't you want to save your skin?"

Winslow hung up the phone, took his head in his hands and slid low behind the Teddy Roosevelt desk.

"What the hell am I doing here?"

23

JUAN UNROLLED HIS YO-YO while he watched Manuel apply a strip of dead fish to his hook.

"Hurry up and get that in the water, it stinks," Vilma said.

"But the fish will love it." Juan said.

There was no weed line today, and the flotilla of Portuguese men-of-war had disappeared. Juan pointed to a huge flock of birds hovering in the distance. He remembered the buzzards that soared above Havana, how they would attack rats that ambled through open gutters, or feast on roadkill.

Several of the birds dove into the water, then circled around and dove in again.

"With any luck, we'll drift into whatever they're eating," Manuel said.

"We need some *food*," Vilma said.

They lowered their hand lines into the purple depths. The bait lingered on the surface, just as Ernesto's corpse had lingered for nearly an hour this morning. Juan had watched his body swirl in the eddies and twist at awkward angles as it was lifted high on the waves.

Vilma passed the time alternating between humming and singing. Her lyrics now stirred a sense of familiarity in Juan.

> *"I don't want the flowers to know about*
> *The torments that life throws at me.*
> *If they knew what I am suffering*
> *They too would weep for my sorrow."*

"What song is that?" Juan asked. "I know it from somewhere."

"It's called *Silencio*," Manuel said. "It's my favorite bolero."

"I'm impressed," Vilma said.

The sun had risen to its noontime peak, its reflection on the water blinding. But the air remained cooler than the days before. Juan shivered, estimating that the wind change and increased velocity had lowered the temperature by ten degrees.

"Look!" Maria pointed to a sailfish that had broken the surface. His sail waved over as he rolled. "He's riding the waves."

"Can we catch him?" Vilma asked.

"Not with these things," Manuel said. "He'd take all our line."

Juan suddenly saw a school of stubby blue fish jump into the air. He hunkered down and hoped for a tug on his line, but they drifted beyond where the sailfish had been without a bite.

"I thought we'd catch something there for sure," he said.

A black bill rose from below, slapped the water and re-ignited the blue fish, which skidded across the surface like skipping stones.

Juan's arms suddenly jerked. "Hey! I've got something." He fought with the yo-yo, but the fish pulled so hard that he nearly fumbled it overboard.

"Hold on!"

His hands burned from the friction as he tried to stop the disc from spinning, and then his fish broke the water.

"It's a tuna!" Manuel cried out. "A perfect little one!"

"If this son-of-a-bitch is small, I'd hate to get a big one," Juan said.

Juan could not stop the spin of the yo-yo, and Juan feared that he would not only lose the fish but all his line, too. He sensed a change and shifted position. The little tuna broke the surface, followed by a large black silhouette that exploded through the water.

"Sailfish!" Manuel shouted. "It's chasing the tuna. Wind it in, Juan. Wind, wind, wind!"

The sailfish moved with lightning speed, incredibly fast and agile. Both fish disappeared below the surface, but Juan could still feel pressure on the line.

"I still have her!"

When the sailfish surfaced again, it had the tuna crossways in its mouth.

"Ayy, no!" Manuel said. "Break the line, don't let him take it!"

Juan pulled up sharply trying to break the fish off, but the yo-yo quickly free spooled down to the knot, the line pulled tight and snapped, and Juan fell backwards with the empty spool still in his hand.

"Shit!" He threw the yo-yo onto the deck.

Manuel looked into the bags tied to the back of the raft.

"That's it, there's no extra line."

Juan took a deep breath. *Great, we're down to one yo-yo.*

On the northwestern horizon a thin dark line separated the water from the sky. For an instant Juan thought it was land, then realized it was a long black squall line.

Juan thought the squall looked like a smoky sea snake slithering in the distance.

THE WHITE HOUSE WAS surrounded by so many TV trucks and reporters that it looked like it was under siege. Deep in the heart of the building, the Press Room was packed beyond capacity. If a Fire Marshall dared to step foot inside the room, he could close the whole Press Conference down. Nobody aside from the voracious White House correspondents wanted to be here right now, especially the Press Secretary.

Harvey Teitlebaum strode toward the podium that bore the presidential seal, the press corps screaming questions even before he stopped. Harvey ignored them, removed his notes, looked tentatively around the room and held his hands up.

"All right...quiet, quiet, please."

The room settled down.

"Today's briefing will focus on the allegations made this morning by Senator Robert Dunleavy. First, I'll read a statement and then I'll take questions."

An explosion of camera flashes blinded Harvey for a moment, and the sound of their clicking shutters, and winding film made him feel like he was in a horror movie with giant insects descending upon him.

"First of all, what Senator Dunleavy said this morning was partially accurate. Winslow Oil did buy the balance of Southern Oil Company's holdings out of bankruptcy in 1987. But, that's where Senator Dunleavy's accuracy ends, and a completely misguided hypothesis begins." Teitlebaum quickly glanced around and balled his fists to fight off his nerves.

"Southern Oil had been in business since 1940, and their assets included twenty-four oil field leases scattered throughout Northern Mexico, and Western Texas, along with two small, but functioning refineries in Houston. The company had once owned some assets in Cuba that were nationalized by the Cuban Government in 1960. All of this is well documented in court records stemming from claims filed against Southern Oil by banks that had financed these assets." A wave rumbled through the Press Corps, and another explosion of flashes blinded him.

"These loans were for the acquisition of oil fields, and the remains of an old refinery east of Havana. When Southern purchased them, the fields had not produced a drop of oil in five years, and the refinery had been abandoned since 1953. Southern Oil's goal had been to drill new wells, and re-build the refinery, which was under construction when Castro took power in 1959.

"The president strongly rejects any linkage between his foreign policy initiative toward Cuba, and any former assets that Southern Oil may have held there over 40 years ago, and to that end, will support Senator Dunleavy's request for a Special Investigation. However, these allegations are completely groundless, and the president has every confidence that they will be dropped quickly once the truth comes to light. Now, I'll take a few questions."

As soon as he mentioned 'questions' the room erupted, which forced Teitlebaum to take a step back from the podium. He leaned into the sound as if it were a gale force wind, and then pointed to someone in the front row. "Daniel," he said.

"Can you confirm that the president has retained Myron Snider as his defense counsel?"

"Yes, he has retained Mr. Snider, but as an advisor, not as defense counsel." He pointed to another. "Greg?"

"Has the president considered resigning over these allegations?"

Teitlebaum ignored the question and pointed to another journalist.

"How is President Winslow taking these accusations?"

The vision of Winslow collapsing into the chair in the Oval Office, and mumbling the words, '…this will ruin me…' played in his mind, but Teitlebaum smiled. "Of course he's upset, but he knows the truth will clear the accusation up quickly, and he's determined not to let it affect his commitment to the American people."

Teitlebaum pointed to a woman in the middle of the crowd. "Regina?"

"How will this affect the plight of the Exodus refugees in Miami?"

"The president is determined to find a solution to the crisis in Florida, and to ensure the preservation of the Migration Accords with Cuba to prevent additional illegal migration."

After responding to each question, Teitlebaum searched the room for journalists that he hoped would be reasonable, and held his breath while they lobbed the next potential grenade.

"Is the president involved in the day to day operations of Winslow Oil?"

"Absolutely not. He placed all his investments into a blind trust before he took office. He took an indefinite leave of absence from his position on the board of Directors at Winslow Oil when he became the Governor of Texas in 1990, and has had no involvement in the operations or management decisions of the company since then."

"Did Southern Oil, or their banks, file a lawsuit at The Hague when Cuba nationalized their assets? And, if so, did Winslow Oil perfect these claims after the acquisition?"

"I don't know the answer to that question, but will find out." He paused. "Yes, Elizabeth?"

"Have the Democrats said who they will use for the Special Investigator?"

"Not that I have heard, but the president has stated that it should be someone who is thorough, diligent and brutally honest so this matter can be aired quickly and put to rest. David?"

"Why is the Administration interested in embracing a brutal communist dictator with such a terrible human rights record?"

Teitlebaum felt like he was on a roll now, and he considered each question as a personal challenge. "The president does not want to 'embrace' Mr. Castro, but he *is* interested in adopting a new approach to bring about positive change in Cuba. The last nine presidents have continued the same aggressive policy, and all that has happened is we have made innocent Cuban people suffer, and upset the rest of the world by imposing sanctions and penalties on them for trading with Cuba. The president was interested in this as another positive step forward to improve global relations, while also preventing Cuba from being pushed into the hands of another unfriendly nation, similar to what happened with the Soviet Union in 1960.

"The Exodus has complicated that initiative, but further emphasizes the need to establish a better policy toward Cuba," Teitlebaum paused and panned the room. "Yes, Ron?"

"Nixon resigned after Watergate, President Clinton was impeached because of his conduct related to various scandals, and President Reagan was mired in Iran-Contra for years. Will that be the same result for Cubagate?"

"Cubagate?" As the word left Teitlelbaum's mouth, he immediately regretted saying it, but with the word uttered, the incident was so-named. "No way. This is totally different," he said. *I hope.*

FROM HIS BED in room 127 of the Green Acres Retirement Home, in Worcester, Massachusetts, Warner Haslett lifted the remote control with a shaky hand, and turned the small television set off. He turned to his roommate, who was lying in the bed next to his, and shook his wrinkled head.

"Heh! He's right, Robey. All that stuff is worthless!"

Robey Johnson's lips peeled back to reveal his toothless gums. "What the hell you talking about, you old fool?" Robey's cataract covered eyes looked like white marbles in a shrunken coconut.

"Fool? They're talking about my old comm-pp-an-ee—" Warner began to cough—the wrinkles on his ancient body quivered with each hack. The coughing, however, could not stop his old mind from turning back to his glory days. Just hearing the name 'Southern Oil' had stirred Warner's most memorable years from his nearly forgotten past. In his mind's eye, he still saw himself as the aggressive young point man responsible to report to the big shots back in Houston on their latest acquisition.

"It's the Pilar! I ran the damn plaaaacc-aahhg-uuggh—" He started to cough and sputter all over again.

"All right, Warner, just don't...Goddamn! Stop that coughing!" Robey lifted his panic button with his ebony hand. "I'll call the nurse if you don't cut that out, Warner. Damn fool talk… Hey! You breathing over there?"

Warner carefully drew in a shallow breath and tried to settle what was left of his remaining lung. He squinted at his younger roommate.

I was there you old son-of-a-bitch. That was my operation!

A huge smile came over Robey Johnson. He started to chuckle, but he sucked in too deeply and began a slow cough that escalated into one that rivaled Warner's. Unconcerned for Robey's welfare, Warner had closed his eyes, and his mind was back in Havana, going from the Pilar Oil Fields to the dancing girls in the private clubs.

I was there all right.

Robey then fell into a deep sleep.

24

TERRI TURNER WAS amazed at the landscape's natural beauty as she flew toward the Cuban mainland, but aside from a vague recognition, her mind was far away. She had nearly made it to the Bahamas when the president called.

"You've got to come back," he said.

"What—"

And then he told her how Senator Dunleavy had thrown him to the wolves and how the wolves were reacting.

"If anyone finds out you're heading to Cuba or *in* Cuba, the press will eat me alive."

She hesitated long enough to catch her breath and allow her instinct to catch up with her sense of caution.

"I can't just blow him off, George. That would be asking for disaster."

"Going to Cuba *ensures* disaster, Terri!"

Her mind spun with the ramifications, but as the cyclone twirled, the answer became clear.

"I understand," she said. "But hold on, listen to me. If I snub Castro, he'll expose me to the press, and it'll fuel his revenge and *ensure* another exodus. It will be exactly the same result as when the glimmer twins went after him last month, except this time he'll relish the opportunity to throw *you* to the wolves."

"But—"

"This is our only chance, George. Forget about Castro. If we can't immediately refute Dunleavy's accusations, we'll be buried in an investigation and scandal for years to come."

"Danny Besing can refute the whole thing, it's all in the—"

"As the CEO of Winslow Oil, Danny Besing's opinion doesn't matter. The truth won't matter. Between Castro having the chance to blow my cover, the emergency session, and now this…"

"No, Terri—get back here now—tell the pilot—"

"Listen to me, George, I have to try. It's our only hope." Turner's voice had calmed to a near whisper. She sensed Winslow wanted to argue further, but he'd either run out of steam or realized she was right.

"We have no choice," she said. "Going down with your guns blazing is better than being dragged to slaughter."

There was a long silence.

"Okay, Terri," he said finally. "My entire presidency is in your hands." He hung up.

After her plane refueled in Nassau, she was back in the air trying to digest the new complication in her rapidly deteriorating world. What had begun as an initiative to stabilize one of the most volatile governments in the hemisphere, simultaneously helping the eleven million Cuban citizens take a step toward freedom, had soured faster than a gallon of milk under the blazing sun.

No good deed goes unpunished.

A sudden inspiration caused her to grab the sat-phone.

"Winslow Oil," the perky Texas voice answered.

"This is Terri Turner, get me Danny Besing."

"Mr. Besing's in a meeting with—oh, never mind—hold on, Ms. Turner."

A few minutes elapsed until Besing came on the line. "Terri, we're working on a battle plan against these allegations."

"Good. Go through the acquisition studies, I'm sure there was a summary on Southern's failed operations in Cuba. You've got to find it, Danny. Dig through everything."

"I know, we—"

"And there's got to be somebody who used to work at Southern Oil who knows the details on those Cuban assets. Turn over every rock—wait, did we hire anybody after the acquisition?"

"Yeah, some of the people running the refinery here in Houston, I think some of the people in Mexico, but hell, there hasn't been anybody in Cuba for 40 years."

"I don't care. Talk to everyone, maybe somebody will remember something, or someone. This is life or death."

Once they disconnected Turner had to shift gears and refocus on the meeting with Castro. Her State Department briefing indicated that Varadero was a lush seaside resort two hours outside Havana. Hundreds of millions of dollars of foreign investment had been spent there over the past decade.

As the Falcon 50 jet reached the coast, the azure water, virgin green islets, and talcum powder beaches that lined the peninsula somehow eased the tension she felt coming to negotiate with one of history's shrewdest dictators. The flight had been bumpy and she was anxious to get her feet back on the ground, so she put her notes away and took in the view from the small window.

"We'll be on the ground in two minutes, ma'am," the pilot said over the intercom. "The tower says there's a car waiting for you."

A chill ran through her.

Turner openly gawked at the new mega-resorts that were comfortably spaced along the broad shore beyond a buffer of lush greenery. The Canadian, European, and Mexican hotel chains far exceeded her expectations.

Too bad this isn't for fun.

She sighed, and for some reason her thoughts turned to the night Winslow drove her home after they drank their sorrows away when his father died. He had shocked her to the core by kissing her, but then just dropped her off when she was certain he would come up.

She'd let it go, chalked it up to the bucket of martinis. Wondering why the memory occurred to her now, she concluded that it was the last time she had seen George so vulnerable until today. First losing his father, now at risk of losing his presidency.

The aircraft came to rest on the tarmac and settled to a stop behind the small, modern looking terminal. A limousine instantly appeared next to the unmarked plane. Turner gathered her briefcase, brushed her hair, chugged a bottle of Evian, reapplied lipstick and walked down the plane's short stairway.

Here goes everything.

"Miss Turner?"

She nodded and stepped into the limousine's open door.

Inside, the driver and another serious-faced man checked her identification and ran a small metal detector over her. The men were short, had dark hair and moustaches, and wore identical dark suits with white shirts. She was certain they were both MININT.

"Your briefcase?" After a quick perusal, he gave a curt nod then openly scanned her figure. She was carrying a coat and dressed casually in a tan knee-length skirt and a pale blue open-collared shirt. Andrew's Air Force Base had been overcast and twenty-eight degrees this morning, and arriving to an eighty-degree afternoon had already resulted in a sticky sheen of perspiration.

The president's been accused of setting foreign policy for personal gain, I'm on a secret mission to Cuba, success is a necessity not an option, I don't speak Spanish, and I'm in a car with security police on my way to meet Fidel Castro. Turner didn't quite smile, but her sense of adventure was fully aroused.

Castro's Colonial-Spanish villa sat on top of a bluff overlooking the turquoise sea. It was huge—hadn't it been originally built by the DuPont family? The villa was surrounded by tropical vegetation, a golf course, lawns, and a cadre of security personnel. A uniformed man opened the car door and stood at attention.

Her heart raced when she stepped inside the villa's cavernous foyer to find Fidel Castro at its center. He said nothing. His eyes pierced her.

She was going to talk him out of launching another boatlift, right? Salvage her president's administration? *And* find some thread of common interest that could establish a platform of trust for the future? Damn right.

She swallowed hard and walked toward her host.

SENATOR ROBERT SPINELLI sat back in his chair and turned C-SPAN off.

"How's the water now, Mr. President?"

Teitlebaum's Press Conference had gone as expected, although he was surprised that Winslow agreed to a Special Investigator so quickly. The press secretary's use of the term 'investigator' instead of 'prosecutor' was not lost on Spinelli, but he was satisfied that things were playing out as designed. Regardless of the outcome, Winslow would be embroiled in a colossal mess for months to come, which Spinelli felt would keep him off his turf until the Exodus situation blew over.

If politics were an art form, Spinelli considered himself the Picasso of the Hill. Although he would never admit it, he absolutely loved the "Spinmaster" nickname the press had given him years ago.

With Cubagate now beginning to gain momentum, and the emergency session back on track, Spinelli figured he was in the catbird seat. The idea of the session was a masterstroke that would give him headlines in a traditionally quiet season and keep him at the epicenter of the national spotlight, though the president's scandal would dilute that attention somewhat.

While trashing a fellow Republican was distasteful, Spinelli wasted little remorse on the situation. Aside from their difference in opinion over Cuba, Winslow had interviewed him as a potential candidate for his Veep but passed him up for Governor Pulaski from New York. Spinelli considered two governors in the White House the worst form of cronyism.

The press's appetite for the emergency session was partially driven by their interest in sensationalizing the rift in the Republican Party. It gave the issue the aura of a soap opera in which he was the star. Cubagate would now thrust the issue squarely into the center of the national stage. With the emergency session set for tomorrow, he'd be riding high going into the next congressional session, which was as good as gold because it meant he would be in demand to support new legislation. In Washington, value meant power, and power was the name of the game.

Dunleavy had called six times this afternoon, but Spinelli was more interested in checking the Internet's coverage of the Press Conference than in holding his hand. On the bottom of his monitor an irritating light blinked at high speed. Spinelli hated that light because it meant he had urgent e-mails and because it would not stop blinking until they were opened. He moved his mouse over and stabbed the irritant so it wouldn't drive him crazy while he read the news.

Seven e-mails from Dunleavy! Good God man, get a grip.

Two others were from Hector San Martin and one was from José Mas Fina. Between the phone messages and e-mails, Spinelli's curiosity was aroused. His phone rang just as he was about to open one of Dunleavy's messages.

"Yes, Emery?"

"Senator Dunleavy's calling again. He claims it's urgent."

"What a pain in the…all right, put him on."

The phone clicked. "Don't you return calls?" Dunleavy said.

"I—"

"We've got problems."

"If this is about the emergency—"

"Forget the damn refugees! I've been on the phone with Mas Fina ever since the press conference. One of their sources in Havana claims a high-ranking U.S. official is there in secret meetings with Castro."

The news hit him like a blunt object. "What? Who the hell's in Havana?"

"Nobody! At least nobody's supposed to be. But *somebody's* there, dammit. Apparently Fidel's been in a frenzy getting prepped, Raúl's running around like a scalded chicken, and Sanchez from MININT worked all night. Something's up, and it's not good for the cause."

"Don't be so sure. If true, this really could sink Winslow. What did Mas Fina say? Who the hell's down there?"

"He wasn't sure. His pigeon works in Castro's office, but the clown wasn't sure who was coming down. He said it was something like 'Jefe Top Brass'."

"What?"

"Supposedly this guy called out of the blue last night and requested a meeting with Fidel for today. Castro freaked out and booted the Canadian Ambassador in order to brainstorm with Raúl, Allasandre, and Sanchez."

"That's crazy. Jefe Top Brass? Who the hell's that? Mas Fina didn't have anything more?" Spinelli chewed on a fingernail.

"All he said was someone from Washington. It can't be good with him there covertly. Something's rotten in Havana, and Mas Fina's going nuts."

Spinelli tuned Dunleavy out and focused on the information. 'Jefe Top Brass'; Washington, President of the United States? *Who could it be?*

He racked his brain, and then it came to him.

The lunch meeting. Terri Turner.

"Chief of Staff! Not Jefe Top Brass!"

"Turner? In Havana?"

"Son-of-a-bitch! Winslow must be trying an end-run. We'll bury him with Cubagate now." He slapped his palm on the table.

"Hold on, that's not all. Governor Cox called to say that Winslow is coming to Miami tomorrow for an unscheduled visit of the refugee camp."

"What?"

"Can you believe that? With the emergency session scheduled for tomorrow and the press swarming him like flies on roadkill, he's flying right into the center of the storm."

Sweat broke out on Spinelli's scalp below the hair folded over from above his ear. *He's going to release funds and steal our thunder.*

"Son-of-a-bitch!" Spinelli yelled.

"I'm on my way to Miami," Dunleavy said. "We should reschedule the emergency session until next week."

"If Winslow gives Federal aid, we'll cancel the damn session," Spinelli said. "If Turner's in Cuba, we'll alert the press. The Special Prosecutor will have a field day."

Spinelli had not been off the phone for two seconds when his intercom buzzed again.

"What?"

"Hector San Martin's on line three."

"Oh crap. All right, put him through." He bit his knuckle.

"Do you know about—"

"Yes, Hector," Spinelli said. "I'm on top of it. I think its Terri Turner. I'm on my way to the White House right now. I'll call you later. By the way, I'm glad you're happy about Cubagate." He hung up without waiting for a reply.

He stood up and took his coat, but the phone rang again.

"What?!"

"José Mas Fina."

"For the love of…" He threw his coat down. "Yes, José, I know about the trip. It's Terri Turner, chief of staff to the president."

"What's she doing there with the Devil?"

"I'm on my way to the White House to find out. I'll let you know."

"Bludgeon him with Cubagate! The emergency session's scheduled for tomorrow, and you're going to look like a fool! And you know how that would make the CAC look—how that would make *me* look!"

Spinelli bristled at Mas Fina's tone. "I'm sure it's nothing. The president is waiting for me. I promise to call you shortly." Spinelli's lies were believable, he hoped, but he doubted he was keeping the anxiety out of his voice.

"Shortly, like one hour. Do you know Winslow's coming here tomorrow? Ay yi, something bad is happening and you and Dunleavy are clueless!"

Spinelli hung up. Largest contributor or not, nobody talks to me like I'm a lackey. He grabbed his coat and ran from the office afraid the phone would ring again.

25

CASTRO STEPPED FORWARD and took Turner's hand.

He looked frail and older than in recent pictures. His skin was blotched with liver spots, his beard scraggly and gray. Only his eyes were fierce—sharp and laid low beneath the hooded veil of his dark brow.

"Miss Turner."

"Mr. President. Thank you for seeing me."

"Your call was a surprise, and my curiosity overcame the anger left from your last delegation."

"You may find what I've come to discuss a greater surprise, so I suggest we get started."

Castro placed a gentle hand on Turner's back and guided her down a labyrinth of hallways, through exquisitely furnished rooms to a corner chamber that was decorated with oil paintings of Cuban landscapes. Hundreds of books filled dark wooden shelves, and two plush leather armchairs sat adjacent to individual tables, each set with pitchers of water, note pads and a stock of writing utensils. It appeared to be Castro's study. A faint smell of old cigar smoke permeated the air despite the steady breeze that blew through the two sets of open French doors.

They seated themselves facing each other, and Turner realized her host was waiting for her to speak.

"Mr. President—"

"Fidel." Castro sat back with a smirk.

"All right, Fidel." She smiled. "And I'm Terri. President Winslow has authorized me to speak on his behalf. He was very disappointed with the results of Senators Spinelli and Dunleavy's visit, and he sent me to have a more meaningful discussion on how we can stabilize relations between our countries."

"Terri, I'm well versed on your government's position and the demands that you require to discontinue your unilateral blockade. I'm sure I could have saved you the trip because I assure you that we'll never agree to outside demands that affect our destiny."

Castro smiled and Turner waited, knowing there would be more.

"Now, I'll be happy to engage in an intellectual discussion with you, if you're interested, but my position is non-negotiable, which I'm sure Washington realizes after 42 years."

Turner had noticed the animated facial expressions and body gestures Castro used as he talked—they emphasized his words like a form of pantomime. Her host might be old, but he was in complete control of his faculties.

"Frankly, President Winslow is tired of archaic rhetoric. He's interested in ending the embargo so our countries can move forward, and so we can all quit living in the past."

"Yes, but at what price? You'll have to pardon me, but as I've grown older I have fewer patience for games and prefer to speak directly."

"Good. I'm not here to posture. The president asked me to make his case, and if you find it acceptable he'll move immediately to terminate the embargo." *Better not mention the Migration Accords, just yet.*

"That's not possible."

"You haven't even heard—"

"Forgive me. What I mean is that President Winslow *can't* quickly terminate the embargo. That would require an act of Congress, which would extend the debate beyond anything I would describe as immediate. And I suspect that this Special Investigation into Winslow Oil's acquisition of the company that once had assets here may complicate the matter."

Turner was tempted to ask if Castro had seen the press conference but instead she ignored his comment. George Winslow, Sr. had coached her that when gambling, it sometimes works to be aggressive from the outset. He referred to it as "going ugly early."

"You're referring to Helms-Burton," she said. "I can tell you that the Attorney General has informed the president that he will be able to bypass the constraints of the Act if you accept our proposal. The president is willing to move quickly and decisively, Fidel—and Congress wouldn't be able to do anything about it. With some concession on your part, it would be entirely possible."

Castro began to pull on his beard. "You continue to intrigue me, Terri. However, before we discuss the details, I need to understand his motivation. Considering the accusations against him, combined with America's war on terrorism, it seems odd that he would want to pursue such a politically dangerous agenda."

Turner, suddenly filled with nervous energy, stood and walked to the open French doors. They looked across a long manicured lawn to a cliff above the ocean. The view was spectacular. She saw sentries stationed in discreet locations, but their presence did not detract from the beauty. She turned back to face her host, who sat watching her every move.

"I could state the obvious motivations, Fidel—to prevent further innocent deaths through another boatlift, or to curtail illegal immigration through normalized relations. But quite simply? We're interested in moving forward rather than sticking to policies that don't work. America's biggest grievance is gone. Cuba could no longer be considered a pawn of the USSR, because there *is* no longer a USSR."

Turner saw no change in Castro's expression, but he was listening.

"We're at a crossroads. Either we continue a policy that's been ineffective in bringing democracy to Cuba, or we can start with a clean slate."

Castro snorted a belly laugh. "A clean slate! Really, Terri, that *is* funny. I'm sorry, I do appreciate your candor and I believe you're sincere, but your metaphor is amusing."

"Not if you keep our differences in perspective. You've led Cuba for over 43 years, and before that you fought a bloody revolution to wrest control of the country from a corrupt dictator. Since then, the U.S. has had nine different presidents, and the world, for all intents and purposes, has moved from a bi-polar balance of power with both the Soviet Union and the U.S. considered superpowers to only the U.S. holding that status."

"China might disagree, but please, continue."

"The president has a new vision of cooperation in our hemisphere, and that's where he draws his courage to challenge those in Congress who still cling to a Cold War mentality."

After a moment of silence, Castro stood and walked to the desk. Without hesitation he picked up the phone, punched a button and barked a command. Turner followed him with her eyes, wishing again that she spoke Spanish.

"It seems we may be talking for awhile, so I ordered us some food," Castro said.

He turned to the bookshelf next to his desk and scanned the spines of several books with his fingers, squinting at their titles. After a moment he found what he sought, ripped the book from the shelf and raised it above his head.

"Do you know what this is?" He paused for a second. "The history of Cuba before the Revolution, written by a Frenchman and non-biased to anyone—but true to history. It's a very sad story. If Hollywood made it into a movie, it would fail miserably because there is no happy ending." He handed the thick, dusty book to his guest, and Turner's arm sagged under its weight.

"Wiping the slate clean is not nearly as easy for Cuba, regardless of the number of presidents we've had. The American Revolution happened nearly 200 years before ours did, and no, I'm not considering our emancipation from Spain our Revolution. They were replaced by your countrymen, who were every bit as exploitive and manipulative."

She held her tongue.

"I too am a student of history," Castro continued. "I recognize that America has a unique way of electing new leaders every four years, and while I think your two party system hypocritical, from time to time there are initiatives that surprise me."

Turner knew that Castro was an endless orator who tossed off six-hour speeches from the hip, and she fidgeted in her chair trying to figure out a way to cut him off.

"Before the Revolution—"

"Fidel, if we're able to agree on moving forward, I'd love to have the chance to sit down with you to discuss your country's history, but at the moment time is of the essence. We really need to utilize this opportunity to focus on the future."

His face froze, and his eyes narrowed. History, she knew, was a much more comfortable subject for him. The future was an unknown, and he had become an old man.

"The question I came to ask you is whether Cuba's ready for a new relationship with the United States."

Castro rapidly waved his index finger. "No, no, no, Miss Turner. The question is whether America has matured beyond blatant and self-righteous imperialism. With laws like Helms-Burton and the Cuban Democracy Act, your country has continued trying to control us long after we removed your last puppet dictator and expelled your industries from exploiting our resources and people. For all I know, Winslow wants to start by reclaiming his company's former assets here, and keep going from there."

"But—" She stopped before allowing an emotional tide to flood in. *I'm not going to spar with you.* Then, in a calculated move to change the atmosphere, she stood up. "I'm sorry, but where's the nearest restroom?"

Armed with directions, she set out into the corridor and locked herself in a small but ornate bathroom. She needed to regroup more than anything. One advantage of being a woman was that the negotiating philosophy of whoever has the bigger bladder wins didn't apply. Charm had better outflank machismo—she knew she'd lose in a head-to-head debate with him on history.

She returned a few moments later to Castro outside the French doors.

"The villa is as spectacular as the view," she said.

He barely nodded. It dawned on Turner that he was afraid of finally being faced with the opportunity of ending a lifetime of posturing against the United States. The fact that it was harder for Cuba than the U.S. to change policy was true for many reasons, not the least of which was that their deadlock had provided Castro with the perfect scapegoat.

"You have a lot to be proud of in your educational programs, healthcare, and your recent steps toward a market economy." A gust of wind lifted her skirt as she spoke.

Castro eyed her legs as he raised his finger. "We are *not* taking steps toward a market economy, nor will we ever. And, we aren't seeking additional foreign investment either. We have carefully chosen where foreign companies can invest, just as we cautiously determine which occupations can be independent from the government. Everything is planned, controlled, and monitored."

"President Winslow is sensitive to your desire not to repeat the mistakes of the past, and we have no intention of going down that road. History's not been Cuba's friend, and your people have suffered enough."

"You have no idea how our people have suffered. Everyone outside of Cuba was certain that we would collapse after the fall of the socialist bloc, but we haven't. Our currency experienced an extraordinary devaluation and the budget deficit ballooned to a near fatal proportion. But throughout that Special Period nobody lost their job, and health care didn't suffer."

She managed not to comment.

"The heroes of the Special Period are the people. This genuine miracle would not have been possible without the unity of socialism."

Castro was not a man to challenge verbally, and Turner did not want to push the discussion too quickly.

"The entire fate of our homeland was at stake during these years when our oppressors promoted slanderous campaigns against us and attempted to cut off our ability to purchase even food and medicine. Yet still we survive."

Castro finally took a breath, and as his emotion subsided she said, "The Cubans have survived because they are a strong people."

He gave her a look—testing her sincerity? And then, apparently satisfied that she meant what she'd said, surprised her.

"So, normalized relations would be cathartic for America? The next step forward after the Elian Gonzalez debacle? One of the only reasons we're talking right now is because of the moral integrity the American people demonstrated by supporting that the young boy be reunited with his father."

The value of an impartial legal system was on the tip of Turner's tongue, but again she bit down.

"That and the assistance you offered after Hurricane Michelle," he said, "made me believe for the first time that perhaps I might see a change in our relations during my lifetime."

A glimmer of light!

"President Winslow is willing to stick his neck out further than any of his predecessors to buck this long-standing policy for something other than political gain. America *has* matured beyond the imperialistic tendencies that lingered during the last century, that's what this is all about."

She finished by staring Castro straight in the eye, wishing she could climb into his skull and read his thoughts.

"Why don't we return to the library," he said. "You can tell me what you've come to say." Castro's hands finally sat idle by his side, his eyes almost soft in the late afternoon light.

HUNCHED OVER IN the back of his limousine, Robert Spinelli felt cold, but the curious glances from pedestrians boosted his self-esteem. He dialed the White House on his cell phone. *Screw protocol.*

"This is Senator Spinelli. Please connect me to the chief of staff."

"I'll connect you to her assistant, Senator. One moment please."

White House operators are always so damn pleasant.

"Hello, Ms. Turner's office."

"Hi, Karla, this is Senator Spinelli. Is she busy?"

"Hello, Senator. Yes, I'm afraid she's going to be very difficult to reach today, but I'll tell her you called."

"Is she at the White House, or traveling?"

"She's in meetings all day, sir."

"Listen, I need to speak with her as soon as possible. Tell her it's an emergency. Send me back to the operator."

Muzak temporarily filled his ear. "Hello?"

"This is Senator Spinelli again. Connect me with the Oval Office."

The phone rang once and Sally Miles answered. No, the president was not available either.

"What's his schedule look like, I'm on my way there and need a moment with him. I have some information that may help him with the democrat's accusations."

"That's impossible, Senator, he's double booked."

Spinelli bit his knuckle. "How about Terri Turner, have you seen her today?"

"No sir, I haven't seen Ms. Turner today."

Turner's the chief of staff, she must see the president twenty times a day. Hell, she probably blows him under the desk.

"All right, tell the president I'm on my way, and I'm prepared to wait until he can see me. It's of the utmost importance. Transfer me to Terri's assistant."

Again with the muzak.

"Hey, Karla, Spinelli again. The president just told me Terri's in Cuba. Will you ask her to call me when you hear from her?" He held his breath.

She hesitated a second too long. "I wouldn't know about that, sir, but I'll have Ms. Turner call you as soon as I hear from her."

"Good. Tell her we need to talk about Cubagate, Helms-Burton, and the Trading with the Enemy Act. Got it?"

There was no reply, but Spinelli could hear the woman breathing.

"Now transfer me back to the Oval Office."

He didn't even notice the muzak now.

"I'll be there in five minutes. Give the president this message: Congress controls Helms-Burton, and having secret meetings with Castro will not help your situation. Got it?"

"Yes, sir, I'll try—"

Spinelli slammed the phone down. His blood was boiling. Nothing had been confirmed, but he knew he was right. *Turner's in Cuba! Son-of-a-bitch!*

ARTURO DIAS RAN down Dixie Highway with his buddies. Some carried sticks, others baseball bats, and Arturo carried a tire iron. The afternoon light was on the wane, eclipsed by the dark clouds that had closed in overhead. No rain had yet fallen, but it was as imminent as the destruction that was soon to descend on South Miami.

One of the younger men in the group sped up alongside Arturo.

"What happened? I thought we were supposed to wait for dark?"

Arturo determined to reach Dadeland before it was too late.

"Rico sent word," he said. "You hear those sirens?"

The younger guy nodded as he ran easily next to Arturo.

"Shit's going down, man...Rico told me... a shitload more Cubans...on their way." He rubbed his sleeve over his sweaty face. "Now's the time...brother!"

As he passed a phone booth, Arturo swung the tire iron and broke its glass. Others followed his lead and pummeled the coin box until change spilled into the street. A police car barreled past them. The officer shouted something unintelligible over the loudspeaker but didn't bother to slow down. Arturo watched the police car turn right into Dadeland's parking lot.

"Fuck!" A larger group of shadowy men headed toward the mall. They hassled cars and threw rocks at the Kentucky Fried Chicken.

"Go! Go! Go!" Arturo yelled.

Motherfuckers ain't gonna get there before me.

26

AS THE LIGHT grew dim, the conditions in the Florida Straits deteriorated. The thin black squall line on the western horizon had become all encompassing and along with the storm front brought high winds and a severe drop in temperature. The sky was now a leaden gray, and waves that rolled predictably now came from all directions. Everyone was queasy, and Vilma had been seasick for the first time in her life.

Juan and Maria scuttled around securing every loose item. The coming storm reminded Juan of a hurricane that hit Havana when he was a teenager. The rain and seawater had created flash floods in the streets perpendicular to the sea wall. He had tried to run across a flooded street as he played chicken with his friends, but the fun came to a sudden stop when he got his foot stuck in a drainage grate in the road, and Juan watched in horror as the floodwaters rose around him. The more he fought to get free, the deeper his leg sank into the twisted rubbish, tree branches, and refuse in the grate. Everything he and his friends tried only made the situation worse.

Mingi, Juan's best friend, dove down repeatedly to try lifting the grate but couldn't hold himself in the velocity of the passing water. The intensity of the flood finally knocked Juan down and he was unable to fight his way back up. He still remembered the sense of complete helplessness as he was pushed backwards by the powerful flow. It took four adults to wrest his leg free, and since that night Juan had avoided the water religiously.

By the look of things, tonight's storm was going to hit just like that one had. But unlike that night when he had been cruising the streets, out for a good time, he was now adrift on the ocean with nobody capable of rescuing him if he got into trouble again.

Manuel double-tied himself to each side of what they had called the front of the raft, but front no longer applied as the platform spiraled in the multidirectional waters. Vilma lay tied off with her head hung over a side of the raft. Maria was busy helping Juan.

"What about this thing?" she asked, pointing to the large container.

"Tie it down as best you can."

Juan watched her try to ignore the fact that the rope in her hand was the same one that had dragged Ernesto to his death. The wind blew her dress open and exposed her colorful swimsuit, but modesty was now a forgotten luxury. After three days of performing bodily functions over the side and existing together aboard the eighty-square-foot platform, there was little left to the imagination.

"It's a bad one," Vilma said.

Both Juan and Manuel checked the black clouds that moved toward them, which were in stark contrast to the faded blue sky to the east. They looked at each other and Manuel cinched the ropes tighter around his waist.

"We're going to get a lot of rain," Juan said. He checked Vilma's rope, which was slack in his hand. "You need to pull this tight."

"My stomach hurts, the rope rubs so hard."

The sea crashed in from all directions, no longer blue or green but more a whitewashed combination of foam, saragasso grass, and roiling water. The wind howled around them, buffeting the raft from the west and the south, alternating from warm to cold.

A bird flew past them like it was shot from a cannon.

"Do you feel any better?" Maria asked Vilma.

"I won't let this storm beat me, not after what I've been through."

"You made it through the Special Period, you can make it through this," Maria said.

"Special!" Juan said. "Don't you just love how Castro called our starvation special."

"'What does a little hunger matter today to conquer bread and freedom tomorrow.'"

Juan had to laugh. "Even in this shit you quote the Beard?"

Clouds moved in rapidly and eclipsed the remaining light. Lightning provided bright fractures in the darkness, now loud with jaw-clenching cracks of thunder.

"None of it matters. Every day's going to be special in America," Juan said. "Really special, not the bullshit version Castro gave us."

"Nothing's for nothing," Vilma said. "All those things you talk about are available in America, but all anyone ever does there is work. Work, work, and work, and that's not to get rich, that's just to survive."

"How is that different in Cuba? Where we get to wait in line for whatever food that might be available this week?" Juan glanced back at Vilma to see her clutching a dollar bill.

"What's that?"

"My lucky dollar. I kept it from when I was a dancer."

"It looks different, can I see it?" Maria asked. She had a roll of money that had been Ernesto's but had not been able to bring herself to count how much was there. "It says 1958. I wonder if it's still good?"

"Money isn't milk, it doesn't go bad," Juan said. "What are you going to do with one dollar?"

"Buy a *Bolita* ticket. My friends tell me they have huge cash prizes in America."

"See? We're not so different. I dream of winning the *Bolita* there too. They call it a lottery."

"I need money for my operation, not for cars and fast women."

A louder clap of thunder rumbled over the incessant wind and put an abrupt stop to their conversation. Vilma stuffed the bill in her bible, which she put inside the plastic bag. The lightning flashes increased—

And the sky opened up. Rain poured down so hard it felt like gravel. Juan double-checked that everyone was securely strapped down. *It's just like that storm in Havana.*

The group hunkered together as the sea slowly lifted them toward the sky. A small dolphin appeared on a wave near Maria, then it vanished. Juan checked the horizon hoping to see light but could not discern a difference between the ocean and sky. Everything had turned black, lightning providing the only color.

Lightning! The thought struck Juan. We're on the water, supported by metal drums and surrounded by bolts of electricity.

LIGHTS FROM THREE police cruisers flashed in the parking lot, but Buzz Luffer could not find any of his fellow officers. Small groups of hoodlums ran in different directions, some threw rocks, others carried boxes or armfuls of clothing, and some were just running and screaming.

Gunshots erupted, their sounds echoing off the concrete walls.

Buzz's speaker continuously spit out information faster than he could discern their codes, and he found himself running in one direction, then turning and running in another.

I can't chase these bastards! What am I going to do if I arrest one? He grabbed his microphone again. *How many times have I called for help? Ten?*

"Come in dispatch, this is officer 2142 calling for back-up. There are thirty, forty, hell, I don't know, fifty people assaulting Dadeland. Please send..." He stopped, suddenly face to face with a young man carrying a torch.

"Freeze!" He dropped his microphone and fumbled with his nightstick. The kid turned the corner and ran. For all Buzz knew, he could be planning to set the mall on fire.

Shit! Buzz took after him. The speaker on his epaulet continued to spew calls from the dispatcher, and his microphone swung wildly behind him, but he heard no reply to his call for assistance. When he rounded the corner he didn't see the kid, but there were a lot of them dressed the same way on the street.

Riots had broken out all over Miami, and the police were out-numbered in every respect. "...10-32 at 219 Opa Locka Boulevard," the speaker sounded. *That's a man with a gun, all the way across town!*

"...Officers please respond to a code 10-34 at Sunniland on Dixie Highway."

10-34 was a *riot,* right?

Buzz couldn't remember. He was still looking for the kid with the torch, and thought he had disappeared behind a large glass showcase filled with electronic gear.

"...Calling all officers in the vicinity of Dadeland Mall, Signal 25," the dispatcher said. "Officer is reported wounded in front of Burdines, ambulance en route. Suspect fled on foot into the mall...."

Buzz stopped in his tracks. *The abandoned cruisers— someone's been shot?*

He turned back toward Burdines but ran straight into a group of men brandishing clubs.

VILMA WATCHED MANUEL'S features twist as his attention had shifted from the churning black clouds to Juan. He put his hand on the young man's back.

"We'll be all right, you can handle this."

His attitude relieved Vilma's concern about the deteriorating conditions. *That's the spirit, Manuel. What will be will be, and there's nothing we can do to change it.*

That sentiment aside, Vilma glanced up at the fleet of thunderheads that marched toward them like the four horses of the apocalypse. She said a prayer and buttoned up her read sweater.

Vilma then studied Manuel's face. It was blood red with sunburn, and his nose had peeled and was raw. She looked at his hands, wrinkled and worn from a lifetime in the cane fields, his fingers permanently bent from arthritis. She knew that determination and survival were staples in the routine of any *campesino* who had lived to his age. He was not a quitter, and he would never reveal fear or doubt, no matter what he felt inside. She felt proud to know him, and even though he had abandoned Cuba she respected his desire to be with his family. He had spent his life serving the Revolution, so it was an urge she understood.

She took Manuel's rough-textured hand in hers, which no doubt surprised him but he didn't resist. She smiled at him and he returned the gesture. Then with a glance toward the darkening horizon, he squeezed her hand and bowed his head. She bowed hers and prayed.

When she looked up again a bolt of lightning shot down through the nearest cloud. Vilma took Maria's hand and looked into her eyes. Sad as they were, there remained the will to survive. She squeezed Maria's hands in hers and got a bit of a smile. Then, in the howl of the wind, she heard a sound that nearly caused her heart to stop. She listened again, waited, but now only heard the wind.

A moment ago she had thought she heard her husband's voice. She shivered and let go of Maria's hands.

WHILE AFTERNOON TURNED to evening, Fidel Castro and Terri Turner hammered out the rough parameters that could normalize relations between the United States and Cuba. Castro had been antagonistic when Turner initially outlined what President Winslow needed to bypass Helms-Burton and terminate the embargo. He stormed out of the room to consult with others over the telephone.

Since she was not supposed to be in Cuba, Turner had been instructed not to call Washington on a landline, cell phone, or satellite phone. She would have liked to call, more for moral support than anything else. Her agenda was simple, and there was no negotiating room. Given the existing legislation if Castro wouldn't agree, the discussion was doomed to die a fast, painful death.

With his consultations made, the two of them debated the issues further, in greater detail. Eventually it became clear that the U.S. was requiring a fraction of what had been demanded in the past, and Castro became more serious. Like a cat with nine lives the deal died many deaths, but in the end Turner's persistence paid off.

The framework for an Agreement was intentionally broad, and detractors would condemn it as vague, with much being gambled on the evolutionary relationship of the post-normalized era. Both sides required assurances on issues having special significance to them but realized that public opinion would play a major role in the success of the proposed new relationship. The mere fact that it would be counterproductive for either side to speak negatively of the other was an incredible departure from the last forty-plus years of hostility. Turner considered that a positive detail for the United States since Castro had never been shy about criticizing his archenemy.

"How will this affect the debate on repatriating the Exodus refugees?" Castro said.

"We'll consider the Exodus an anomaly in the Migration Accords," Turner said. "With normalized relations we'll establish a more cohesive policy towards emigration." She held her breath and awaited the response.

A grumble emanated deep within Castro's throat. Turner did not imagine cataclysmic possibilities, but she feared he would hold fast to his last bit of leverage.

Castro finally grunted, his eyes veiled below his brow, again the lion in the grass.

"We'll see what happens with your Congress."

"Fine, but we have to keep the Migration Accords in place until we can establish a new Agreement. That will allow the president to help the Exodus refugees."

"So much for the emergency session of Congress." Castro smiled.

We both get our revenge. The image of Spinelli in a rage popped into her head, and she smiled.

"Bringing families back together will heal many wounds," she said. "That alone will send a strong message that we both hold human and individual rights in the highest regard."

"We can't afford the luxury to focus on individuals," Castro said. "Our system provides equal services to everyone, not just those wealthy enough to afford specialists. That won't change."

We'll see.

"Our people have endured a long isolation, Terri, and 500 years of foreign domination. Patience is a virtue we will not retire." Castro looked past his guest toward storm clouds on the horizon.

The short but meaningful list of U.S. requirements necessary to terminate the embargo had been hard for him to swallow, but compared with the impossible litany of the past, it was an opportunity that could hardly be replicated. Castro mumbled something about it coinciding with the timing of his plans, and eventually agreed.

Turner was numb. She stood and stretched her legs. It had been a long day—but the most interesting day of her life.

"What about this Cubagate?" Castro asked. "Won't this agreement complicate that?"

Just hearing the term made Turner cringe. *Good question.*

"Would you mind looking into the status of the assets once owned by Southern Oil here? Our records showed that they were dry wells and a rundown refinery with no value. If you could verify that, it might help the president prove the accusations are groundless."

"We'll investigate the matter." His eyes glistened. "Now that we're finished, Terri, allow me to pour us some aged rum to celebrate. Havana Club, eighteen years old."

He removed a decanter of amber rum and two glasses from a cupboard below a bookshelf.

With each glass half-full of rum, neat, they held them aloft in toast. Turner's smile sparkled in the cool light. Although it was hot in her throat, the amber liquid was smoother than she expected, unlike any rum she had ever tasted.

"This is amazing, Fidel."

"Indeed it is," Castro said. "Now how shall we formalize these discussions?"

"We need to finalize an Agreement as soon as possible, and the president would like to come here for a formal ceremony."

Castro did his best to mask how much this proposal pleased him—the President of the United States coming to him to end the embargo.

"That would be acceptable," he said. "We can have a ceremony to commemorate the event in a month or so."

Turner smiled, knowing she was about to blow Castro's mind.

"The president can't wait a month. He wants to come here in a couple of days."

"Days! How can we be ready in a couple days? It will take weeks to finalize the Agreement."

"It only needs to be a couple of pages. With the issue of repatriating the Exodus refugees on fire at home and the false accusations about Winslow Oil's assets here, we need to get this done fast, or the fate of those fifty thousand people will be in jeopardy. Not to mention that I'm here without Congress's knowledge. If we don't move quickly, with you making the agreed upon announcements, the Senate will block our efforts and paralyze the entire plan."

Castro sagged in his chair ever so slightly.

"We have to keep silent while our teams finalize the Agreement to our mutual satisfaction," she said. "Let's plan to meet again to codify everything and make the announcement two days from now?"

"Two days?" Castro's face revealed nothing, and she wasn't sure she saw goose bumps on his arms.

"The Attorney General will draft the Agreement and have it to you by tomorrow morning," she said.

"In that case you'd better go. The rum can age another two days."

27

WITH HIS HANDS ON HIS KNEES, ARTURO tried to catch his breath.

"Wait! You punks stay with me."

He scanned the parking lot as he rested. People ran in all directions, most of them shoppers caught in the riot. Arturo grinned. *I don't know where you people think you're going, this whole town's gonna burn!*

"All right, let's go!" He ran ahead—it was smash-and-grab time, and he was going to get to the booty before anyone else. He swung the tire iron over his head like an Indian brandishing a tomahawk, screaming at the top of his lungs and terrifying an elderly woman who lurched out of Burdines.

The old woman fell down and Arturo jumped over her. As he rounded the corner, a skinny cop holding a billy club turned to face him twenty feet away. Arturo stopped cold, with his cohorts bunched up behind him. He could see the glass display case behind the lone cop, and he gave a sharp glance to his friends.

"AAAGGGHHH!" Arturo yelled, lifted the steel rod over his head and rushed toward the cop, his eyes looking past him into the illuminated window.

The officer dropped the billy club and reached for his gun. He yelled something, but Arturo was deafened by his own scream—a flame leapt out and hit him—the sound shattered his eardrums.

A bullet ripped into Arturo's abdomen, then another into his shoulder, and another past him into the concrete wall. Arturo's legs buckled and as he spun toward the ground, his world flashed before him like a kaleidoscope. His face hit the concrete with a thud and he flopped on the sidewalk shrieking from the pain and the sight of his blood squirting out from the fire in his gut.

The cop ran up to Arturo and looked down on him. Arturo's friends had scattered to the wind. The sound of sirens, the cop's microphone, glass breaking and people shouting could be heard as Arturo's screams quieted and finally stopped.

The last thing he saw was the cop standing frozen above him.

STILL LOOKING DOWN on Arturo, BUZZ turned and threw up.

TURNER HURRIEDLY LEFT the villa, and Fidel watched in disbelief as the car pulled away. The Americans had dropped nearly every single requirement they had championed for the last 42 years. He'd only had to agree to very few conditions, some of which he had been prepared to do in less time than they required anyway.

Back inside, he hurried to the other side of the house where Raúl sat in the communications room. He had listened to the entire discussion and was also in shock. Fidel threw the door open and stared at Raúl. The brothers laughed and embraced each other, feeling a joy they had not experienced in decades.

THE RIDE TO the airport went by quickly, and Turner's jet roared down the runway minutes after arriving. There was no time to stare at the mega-hotels now. She called the president on the satellite phone.

"I was beginning to think they threw you in jail. What happened?"

"We're just trying to get out of here at the moment. There's a nasty storm brewing and this toy jet's blowing around like a tumble weed in a West Texas windstorm." She tried to find the appropriate words, but her excitement rose like the weather outside her window and they all spilled out in a rush. "We had a GREAT meeting. I mean aside from the history lessons, bravado, veiled threats, and brinkmanship. It took some serious CPR but it *worked*, it was worth it! Castro agreed to EVERTHING!"

"The Migration Accords?"

"The whole enchilada. Ending the embargo and normalizing relations."

"That's… amazing!"

"Fidel argued over the requirements, but he's no fool, it's a fraction of what's been demanded in the past."

"Fidel? You two got cozy quick."

"We even had a glass of his best rum to celebrate. He about choked when I told him you wanted to come down in two days. I know he was envisioning a big public relations coup with America coming to him, the international press all in attendance and the Plaza de la Revolución packed with dignitaries. I'm sure he'll still work the press into a frenzy but he won't have much time to do it."

"Will he keep his mouth shut until the details are worked out?"

"He knows it's a dead deal if he blows our cover."

"How about Southern Oil's assets? Did he know anything about them?"

"No, but he's going to look into it."

Winslow was quiet for a moment. "Here's a news flash for you. Congress postponed the emergency session. They think I'm releasing Federal funds while in Miami tomorrow. And Roy Perkins told me that Dunleavy had some silent partners on this Cubagate bullshit."

"There's a surprise."

"Plus, our friend the Spinmaster smells a rat. He sat outside my office under the guise that he could help me with the allegations, but when I wouldn't let him in, he left—screaming that he knew you were in Cuba. I don't know where he's getting his information, but he's right on our asses."

"He could ruin everything." She took a deep breath. "What's the latest on Dunleavy's accusations?"

"I'm meeting with Snider in an hour. My Special Investigator ought to have an aggressive strategy to overwhelm them with information. I don't know, we'll see."

"Are you set for tomorrow? You still going to do it?"

The satellite line crackled and Turner looked out the window for the first time since she took off. The black and pink horizon was foreboding and a nasty storm was building fast. Winslow laid out the schedule for the morning in Miami, the tour of the camps, and then a press conference with Governor Cox.

The president couldn't wait to make the announcement, and Turner knew his speech would rock the nation. Their main concern now was how the news would be received in light of the charges that he was manipulating foreign policy for personal gain.

"What's Besing come up with?" she said.

"He says it's all spelled out in the records, that you'd have to be a moron not to understand that the assets are worthless. He's trying to dig up any former Southern executives that may have been in Cuba, but they'd be ancient if any are still alive."

"Speaking of morons, will Dunleavy be in Miami?"

"Are you kidding? Now that he's back in the spotlight, he'll be attached to the governor at the hip."

"All right, I need to call the AG so he can finalize the Agreement. There aren't many changes, and I promised Castro he'd have something by morning." She took a deep breath, then exhaled it slowly. "It might just work."

"Don't count your chickens yet, Terri. Just pray we're still standing after the dust settles."

"We have a good shot for success, unless Spinelli figures it out first. One day won't give him much time to gum up the works, though."

"If anyone can screw us, it'll be the Spinmaster. Great job, Terri, I'll see you in Miami."

"I NEED TO speak to George Winsl-o-oh." A cough interrupted Warner Haslett's last syllable.

The doctor stood over him, a brief smile crossed his lips.

"Tell him who you are, Warner. The president'll drop everything to talk to you." Robey Johnson, his roommate, giggled as he spoke.

"Okay, Mr. Haslett, you need to stop this. The nurses say you've been abusive."

"They won't listen, dammit! I need to get him a message." He shook the remote control in his hand as he spoke, his chalky eyes fluttering blindly about the room.

Robey Johnson's smile filled his caramel-skinned face. "You're such a fool. '*I need to get him a message.*' You gotta be kiddin' me, Warner!" A cough choked his laughter.

The doctor looked from one patient to the next, shook his head, and let out a sigh. "Now you start behaving, Mr. Haslett, or we'll have to sedate you."

"I tell you he'd like to hear from me. I could help him, Doctor, ah, Doctor—"

"Keller," the Doctor said. He then left the room.

Robey finished his coughing spell and sailed on. "They gonna send some secret agents here, and you gonna get booted out on yo ass, you old fool."

"I'm calling the White House, dammit, I'll show you...." Warner held the remote control up to his ear as if it were the phone.

Robey couldn't stop the laugh, then his lungs constricted and he started to cough again.

"Son-of-a—" Warner tried to replace the remote control onto the table but dropped it on the floor.

Robey hacked and sputtered until he caught his breath. "I knew you'd start slippin' before me."

Warner ignored him—a stranger stood in the doorway. The man was dressed in a suit and looked important like a doctor, but better than the ones around Green Acres.

"Excuse me, gentlemen. Would one of you happen to be Warner Haslett?"

Warner and Robey exchanged a quick glance. Warner's brow bent into a deep wrinkle. "Who wants to know?"

"Oh, I'm sorry. My name is Jeff Dole. I work for a company called Winslow Oil. We're looking for a man named Warner Haslett who used to manage Southern Oil Company's refinery in Havana, Cuba, in the 1950's." The well-dressed young man stared at the two octogenarians with a healthy amount of doubt on his face.

The old men again exchanged a glance. This time, Robey's eyes were so wide they were completely round, and Warner's were thin to match his smile.

28

TTAA00 KEYW 132142
FLC087-132250

BULLETIN – EAS ACTIVATION REQUESTED
TORNADO-WATERSPOUT WARNING
NATIONAL WEATHER SERVICE KEY WEST FL
2130 PM EDT TH FEB 13 2001

THE NATIONAL WEATHER SERVICE IN KEY WEST HAS
ISSUED A

*TORNADO-WATERSPOUT WARNING FOR
SOUTHERN FLORIDA...THE LOWER KEYS IN MONROE
COUNTY AND ADJACENT COASTAL WATERS

*UNTIL FRI FEB 14 100 AM
*AT 2127 PM EDT...DOPPLER RADAR AND SPOTTER
REPORTS DETECTED SEVERAL WATERSPOUTS 27-45
MILES SOUTHWEST OF KEY WEST...MOVING EAST.
THESE
WATERSPOUTS SEVERE IN NATURE...F0-F2
STRENGTH

EXTREMELY HAZARDOUS TO WATERCRAFT OF ALL
SIZES.

IF YOU ARE IN THIS AREA RETURN TO LAND
IMMEDIATELY

THE RAFT HAD BEEN PUMMELLED by waves that chopped and lifted it high only to slam it down at sharp angles. The lack of the sixth drum caused a structural weakness that twisted and buckled the platform in the churning sea.

"It won't take much more of this!" Juan shouted.

Manuel leaned close to Juan and yelled. "We've got to get rid of the back section."

"You're crazy, old man!"

"There's no choice. The back is twisting so bad, we'll capsize."

The screech from wind made Manuel's voice hard to hear. Another large wave rolled over them, and while they held on, everyone watched the seam on the back third of the deck, the ropes stretched and the edges of the boards crunched together. It looked ready to snap.

The rain had temporarily stopped, but the air was cold and the wind howled unceasingly. The seesaw shift from warm to cold had produced massive anvil-shaped clouds that poured down sheets of rain and hurled bolts of lightning in all directions.

They were strapped to a roller coaster with only tattered ropes and raw fingers to hold themselves aboard.

Juan sucked in a sharp breath, amazed by the raft's rapid deterioration yet no longer afraid. His fear had been replaced by an icy resolve.

"All right, old man, let's try it."

He loosened his waist rope and crawled onto the bucking back third. Maria moved into the center where the others were huddled to stay away from the edge and grasp of the violent waves. Juan untied her rope from the back and handed it to her to reattach in the center. She scrambled to tie herself down as another wave hoisted them high—and twisted the raft on its end.

Maria fell onto her side, frantically grabbed for the platform's edge and fought to hold on. She dug her fingernails into the wood, but as slid down the platform it ripped the nail clean off her index finger and left a trail of blood in its path. Her shriek was cut short when the raft dropped flat, and Vilma grabbed Maria's rope.

"Hang on! We'll make it!"

The waves came from all angles. Juan fought to balance himself and salvage their few supplies. The large water container, half full, was a giant impediment to get around. Aside from one five-gallon jug it was the only water they had left. Brutal waves twisted the raft in various directions as the maelstrom continued to build.

The sky changed constantly from black to grey, then to black again as low rain-soaked clouds roared past.

The drums in the center were attached to the back platform with the same ropes, which made it impossible to simply cut the back third free.

"If we cut the ropes in the center, all the drums will come loose," Juan said.

"You can't cut them then re-tie them quickly?" Manuel asked.

"Are you crazy?!"

Juan's blood raced through his heart so fast he couldn't concentrate. When the next wave slammed the raft and it buckled again, he knew there was no choice.

"Hold on to me!"

He cinched the rope tightly around his waist, then hung over the side and tried to cut the ropes on the far end of the drum. The angle was impossible, and waves grabbed at him and tried to pull him down.

This is insane. How am I supposed to do this?

As the solution crystallized in his mind, Juan began to shake. A sense of sheer terror shook him to his core, for in the center of his being were the moments when his foot had been stuck in the drain and water had pressed him into the raging torrent.

Another wave slapped the raft sideways and the ropes stretched like rubber bands.

That's it. Juan muscled his fear aside.

"I have to go underneath, I'll untie the knots then retie the ropes when that piece of shit's gone."

Nobody said a word, but everyone knew he could not swim.

"We'll keep hold of you," Manuel said. They all grabbed a section of his rope.

"It's pitch black under there, how will you see?" Maria yelled.

Juan ignored her and fought off the inner scream that shouted he was about to die.

He slipped off the edge and disappeared into the inky blackness. Under the raft he quickly found an airspace next to the drum. The water slammed him around, and it took all of his strength to hang on.

"I'm okay!"

The rush of wind and water was the only reply. His hands shook, and his breaths came in short, rapid spurts. *Concentrate, focus on the knots!*

He groped around blindly until he found each knot that connected the drum to the center platform. Ernesto had used slipknots when he retied them yesterday. He grabbed hold of the first knot and twisted it loose.

A wave lifted the raft and Juan with it, and he felt the single drum twist at a different angle than the others. Protected from the wind, the screech of wood against wood nearly deafened him. Manuel had been right, even if they didn't capsize, the pressure of the wood crunching against itself would rip the raft apart.

With no time for analysis, Juan decided to untie the entire section of platform instead of first releasing the drum. He hoped it would do the job faster.

If I can untie the knots and get back on board fast enough to retie them up there, the middle drums won't come apart, otherwise the whole thing will break apart.

It was a huge risk, but there was no other option.

Another wave lifted them high and the platform crashed down on top of him, the edge of the drum smashed against his head and sliced a deep gash across his forehead. Juan's vision blurred and he saw stars. Blood rushed down his face. It burned his eyes—he tasted it and had an instantaneous concern about sharks.

I've got to get this done and get out of here.

He reached up and groped his way down the seam, pulling the tag end of each knot as he went. The back section instantly separated from the rest and the empty platform flipped onto its side.

The web of ropes pulled away fast—faster than Juan expected. He heard a woman's shriek over the wind as he struggled to get out from underneath and back on board before the ropes came all the way apart. He ducked the rogue drum—but as it twisted away, the back corner of the remaining deck smashed the side of his head.

Juan blacked out and went limp.

He came to and saw lightning flash above him. In the next flash he saw that the loose ropes from the next two drums now hung free. An upward pull lifted his body—God was yanking him into the afterlife.

Remarkably, God was a beautiful woman.

In fact, she looked familiar.

Now Juan saw Maria on her knees at the edge of the raft. She pulled the rope wrapped around his chest while Manuel pulled her. He took hold of the platform, and with the help of the others dragged himself on board. The back section was still connected by a loose spider web of ropes, and Juan struggled to retie them before their world collapsed.

Manuel held the ropes tight while Juan fumbled with the knots. The back third of the platform continued to drag behind them, and it pulled hard and jerked the raft in the waves. Water poured over the deck where Maria and Vilma kicked and pushed at the rogue section.

"Come on, you bastard!" Juan yelled.

"Hang on!" Manuel shouted. Then he looked toward the sky and froze. The ropes slipped from his hands, and his eyes spread wide as saucers. "Juuaaaan!"

With one last knot to tie, he saw terror on the old man's face and heard his scream through the rising wind.

Beyond him was an incomprehensible sight.

From the purple hulk of clouds a white cylinder descended directly in their path. Broad and pulsating, the column palpitated from heaven to sea, carving the frenzied waves in half.

Juan dropped the last rope.

A huge waterspout swung wildly from the sky at the same instant lightning strobed with electricity struck. The noise paralyzed Juan as the waterspout came slowly toward them. He grabbed one of the oars and paddled wildly away from its path. Who was it that told him a waterspout was a tornado over water?

The raft lurched to the left, then the right, but the water-filled tornado tacked toward them with an unearthly screech, the spout spraying water in all directions as it gouged its way through the surf. Raw centrifugal force sucked the raft closer, no matter how hard Juan had paddled. The spout's tip lifted up like a giant drill bit that swirled in a rotation of destructive liquid power.

The group fell together, tied in a bunch to the deck. The spout continued to rise above the waves, just twenty feet from the raft. Juan willed it to rise over them.

"Be gone, devil!" Vilma screamed.

Water flew through the wind like shrapnel. Juan, focused on the beast hovering closer, barely noticed the sting.

Manuel closed his eyes as the immense column lifted above them. The screech of water ripped through the air— sounded like the rusty gates of hell had swung open to suck them in. The spiraling winds were filled with a thousand feet of speeding liquid, capable of destroying anything in its path.

The spout recovered from its skid off the waves and began to descend upon the edge of the raft like a giant vacuum cleaner.

"No!" Vilma covered her face with her forearm.

The oar was ripped from Juan's hand and disappeared into the cylinder.

The suction lifted the raft off the water and the group hung on, their bodies connected to the airborne platform with frail twine cords except for Juan, floating in a state of weightlessness—and then came an astonishing pull from the rope.

The waterspout pitched the platform into the air and lifted Vilma onto its peak. Gravity pulled her headfirst into Maria's gut just before the spout sucked Vilma back up off the raft's outer edge into its vortex.

No human sound marked Vilma's disappearance. A split second after Juan saw Vilma vanish into the spiraling cylinder, the ragged edge of her waist rope was spit back at the raft.

The raft bounced off the spout's outer edge and was thrust back across wave tops like a skipping stone, careening, cartwheeling, and then miraculously skidding to rest upright fifty feet outside the cylinder's path.

It came to a stop without a soul on board.

With the air punched out of his lungs, Juan flailed in the roiling water toward one of the ropes—grabbed it—pulled himself back on board—

Nobody was there.

He found another one of the ropes and pulled it, only to find it had snapped.

He got on his knees and grabbed another, pulled it frantically, but again there was nothing.

There! One last rope, but like the others, it too was severed clean.

"Maria! Manuel!" Juan stood and screamed their names, again and again. He heard nothing in reply. Even the howl of the waterspout had faded away.

"Juan!" A voice sounded from the darkness.

It was Maria. He could hear her as she struggled in the water.

"Help me, I've got Manuel!"

Juan grabbed the longest rope and threw it toward her voice. He heard splashing, and the rope went taut. He pulled on the rope as hard as he could, which seemed weak to him but Maria and Manuel slowly emerged from the darkness. And somehow he managed to help them on board.

Maria immediately collapsed on the deck.

"What about Vilma?" Manuel asked.

"She's gone," Juan said. "The spout, it sucked her in-I've shouted for her a hundred times—it doesn't makes sense!"

Even though he knew she couldn't swim, he continued to call her name, but to no avail. Maria lay curled in the fetal position. She clutched her knees and groaned. Juan and Manuel called Vilma's name until they were hoarse, then reluctantly conceded her to the sea.

Juan checked each rope on the platform, and remarkably, they were still in one piece. The food was gone, the large water container was gone, and they had one half-full five-gallon jug and one empty one, along with their small bag of possessions. The rain continued to come down hard.

He used what rope was left to retie the others to the raft.

I can't believe Vilma's gone. I can't believe this has fucking happened to us!

Juan slowly fell to his knees as a familiar sense of abandonment overcame him. The movement made him dizzy, and he felt a slight throb—the gash on his forehead. The bleeding had stopped, but the wound felt swollen. Thinking he could taste salt and blood in his mouth, he spit into the waves to rid himself of the flavor of pain and death.

"I never thought you wouldn't make it, Vilma." Guilt tore at his stomach. Then he bent over to check Maria. He cinched her rope up tightly, noticed a dark stain on her dress but didn't investigate—what could he do about it? She moaned, he hoped from shock not pain.

I won't let you down, Ernesto.

29

THE SECRET SERVICE AGENTS nervously watched the refugees press hard against makeshift fences and yell words they could not understand. Governor Cox, familiar with Cuban slang, hoped the audio would be edited from the evening news. Representative Ortega who understood every word, feared they might break through the fence at any moment. Senator Dunleavy focused exclusively on the network cameramen.

The entourage walked through a fenced aisle between the endless rows of white tents. The male refugees were on one side and the females on the other. Families were separated but could see each other through the chain-link, which only increased their agitation. The Dade County and State of Florida Task Forces had decided upon this design as the number of immigrants rapidly escalated during the Exodus. Their rationale had been that it was the best way to ensure the women's' privacy and safety, and federal aid would soon come.

No aid had come yet, but with the president here now, expectations were high. "Better late than never," Governor Cox had been quoted in the Miami Herald.

Winslow walked confidently toward the stage. He was wearing khaki pants and shirt with a lightweight windbreaker bearing the presidential seal. Even though it was winter, the weather was warm and the sky had cleared up considerably after last night's storm blew over.

"See what I've been talking about?" Governor Cox said.

Winslow stopped and looked back down along the tents. Angry men, many stripped down to their shorts, were on one side of the aisle, women and children were on the other. Collectively, they were filthy and looked like caged animals. The scene might have been a refugee camp in Somalia.

"Not a pretty sight, is it?" Winslow said.

"Pathetic." Dunleavy answered for the governor. "These people should have been released weeks ago."

"Could you imagine having to flee your home to find freedom?" Winslow asked.

"I fled Cuba, Mr. President," Representative Carmen Ortega said. "Not on a boat or a raft like these people, but I fled just the same."

Winslow glanced at her but did not respond. He remembered her election campaign sensationalizing her family's exodus. In reality, her father had lost his American sponsored business and vast fortune to the Revolution just after diplomatic relations were severed in 1962. He came to America seeking to plot Castro's overthrow. Carmen Ortega was an infant at that time.

A huddle of suits approached the stage, and the president saw Senator Spinelli in their midst. He turned to Terri Turner.

"Let's take a minute."

They stepped off the stage and into the limousine parked behind it, which was immediately surrounded by Secret Service Agents. "I talked to the AG while you were touring the tents," Turner said. "He heard from Havana, they made a few changes but nothing major. No deal killers."

"All right, so I guess that's it. We'll move forward."

They shared a long smile.

"José Mas Fina is here with Spinelli," Turner said. "They must smell a rat, they're not just here for a photo-op."

"Make sure the detail keeps a close eye on them," Winslow said, nodding toward Secret Service agents.

"What are you going to say about Dunleavy's accusation? Aside from Harvey's press conference, you haven't said a word."

The president shrugged, a hint of a smile turning his lips.

"I haven't decided yet. Snider told me to stick to the old axiom of the best defense being a good offense."

"Well, you're the quarterback, you better throw a bomb."

"More like a Hail Mary."

MARIA LAY COMATOSE in the fetal position. She faced the pink glow on the horizon and finally stirred when she felt the heat of the sun on her cheek. A stab of pain tore through her abdomen—a little one, not like the ones from last night—and she shut her eyes tightly. But with her eyes closed, she again saw the storm's surreal lightning flashes and shrieking winds—and then, worse, the image of the raft lifted up onto its side, which launched Vilma into her stomach and caused that first stab of pain....

A dark red stain now extended from her waist to her knees. Far worse was the emptiness she felt inside her entire body, not just her belly. Last night she had ground her teeth so hard that her jaw now ached. With her eyes pinched tightly closed, the tears still managed to slip past her quivering eyelids.

Manuel and Juan lay balled up in sleep. Juan had a nasty gash across his forehead caked with dried blood. *You saved our lives, Juan.*

Maria rolled onto her knees—her stomach convulsed as she moved.

As she slipped over the edge into the sea she felt a viscous sensation between her legs. The ocean felt cold at first, but it slowly helped to numb and soothe her tired body. She stared at the bloodied tips of her fingers, nails ripped, and her mind wandered back to the storm and to the unfathomable losses.

She closed her eyes. *I could let go right now and it would all be over.*

Her ragged fingers slid closer to the edge. One hand fell away, and her free arm floated peacefully. Her breathing slowed as she released her remaining fingers from the raft.

She drifted freely, her body shifted in the water, and she sank slowly to her nose.

Another pain tore at her abdomen. Maria flinched—then grabbed the deck with both hands and bit down until the pain passed. She lifted her dress and pulled down the bottom of her bathing suit and kneaded it clean.

A dark red sheen surrounded her in the water. Again she bit her lip to hold back the tears.

Is this my reward, God? For my life...for the lies?

She looked at the two men, then past them across the endless blue ocean, her heart empty. Neither Juan nor Manuel awoke as she pulled herself back on board. Thoroughly soaked and whittled down to a fraction of herself, Maria passed out from the loss of blood and her inconsolable sense of loss and desolation.

30

"YOU PEOPLE DIDN'T come to America to live in tents." Winslow's voice echoed over the loudspeakers that had been erected throughout the compound inside Homestead Air Reserve Base. He paused to allow the translator to restate his words in Spanish.

"You came here to seek your dreams, and to escape the conditions you lived under at home. The Cuban government has made many advancements in the shadow of our 42-year embargo, largely because our allies have ignored our requests to sanction the Castro regime, but those advancements are obviously not enough. The embargo's been successful in keeping Cuba economically weak, but it has not brought about the change in political philosophy that was originally sought. Most people who have left Cuba have done so for economic reasons, not ideological ones, so promoting economic starvation there has been a long term, failed policy."

A polite if somewhat confused applause sounded from the tents. Winslow risked a quick look at Spinelli and saw his jaw thrust forward like a bulldog's.

"Most of America's former foes have become ghosts on the pages of history. Today, we face different kinds of adversaries, ones who plot in the shadows, gypsies who operate outside of nation-states. Weak and oppressed countries become targets for these adversaries who pay vast sums to buy safe harbor, and then their evil flourishes within the host country like a parasite. Cuba has proven itself vulnerable to this type of relationship in the past, and since their isolation has left them so economically weak, they continue to be a logical target for our enemies today.

"The history of our relationship with your country has been difficult." He gestured to the tents. "It's been marked with heroics and passion, but it's also been tainted by imperialist actions from an age gone by, going back nearly 200 years to the Monroe Doctrine. And even though there's been significant friction between our governments, there has always been a strong affinity between our peoples. And that is part of the reason we are here today.

"In this new era we must use our experience and knowledge to chart a course for achieving our goals in the hemisphere and to preventing our shadow adversaries from lodging themselves within the region." He waited for the polite applause to subside before continuing.

"You people have suffered great hardship in abandoning your lives. You survived a harrowing journey and now you've been apart from your families for a month, not sure if you will ever be accepted into America. On behalf of the American people, I apologize for these conditions, but unfortunately, we could not absorb so many of you all at once. The people of Florida alone have carried the burden since your arrival, and to them we're grateful." Out of the corner of his eye, he saw Governor Cox take a slight bow for the cameras.

"Moreover, Miami has endured heightened tensions, and I'd like to express my compliments to Mayor Martinez for restoring order after yesterday's problems. I'd also like to ask the people of Miami to remain calm while the solution is finalized.

"I'm here today to make a promise. A promise that I'll work with Governor Cox to help expedite your processing so you can enjoy the freedom that you risked your lives to attain." He caught Turner's eye as loud applause sounded after his statement was translated.

"But I'm not stopping there."

The statement wiped the smug smiles from Spinelli and Mas Fina's faces.

"The stalemate between Cuba and America has gone on too long. Many of you came here as a result of the failed negotiations that I endorsed with President Castro. You gave up hope, and I'll bet there's many more like you who've given up hope too. Once hope is lost, people do desperate things, and I don't want America to contribute to the desperation of the Cuban people any longer."

A wave of confusion passed over the stage as the president's statement sank in.

"Even though some have attempted to block my initiative toward Cuba with false accusations, I've agreed to meet with President Castro to try and end the hostilities between our countries, and to potentially normalize relations so the suffering can end."

An implosion of breath could be heard across the stage, which after the translation was followed by an explosion of cheers from the tents.

"Forty-two years of embargo has not produced an end to justify the means, so I see no benefit in continuing this policy. If we're able to agree on some mutually constructive changes that will allow our countries to peacefully coexist, that will lead to an improvement of the living conditions in Cuba *and* will allow free and open travel, investment, cultural exchanges, tourism, and a mutually beneficial relationship, then I'll call for an end to the embargo."

Thunderous cheers from the tents drowned out the clamoring on the stage.

"The best way we can change the situation inside Cuba is by engaging the Cuban people," Winslow said when the noise died down. "History has proven that change will come faster through exposure to the bright light of encouragement than through the darkness of animosity. I feel strongly that this is the best course to improve the human rights conditions in your country, so tomorrow I'm flying to Havana to meet with President Castro and I hope to return with good news for the world."

The roar of applause and whistles drowned out the few shouts of disapproval, including that of José Mas Fina—who, Winslow saw was being restrained by the Secret Service. Spinelli and Dunleavy looked crestfallen. They had cancelled the emergency session in anticipation of Winslow releasing federal aid, but could never have anticipated what had just transpired.

"U.S.A.! U.S.A.! U.S.A.!"

The crowd's spontaneous chant sent a bolt of electricity through President Winslow. He had made the right decision.

"Please be patient while we work with Governor Cox to facilitate your situation, and if we are successful tomorrow, you may soon have the option to stay here, or return home to a new environment of cooperation between our countries. Thank you, and may God bless us all."

"U.S.A.! U.S.A.! U.S.A!"

Turner tugged at Winslow's arm and tried to steer him off the stage, but the president smiled and waved his arms, and the crowd cheered even louder. Finally, surrounded like prizefighters by Secret Service agents, Winslow and Turner moved off the stage. The press swarmed them, drowning out each other's questions in their frenzy for answers. Winslow pressed on to the sanctuary of his car. The thunderous ovation from the fifty thousand Cuban émigrés had not let up, and together with the press and stunned politicians, the atmosphere equated to pure chaos.

Reporters engulfed his limousine, anxious for a statement, but the car inched forward in the midst of the flashing lights of his motorcade. When the limousine suddenly stopped, the president saw Spinelli in the middle of the road, blocking their path. The expression on his face was desperate.

Winslow decided to face him.

"Let him in."

"What are you doing?" Turner asked, but Winslow held up his hand.

Once inside, Spinelli sat hunched over across from them.

"With all due respect, Mr. President, are you insane?"

"Actually—"

"You don't have the authority to end the embargo, only Congress can do that. Are you familiar with the Helms-Burton—"

"Don't wave your goddamn finger at me, Senator. I'm fully cognizant of my constraints. I've got no choice but to rectify the mess *you* made, so think about that before you go stirring up the hornet's nest. Good day."

The Secret Service took their cue, the door was opened, and Senator Robert Spinelli was removed like an unwanted hitchhiker.

LUNCH WAS SERVED on china that was once fine but showed its age with a chip here and an embedded crack there. Fried pork was accompanied by yellow rice, yucca, plantain, black beans, and several plates of bread.

"We should consider this a pivotal advancement of the Revolution," Fidel said.

"I heard every word in Varadero, and I think Winslow is trying to save his own skin," Raúl said. "Perhaps the American press is right and he does want his oil fields back. He could be the worst imperialist yet."

Fidel laughed. He was full of confidence for reasons he could not explain, but he had learned a half century ago to trust his instincts.

"Raúl may be right," Sanchez, the Minister of MININT said.

"Of course the military and secret police suspect a conspiracy," Castro said. "I would be disappointed if you didn't."

"Huh! After all these years of your preparing us to fight from door to door to repel the American horde, now I'm the one consumed with conspiracy theories?" Sanchez said.

Many lesser ministers would find themselves in jail for such an aggressive statement, but Sanchez was one of the few whose counsel Castro trusted. He waved off the question and asked one of his own.

"What have you learned about Southern Oil's former properties?"

"Completely worthless." Sanchez smiled. "At least as far as they know."

"What's that supposed to mean?"

"The refinery is a wreck, too antiquated to refurbish, and their original wells are dry."

"But?"

"But new wells were drilled on their former land that are functional and have been productive for over 20 years."

Castro sat back in his chair, a smile growing on his lips.

"You find this amusing?" Raúl said.

"Not at all, my brother. But with this information, we have two interesting options. Either we help Winslow by stating that their former property is no good, or we destroy him by telling the world that it's highly valuable."

Sanchez smiled broadly.

"I believe Winslow and Turner are sincere," Ricardo Allasandre said.

All eyes turned to the Foreign Minister, who had formerly been the Cuban Ambassador to the United Nations. He had spent more time in the United States than the rest of them combined.

"Based on America's political trends toward the world after declaring war on terrorism and the growing sentiment against the embargo after the Elian Gonzalez case, I can imagine a forward thinking president risking short term upheaval for long term victory."

"So they've developed a guilty conscience?" Raúl asked.

Castro launched forward in his chair, pointing his index finger at his brother.

"Precisely, the American people *do* have a guilty conscience! That's because they have moral integrity, it's their politicians we can't trust!"

"They've done nothing but pass aggressive legislation designed to make us suffer. How does that depict a positive political trend?" Sanchez asked.

"As an autocrat, you wouldn't understand the finer details of political posturing," Allasandre said.

Castro snorted a laugh, then began to cough.

"Aggressive legislation is easy to pass against long standing enemies," Allasandre said. "Most American politicians are too cowardly to change their paradigms, especially when it comes to a policy that's existed for 42 years. It's not so different than the discussion we're having right now."

"What's that supposed to mean?"

"In light of last month's humiliation, it would be easier to ignore their advances and launch our human waste toward their shores as we originally planned." Allasandre paused and looked into each waiting eye. "For the Americans it's much more difficult to change, they have public opinion and opposing parties to contend with. This feels different."

Sanchez grunted and offered his own version of a dismissive hand gesture. Raúl looked toward his brother.

"What Ricardo says is true," Castro said. "I believe Winslow's crusade to right their listing ship of international relations has finally docked in Havana. Plus, American politicians probably think our people's exposure to their ideology will soften the Revolution. Believe it, Sanchez, the world is changing very fast these days."

"We've survived their blockade and they know we'll never surrender, so maybe it's true, maybe they have given up on their antagonistic policies," Raúl said.

Castro felt as if he were again the guerilla strategist high in the mountains of the Sierra Maestra.

"Winslow has put himself out on a political limb. If he doesn't cooperate with us, he'll find a noose waiting for him at the end. The American press and Winslow's political enemies are screaming bloody murder over this Cubagate. Coming here will either save him, or finish him off. So whether he realizes it or not, he has put his fate in our hands."

"What reports have come in from Miami since Winslow's speech this morning? Any more rioting?" Raúl asked.

Sanchez' eyes wavered. "The reports have been mixed. No more big riots. The refugees were jubilant, but demonstrations opposing the trip broke out immediately with picketing and looting."

"Aha! You see?" Castro said. "A perfect backdrop for tomorrow's meeting."

In his youth Fidel Castro considered himself a lion, stalking and devouring prey. Over time he learned to become a fox. And now, having let the Americans think they were getting what they wanted, he intended to manipulate the end game of their bitter relationship and preside over the birth of a new era. He had not yet shared the one concession that the American deal was based upon, and Raúl as instructed had kept his mouth shut. Castro had given Washington the signal that he accepted their proposal, now it was time to break the news.

To the patient goes victory.

"Winslow's timing works well with our plans for the future."

"What plans?" Allasandre asked.

"My plans for withdrawing from the day to day operations of government. Publicizing the transition we had planned for next summer will be good for the peace of mind of our people, and it will satisfy the one hurdle Winslow needs to overcome the Helms-Burton Act."

"What are you talking about?"

187

"The only way he can end the embargo is if a transition government has been created that will appear to lead toward elections."

"You agreed to this?" Sanchez was all but shouting, "Allowing them to dictate our political process?"

"Of course not. When Turner came begging I made it clear that we'd never agree to America, or anyone, determining policy within Cuba. Once I believed their intentions were sincere, I told her about our transition plan. She was thrilled that the timing could coincide with their desire to end the embargo."

"You told her of our plans?"

Castro felt blood rush to his face.

"I revealed our plans as a calculated move in a chess game with an American emissary on a covert mission searching for a way to end the embargo that's strangled our country for decades. It was like dangling a piece of cheese in front of a rat. Just because she saw it doesn't mean she'll ever be able to eat it." Castro's stare lingered on Sanchez, who for all his power knew when to keep his mouth shut.

Allasandre was beaming, and Raúl stared out toward the José Marti monument.

"So what about tomorrow?" the foreign minister asked.

Everything was happening quickly, but Castro hadn't wanted to finalize his plan until he had the Americans where he wanted them. Based on the news of Southern Oil's former assets, he now did.

"What was the name of Southern Oil's refinery prior to the Revolution?" Castro said.

The Minister of the Secret Police pursed his lips, and paged through his notes.

"El Pilar."

Raul smiled. "Named after Hemingway's boat. You won the first ever marlin tournament aboard that boat, brother."

"And tomorrow we shall win again," Castro said. "The international press is coming in by the plane load, and Winslow's entourage arrives in the morning. We will have a joint press conference after our meeting, and it will be one of the finest hours in the Plaza de la Revolución, regardless of the outcome."

"Who will attend the meeting?" Allasandre asked.

"Raúl will be there, and you obviously need to be there, Ricardo. That will be important based on the future—"

"I met President Winslow while I was at the U.N. He was in New York at a conference of Governors," Allasandre said. "I'll be glad to see him again."

Castro said, "I'll leave it to you and Minister Ibarra to review the documents while I handle the final negotiations with Winslow. If everything is not to our liking, then it will be my pleasure to tell the press about Southern Oil's former assets."

"And they don't even realize they are walking into a trap," Sanchez said.

"Exactly. After the humiliation we endured last month, it would be a fitting retribution. And, since Winslow has put himself out on a limb, he's vulnerable to my final demands, lest he wants the noose. The end of the embargo will be a victory for Cuba. Let the world speculate on the linkages, at my age it's a moot point."

"Do you expect other changes?" Sanchez asked.

"Nothing else will change—until I make my final demand. We'll still have our socialist system and the Cuban people will continue to own every important industry, piece of land and strategic property. Americans will be treated the same as any other foreign joint venture partner. Nothing more, nothing less."

"Final demand?" Allasandre said.

"It will be a surprise."

President Castro's voice was strong and convincing, as were his words, but everyone in the room knew that Cuba would never be the same. For better or worse, they were on the eve of one of the most significant events in their country's history, and the revelation had left them all speechless.

31

"ONE JUG OF WATER and two limes," Juan said. "And if we're lucky, maybe we're not too far off course."

The old man studied the horizon. There was nothing but water and sky in every direction.

"How much longer do you think?"

"What's this, day four?" Juan said. "I don't know, could be two or three more."

While they spoke, Maria stared blankly out to sea. She had slept into the early afternoon, and based on the bloodstains on her dress, Juan and Manuel had deduced that the storm had claimed another life. With no signs of further bleeding, the men hoped she was out of danger.

"Can I do anything for you?" Juan said. Maria did not look up.

Juan had awakened with a start this morning after a few hours of restless sleep filled with nightmares. The image of Vilma being sucked into oblivion had played and replayed, as had his absurd attempts to save her and his inability to get anywhere near her. His heart was still heavy with the feeling that her death was his fault—

Stop thinking like that. We'll all die if we don't eat something.

"We need to catch some fish," he said.

"With what?" Manuel said. "Limes?" He was looking at Maria, who was holding her head in her hands.

"She's been through hell." Juan whispered. "I've lost my share of family, but not yanked from my gut." Her optimistic aura had been destroyed, and what remained was still not clear.

As if sensing his stare, Maria lifted her head and turned to them. Juan cringed hoping she hadn't heard his comment. Their eyes met and she looked past him, out toward the horizon. Her bloodshot eyes had run dry of tears. To his surprise she sat up and stretched her arms.

"Do we have any water left?"

Juan handed her the jug and she took a long pull. He watched the bubbles rise in the clear jug. A couple gallons wouldn't last long.

"How about food?" Maria asked.

Juan shook his head.

"I dreamt about pork loin and *palomilla* steak last night," Manuel said.

Maria inhaled a deep breath and blew it out slowly. Dry white spittle clung to the corners of her mouth.

"When I was a little girl in Viñales," she said. "I used to wait in line for food after school while my mother worked in the tobacco fields, before she left us and moved to Havana. We ate whatever I could get at the *bodega,* but it usually wasn't much more than rice. Sometimes we'd get some eggs, or some chicken, or a piece of fish."

Juan glanced at Manuel, surprised more by her sudden chatter than by its odd tone. Maria's expression remained fixed on the horizon, and her voice had a detached quality, as if she was not speaking to them, but just aloud. "Every so often my father would appear in his uniform but he'd be gone in a day or two. When I was fifteen I moved in with my grandmother and still we had little food. Except during the picking season, there was always more food then because the *vaqueros* wanted the pickers to be healthy."

"V*aquero?*" Juan said.

"Tobacco farmer," Manuel whispered.

"My friends wanted to be with older men, I don't know why. We all wore make up and dressed like women not girls. Everyone hung out in town, it was like we were afraid to be alone. Going to dances was fun, hearing music and sometimes we'd have a drink or a cigarette but the boys strutted around like roosters and got into fights."

Her eyes were empty, her voice a monotone.

Is she talking in her sleep?

"When I was sixteen I started seeing the man who had moved next door. I came home from school one day, he was replacing boards on his house. I was bored and offered to help. He was forty-one."

Juan looked at Manuel and raised an eyebrow. The old man, eyes narrowed, shook his head.

"My grandmother thought it was wonderful, and I started to spend a lot of time with him and after a month I moved in with him. Carlos didn't work, he lived off of a pension his family had for some tobacco land the government took, it wasn't much but it was enough."

A small white bird landed on the back of the raft.

Where did you come from, little bird? Juan stared at it while Maria kept talking. Its beak was open and its chest pulsated rapidly. *Did you come off a boat? Maybe you flew from Florida. Are we close to Florida?* He wished he could fly like a bird—rise a mile into the sky to see where they were.

"He could be gone for days at a time, but I didn't care. Until I got pregnant."

Pregnant? Juan heard the word and turned back toward her.

"All at once I was grown up yet scared like a child," Maria was saying. "Terrified, really."

Juan continued to listen but turned back to the bird. It hadn't moved. Then Manuel saw the bird and he poked Juan in the ribs, and nodded.

What?

Manuel nodded toward the bird again.

Ah, I get it, old man.

Juan slowly reached for the remaining oar strapped to the deck, untied the knot and slid the oar free. The little bird's beak was still open and its chest vibrated at a rapid pace.

If I breathed that fast I'd black out.

Juan edged closer to the bird.

"I hoped he'd be excited," Maria said, "but he said he already had a wife and three children in Bahía Honda and there was no way he'd have any more."

The little bird remained perched on the edge of the raft.

How far have you traveled, little one? You may be lost, but you picked the wrong place to land. Juan moved in slowly, raising the oar.

"Carlos demanded I get an abortion. I really wasn't much of a Catholic but I said no anyway. It was scarier than having the baby. But he wouldn't let up, he said if I wouldn't see the doctor he'd beat me in the stomach until he killed the baby." Maria's voice wavered. She continued to stare off toward the horizon, but her hand came up to rest on her bloodstained dress.

"Carlos wouldn't come with me," she said. "It was so painful...."

I'll bet Ernesto never heard this story. Juan's eyes shifted quickly from Maria back to the bird.

WHACK!

The oar slamming onto the deck was so loud it shocked Maria out of her trance. She shrieked, which caused Manuel to jump.

"Gotcha!" Juan said.

He dropped the oar and dove at the little bird, still moving but now in a daze. The assault had broken one of its wings, and a small drop of blood dripped from its beak. Juan grabbed at the bird and missed, grabbed again and got hold of its broken wing.

The little bird dug its beak into the soft skin between Juan's thumb and index finger.

"AAGGHH!"

"Twist his head!" Manuel called out.

With blood running down his hand, Juan grabbed the bird's head with his other hand and began to twist it slowly as if it were a bottle cap.

"Not like that, grab his head and shake his body, like this." Manuel shook his hand in a circle showing Juan how to break the bird's neck.

"*Y, mi madre...*" Juan did as instructed and felt the bird's bones break between his fingers. Anger and pain outweighed remorse. "That's it, you little bastard."

He looked around triumphantly, but his pride was dashed when he saw tears on Maria's cheeks.

"More death," she said.

Y coño. Guilt tore at Juan's heart.

"Vilma was fighting for her life." Maria mentioned her name for the first time.

"We're all fighting for our lives," Manuel said. "And we'll continue to fight."

Juan knew it wasn't the bird she cried for. It was the loss of the baby never to be born, the loss of Ernesto and then Vilma, the growing fear that she too might never escape this ocean. Or maybe even the fear of what might become of her if she did.

He sucked on his hand.

"When you're finished licking your wound," Manual said, "cut the bird up and catch us something to eat."

"I'd give my entire hand for a cigarette." Juan held his arm aloft. The three of them suddenly laughed, and for a brief moment overcame their grief.

32

PRESIDENT WINSLOW AND HIS ENTOURAGE had moved into the top floor of the Royal Palm Hotel in Coconut Grove, and the feeling was that of an armed camp. Connecting suites were filled with a dozen Secret Service agents, Press Secretary, Harvey Teitlebaum, Attorney General, Steve Persico, Terri Turner and President Winslow. An army of aides and assistants came and went, presenting up to the minute polling information, snippets from news wires, and messages from important sources around the country, including senators, congressmen, governors, even lobbyists representing special interest groups.

Televisions in each suite were set to various news stations, and talking heads whispered opinions and the results of impromptu polls as the backdrop to the frenzied environment. Turner met with her aides in the suite furthest from the president to consolidate the reports into a coherent summary.

One of her senior aides walked out of that suite with a serious look on her face, leaving Turner sitting alone to digest the summary garnered from countless phone calls to various Congressional staffers on their bosses' opinions and intentions.

Time to go brief the president.

She walked into the middle suite to find Steve Persico sitting close to the television surrounded by two of his staffers. She stopped to listen, and Persico waved her closer.

"What are you watching?" she said.

"CNN."

"…I don't think it matters at all, Brian," the guest speaker said. "Cubagate will not go away that easily. In fact, with the president going to Havana tomorrow, it would seem to reinforce the accusations."

"Who's that?"

"Some supposed expert from the University of Miami."

"…Even though Winslow Oil has agreed to give away the assets, and not pursue any claims for reparation?"

"President Winslow had no choice but to insist on that. Plus, how do we know the assets in Havana are worthless? We'll need the Cuban government to confirm that, and they aren't exactly forthcoming."

Turner grimaced and continued toward the president's suite. Staffers scurried about, cell phones and house phones all in use. The bedroom door was closed—she pressed her ear against it and heard nothing. She knocked twice and walked inside to find Winslow lying on the bed.

"I'm trying to get some rest, Terri. What's up?"

"The news is as expected. The press isn't letting up on Cubagate, and neither are the Democrats. We've spoken to nearly thirty senators and congressmen so far, and they're holding fast to predictable stances. Some have been supportive off the record, others aghast."

"What do the public polls say?"

"Not much." She'd hedged, not wanting to upset him further. "We're seeing about a 50/50 split on the trip, and a little higher spread on Cubagate."

"In which direction? Are they buying Dunleavy's crap?"

"I'm afraid so, but I spoke with your attorney and he thinks that once the Southern Oil facts are released, the issue will die. That, and hopefully some news from Cuba that the assets are in fact worthless." Turner tried to put a positive spin in her voice, but she could see the president wasn't buying it.

"All we can do is press forward and hope for success." He put his forearm over his eyes as he spoke. "I need a nap before our strategy session tonight."

"You can't now, George. Spinelli's still waiting downstairs."

"Why would I want to see him again?"

Turner sat on the corner of the bed. The president sat up and looked at her.

"He's a shrewd bastard. If he's smart, he'll see the tide is turning against him and jump on board. If not, he'll continue to be a problem once this gets to Congress. Better to find out now," she said.

The sarcastic look she got in return was not what she'd hoped for. A knock interrupted them, and Lee Hewson, Turner's deputy chief of staff, stuck his head in the door.

"There's a call for you, Mr. President. Danny Besing from Southern Oil. Said it was urgent."

"Winslow stood up to take the cell phone from Hewson.

"Hey, Danny, what's going on?"

Turner watched as Winslow's face changed from concerned to blank to amazed.

"Have you checked him out?"

Turner could not hear what Besing was saying.

"What's he like?" Winslow asked. "How old? Is he senile?" A pause, then his face lit up. "Danny, there *is* a God. Hold on, let me get a pen, give me his address and I'll have someone there within the hour.... Great job. If you ever get tired of the oil business, you'd make a hell of a detective." Winslow turned to face his chief of staff.

"Looks like we finally got a break," he said.

THE LOBBY OF THE ROYAL PALM RESORT was engulfed with press and policemen, and barricades had been erected in the streets around the hotel to keep clashing protesters at a safe distance. Newscasters pontificated on calculations of the ratios between angry versus pro-demonstrators and hyped any sign of hysteria to keep viewers riveted to their television sets. Bi-lingual signs illustrated the crowd's differing opinions, but their numbers were close to equal.

Tension was high within the hotel where Secret Service agents and Miami-Dade police officers guarded each entry and inspected the credentials of anyone coming or going. Hotel guests had to produce keys or special passes that had been hastily issued after the president arrived and the circus began. At first the guests were excited to have the president at their hotel, but the excitement wore off as they were stuck square in the middle of the chaos.

Disgruntled Royal Palm guests were less agitated than Senator Robert Spinelli, pacing in the lobby as he held vigil to see the president. At least José Mas Fina and Hector San Martin were a block away behind the police barricade. Winslow's plans had them insane with fury, and their threats about dropping Spinelli like a shriveled mango rang in his ear. *I'll be made a mockery if Winslow succeeds in Cuba, an overnight cold-war relic.*

The elevator door opened, and Paul Scott, the Secret Service Agent in charge of the president's detail emerged. Spinelli threw himself in front of Agent Scott.

"You said I could see him an hour ago! What the hell's going on?"

Agent Scott, his face impassive, said, "I'm here to get you."

"Let's go then, dammit."

Spinelli marched onto the elevator, which carried them to the hotel's penthouse. The agents stopped in mid-conversation to watch the senator storming down the hallway—hair wild, shirttail hanging out from his suit jacket. He rounded a corner and came face to face with Terri Turner.

You!

"Good of you to come, Senator." Turner's smile cut like a knife.

"Don't give me that shit, you two-bit Texas oil-trash. You double-crossed me!"

"You double-crossed yourself, sir."

"What—"

"Let me give you a tip," Turner said. "If you want to be a part of the solution, we can make that happen. However, if you start to rant and rave again, the president will kick you out, *again.*"

Spinelli stopped short of the door. Still furious at Winslow for ejecting him from the limousine, he knew Turner was right. He took a deep breath, raked fingers through his thin hair, and fought to compose himself.

"Who else is in there?" Spinelli said.

"AG Persico."

It took all the experience at positioning, posturing and acting he'd learned wading through the dark cesspools of Capitol Hill to summon the ability to convert emotion into negotiating prowess. His reward was to see the surprise on the president's face in response to his big smile.

33

THE AFTERNOON SUN descended steadily toward the sea. Captain Scott Hawkes checked the clock and saw that it was almost time to change the evening watch. Suddenly the watchman's whistle sounded from the starboard side of the ship—something must have been spotted. The Captain stepped back inside the bridge.

"What's up, Casey?"

"A body, sir. They're sending a RHIB out for it now. And you've got a flash message." The OOD held out an envelope.

Hawkes took it, read the message, and then walked down the two flights of steps, and then across the flight deck and down another set of steps to where the rigid hull inflatable boat was being winched over the starboard rail. He saw the three-person detail climbing down the ladder and into the RHIB.

The ship's engines soon stopped, and its giant hull slowed to nearly a crawl with only momentum to carry it forward.

"There it is, 10:00," a voice sounded from the rail.

"Wish we had a friggin' helo out here," another said.

The twin engines on the orange-hulled RHIB sounded above the breeze as it sped out toward the target.

"You're right on it, Mooney," chief petty officer Jaegle said into the microphone. "Keep that course and you can't miss it—just look for the bright red jacket, or shirt, or whatever the hell it is."

Hawkes walked to the rail squinted in the direction the RHIB was headed. Jaegle leaned into him and pointed toward a red object that rose and fell in the seas. Before long, the detail returned to the Mohawk's starboard corner.

"They say it's a woman, sir," Jaegle said.

The crew had lowered the winch, and the cable clicked steadily as it wound back onto the spool. Captain Hawkes peered over the rail and saw the corpse levitate up toward them.

"It's a woman all right, was anyway," he said as the corpse arrived at the rail. "Hasn't been dead long, she's hardly bloated."

Hawkes met his glance with a stony expression and turned to the deceased. She wore a bright red sweater and appeared too old to have attempted the crossing.

She's got to be at least sixty.

"Take her below," he said. "She's the last one of this deployment." He patted his jacket pocket. "We've got new orders. We're heading back to the base."

Hawkes saw smiles on the men gathered around the corpse. Who could blame them? After what they'd seen in the past couple of weeks, shore leave in Key West would be a welcome relief.

He disappeared back up the stairs.

"THANK YOU FOR seeing me, Mr. President," Spinelli said as he strode across the floor with his hand outstretched.

"Robert."

The door to the adjacent suite closed and Spinelli sat down with the president, the attorney general and Terri Turner. The fact that he was seriously outgunned did nothing to discourage his smirk, or what he considered an opening salvo.

"You're really going out on a limb here, sir."

"We'll see." Winslow's confident expression matched Spinelli's. "Are you with me?"

Spinelli laughed. "I was shocked when you made the announcement this morning. You didn't even consult Congress, or those from your own party who have fought Cuba for so long. And with Cubagate—"

"I gave you your chance and you sabotaged it for personal gain. I have you and Dunleavy to thank for this damn Exodus, and for putting Congress up my ass demanding that we honor the Migration Accords and send the refugees back."

Spinelli sat on the edge of his chair. The president leaned forward in his.

"Dropping the embargo would allow us to keep the Accords, defuse Castro's offensive, and let the Exodus Cubans stay. If you want to fight me, then I'll have no choice but to send the refugees back. Do you really want *that*?"

A half-minute of silence, then Spinelli sailed on.

"I've been on the phone all day with congressmen from both parties who vehemently oppose your trip. You can't succeed. Helms-Burton has too many stipulations. The Executive Office is not empowered to negotiate with Castro, Clinton gave that up."

"I know all about Helms-Burton," Winslow said. "I'm no fool, Robert. Anything I do in Cuba will be within those constraints."

Spinelli sat back. What he'd said was true, he had been on the phone all day—there were a number of senior politicians from both parties willing to go to battle over this situation. Helms-Burton was a maze of booby traps and dead ends, and Winslow would need the dexterity of Indiana Jones to pull off his goal. Spinelli was determined not to let that happen.

"The press is eating you alive. How can you go to Cuba in the midst of this controversy? It's political suicide."

"I'll—"

"Castro's too old to last much longer, especially now that we have him on the ropes," Spinelli said.

"That's the same broken record we've been hearing since 1960."

"You're right, but things have only gotten worse—their communist single-party system has a long record of human rights violations by a dictator of epic proportions—Cuba became the USSR's showcase, for heaven's sake!"

"Exactly, that's why it's time to change our approach. Castro's been training his people for years waiting for the United States to invade them, but it's the Cuban people who have invaded us! Castro's outsmarted us at our own foolish game."

Frustration appeared on Spinelli's face, and the contrived smile was long gone.

"I was just there, the conditions are ripe for collapse. Giving in now makes no sense."

"We're not giving in, and it makes all the sense in the world. If what you say is true, and Castro *is* in trouble, which I doubt, what will happen? Anarchy? Civil War? Cuba becomes a staging ground for terrorists so they *can* start manufacturing biological weapons? Or maybe a greater alignment with some unfriendly nation?"

"We'll install a democratic government—"

"Please, are you kidding? Who, Spinelli? José Mas Fina, or some other wild-eyed expatriate? You think the Cuban people want another puppet moving down from Miami? That may play well at fundraisers, but it's a fool's dream."

"Then who?"

"Any number of hard-liners could fill Castro's void and we'll still be out in the cold. We need to change our policy now, *before* Castro steps down. Hell, the man's 76 years old! We'll stand a better chance of guiding them toward democracy from the inside than we would as a bully."

"If you embrace him now, you'll be giving up everything we've stood for."

"It's time to admit that even though we thought Cuba would collapse after the Soviet Union fell apart, it hasn't. When communism was still the rule in Eastern Europe, we let our citizens travel there because of our faith and confidence in our system, and—"

"Reagan bankrupted them with military spending, damn near bankrupted us too."

Winslow wanted to scream, so he took a deep breath. "Communism wasn't defeated because of an embargo," he said calmly if coldly," but because we introduced a better system through our best ambassadors, the American people. The same thing will happen in Cuba."

"It won't work. On top of giving Castro the final victory, we'll have riots this country hasn't seen since Watts. Besides, it's all moot anyway, Helms-Burton requires an act of Congress to end the embargo."

The president jumped up, which caused Spinelli to flinch.

"What a miserable piece of legislation. All it's done is piss off every other country in the world by imposing trade restrictions on them. How arrogant is that?"

Spinelli slowly stood and walked around the circle of advisors. "You're starting a hell of a fight. These issues won't go away, they've been here for 42 years too: reparations for the nationalized land and industry, free elections, and their human rights violations have only gotten worse. Now they've got a virtual tourism-apartheid working where Cuban citizens aren't even allowed to enter the hotels. You'll be crucified." He stopped, took in a deep breath and then narrowed his eyes. "Consider it fair warning that several congressmen are using the term 'trading with the enemy.'"

"Hogwash."

Spinelli spit out a nervous laugh. "You're a fool. Mark my words, you'll be drawn, quartered, and hung out to dry. Castro's on his heels, and even if your thoughts on his succession merit consideration, flying down there tomorrow will only blow up in your face."

The senator's words sent a chill through the president. He glanced at Turner then Persico, but neither of them jumped in to defend him. He sat back down, stewing over instantaneous visions of nasty headlines. If he could only tell Spinelli that Turner had already all but finalized the deal, but he knew he couldn't trust the man.

"The Exodus Cubans are here illegally—wet foot, dry foot, or not," Winslow said. "I have every right to send them back, and if you force my hand that's exactly what I'll do. How will that fly in Little Havana? You think Elian Gonzalez was a black eye? This will be a decapitation."

Spinelli didn't reply.

"If we're able to negotiate a favorable conclusion to the embargo, we could preserve the Accords *and* let them stay. But if not, Castro's ready to open the floodgates as a payback for your grandstanding, so no matter what, it's going to be a mess."

"He's bluffing."

"Our intel shows otherwise. Did he bluff Carter in 1980? Do you want to take that chance? I don't."

Spinelli's lips curled under, and he bit his knuckle.

"Helms-Burton is the law, and unless Castro disappears, there's nothing to talk about. We'll just have to take our chances on another Exodus."

Winslow balled his hands into fists, stretched them wide and balled them up again.

"You're right about one thing," Spinelli said. "If you try to send them back, there will be riots in Little Havana, throughout Florida, and New Jersey for that matter." He paused and a calm came over him. "If you want to put the gun to your own head, that's your choice."

They stared at each other and neither man blinked. Winslow suddenly changed his tone.

"What do you need to satisfy Helms-Burton?"

The question caught Spinelli off guard, but not for long.

"Castro stepping down for a start. Then the release of jailed dissidents. Free elections, allow a free press—"

"How many jailed dissidents are there now?"

"Last I heard there were over two hundred." Spinelli's voice was gradually recharging with self-righteousness.

"Compare that figure with the number of refugees we see every year. On average, the Coast Guard intercepts *two thousand* Cuban rafters."

Spinelli shrugged.

"That number doesn't impress you? How about this, we've recovered thousands of dead bodies during the Exodus, and the Cuban press has reported another four thousand bodies found in Cuban waters."

"Castro's fault."

"That's thousands of people—*that we know of*—who died trying to reach freedom in this boatlift alone. Would those people be dead if we weren't denying them access to food, medicine, trade, and all the rights afforded to any other nation?"

Spinelli's mouth dropped open, then closed.

"Now, compare that with the 200 political prisoners. Our embargo's keeping all eleven million of them political prisoners. It hasn't worked, Senator, and I'm not going to suck up to the small fraction of Cuban-American hard-liners just to get some votes. I'll bet you right here and now that if the walls come down, those same Cuban-Americans you're representing will change their tune."

"No way, never."

"When they can go home and start doing business there? They'll figure out a more proactive way to bring about change than starving their former countrymen."

"What about Cubagate? That's not going away."

The president didn't respond and when Spinelli looked up, Winslow wished he had a picture of the man's face.

"What the hell are you smiling about?"

"What you refer to as 'Cubagate' is a dead issue."

Spinelli barked a nervous laugh. "I don't think so. Have you seen—?"

"We've found the former manager of Southern Oil's El Pilar refinery and oil fields. He has all of his original reports on the status of the assets at the time of the Revolution. It's just like I've been saying, it's all bullshit."

When the color drained from Spinelli's face, the president knew he had assisted Dunleavy with the so-called Cubagate accusation.

"That's impossible, he'd be—"

"93 years old. Sharp old guy, lives in a nursing home outside of Boston. I spoke to him myself an hour ago. Name's Warner Haslett. You'll be seeing him on the news tonight." The president stood. "Thanks for coming, Senator. It's time to prepare for the future."

"You're still going?"

"Damn right."

"Don't say I didn't warn you. It's going to be an ugly fight."

Silence smothered the room after the senator left. The discovery of Warner Haslett had lifted the president's confidence, but the weight of the pending challenge was growing heavier. Turner stared out the window at the brilliant sunset. Attorney general Persico shook his head.

"What's wrong?" Winslow said.

"Based on our deal, Castro's got up to six months to retire. Congress *will* be able to enforce Helms-Burton and stymie the deal. I hate to say it, but he's right, it could be an ugly fight."

Winslow looked to Turner. "So much for Spinelli being part of the solution."

"You 100% sure about this?" she said. "I know we've cut a good deal, and in time it'll all be clear, but like your Daddy used to say, 'Don't get into a pissing match with a skunk.' Spinelli will not go quietly into the night."

Without speaking another word, the president walked into the bedroom and closed the door. Gut-check time.

34

"WE'RE OUT OF WATER." Juan's lips stuck together as he spoke.

Maria lay flat on her back and stared into the dusky sky.

"I should have drowned instead of Vilma," she said.

Juan only heard her say Vilma's name. "What was that song she was singing, how did it end?"

Manuel turned away.

"You know the rest, old man?"

A slow nod was his answer. "It'll be cold tonight," he said. He closed the top button of his paper-thin shirt. Maria wore Ernesto's jacket, but Manuel was sure to freeze. Juan pulled off his sweater and revealed a tattered t-shirt underneath.

"Take this, old man. I'd rather shake from the cold than from craving cigarettes."

"You'll—"

Juan held his hand up.

The sweater was tight against Manuel's round belly.

The ocean had remained calm throughout the day, although the wind picked up from the dead calm of morning. With no clouds to block the sun, the day's heat had been brutal. Every inch of exposed skin was as red as bougainvillea in spring. Manuel had blisters on his forehead and hands, third degree sunburn made worse by the salt that covered his body like a fine talcum powder.

Juan felt helpless. The longer they survived, the more difficult their survival had become. When the moon emerged over the lip of the horizon, it seemed significantly smaller than its size at their departure. Cumulus clouds hung low and gray, their bottom edges made orange as they caught the last of the day's light. The water turned from a ribbon of lavender to bottomless black, and with the loss of light their world closed in on them and accentuated the sense of isolation.

"Tomorrow's the day," Manuel said.

"Why do you say that?" Juan asked.

"That's the story of my life, short periods of happiness separated by years of suffering. It's been no different out here, and after 65 years, I can sense when the tides are about to change."

"You're—" Juan started, but then he saw Maria's spirits lift. *Crazy.*

She gazed at Manuel, the quarter moon behind him, and her eyes were doe-like. *Any straw of optimism for the desperate.*

Manuel must have seen the hope in Maria's eyes too, because he started to talk about his life after the Revolution, about his family's loss of prosperity, and how he continued to wait for change, to wait for his family, and to wait for happiness.

Always waiting.

Maria hung on Manuel's every word, but Juan stared into the blackness, sad for how the old man let his life pass by.

That's why I won't wait for shit. I don't want to die out here, but I'd rather die trying than live a life like that.

"When's the last time you spoke to your family?" Maria asked.

"Every now and then a letter comes," Manuel said. "Sometimes I get some news from others, but it's been three years since I talked to somebody."

Juan saw Maria wince. Manuel's pain was like hers, worse even, because his entire lifetime had been filled with suffering. It was like dying from a slow disease and your family couldn't speak to you, even though they knew you were suffering. For a moment it seemed worse than her more immediate losses.

"You got a pension for your land, though, didn't you?" Maria said.

"I chased after the government for years, and finally in 1975 I got a letter back saying that I would receive something the next year, but it never came. I gave up. The decades passed by one day at a time.

"Then, last year, the government sent a doctor to examine me. After testing this, and testing that, he told me I was no longer fit to work the land. They forced me out of my house to make room for a younger manager, and they sent me to Havana, stripped of the only thing I had left. You can't keep self-respect if you're not allowed to work."

"At least you were able to come to the city."

"Heh! Purgatory! In the country there's peace. You learn to live with the shortages and solitude. In Havana you're packed together like sugarcane in a bale. All anyone ever talks about is getting to America. Paint-sprayed slogans that criticize the government were everywhere. What the youth gets away with now amazes me. But when I met Juan at the hotel and he told me of his plans to come to America—do you remember?"

"In the restaurant."

"Right."

"I was a busboy there."

"Busboy? You said your brother was the manager, that you were helping him."

"I lied."

Manuel sighed. "Whatever."

"Exactly, old man, whatever. None of it matters now, only surviving this journey."

"You told me about the others: Vilma, Maria, and then Ernesto del Torres. When I heard that name, a puff of wind would have blown me over. You said that Ernesto paid for the entire voyage, that he was your partner."

"I lied about that too. He gave me money, I used it to buy the wood and drums, but he wasn't my partner. I told him everyone paid the same amount."

Juan followed Maria's gaze toward the sky in time to catch a small shooting star, which disappeared as quickly as it had flashed through the dark sky.

"When I heard Ernesto was coming," Manuel said, "I made my mind up without even thinking."

"Why?" Maria turned to face him.

Manuel was quiet for a moment. "When the new Revolutionary government came to Birán to take over the sugar farms, El Presidenté sent a war hero to do his dirty work. It was supposed to reduce resistance. The man who took our land was Ramon del Torres."

"Ahh," Juan said.

"War hero or not, we weren't giving up our farm, so my father tried to fight them, but the troops beat him unconscious. Del Torres had him arrested. They held him 127 days. When he returned, he was emaciated and covered with scars. I guess that's why we didn't get a pension, but at least they let me stay in our house."

A dolphin broke through the black water next to the raft, and spouted water from its blowhole. Moonlight glistened off its skin, and then it disappeared.

"Is that the same dolphin we saw before?" Juan asked.

"You think there's only one?" Maria said.

Her response struck Juan as strange, and he turned to Manuel.

"So, why did you care that Ernesto was on board? You never said anything to him about it."

"I don't know. I was so amazed that he would leave Cuba, the son of a war hero and Politburo member. Part of me wanted to know why, and part of me wanted to hurt Ramon del Torres. I never thought about revenge after we lost the farm, we weren't the only ones. Del Torres meant nothing to me, but when I heard about Ernesto, I was fascinated. Then when I met him, he looked just like his father had when he appeared at our farm. I knew this was my chance."

"Chance for what?"

"To fix in the future what had been destroyed in the past."

"Why didn't you say something?" Maria asked.

"After Ernesto shared your story and then talked about his goal of working in the American sugar industry, it all came together in my mind. I would introduce him to my sons, and they'd give him a job. All those years of waiting suddenly had a purpose. It seemed almost…divine, somehow."

"That's—" A sudden whiff of a putrid odor caused Juan to shut his mouth quickly.

"What's that odor?" Maria asked.

It smelled just like the bloody carcass from the other night. They sat up and scanned the water. It was pitch black, and the constant motion of the waves made it impossible to see anything.

"There! What's that?" Juan pointed to a place where waves broke against something. He took out the oar and paddled closer. Even though the smell was awful, eye-watering awful, it reminded him of food. The rumbling in his stomach had even eclipsed his desire for cigarettes.

The object gradually took shape. It was something large that rose and fell in the gentle swells. *It's too big to be another dead Cubano.*

Maria covered her face with her arm.

"It's a turtle, a huge one," Manuel said. "It's dead."

"Really, old man? You think?"

Manuel held up his hand as if he would slap Juan. "Keep paddling, we're almost there."

"Damn thing's as big as the raft."

"Must be an old leatherback," Manuel said. "Almost seven feet across. She's been dead awhile."

Juan grabbed the edge of its massive shell and slowly spun it around. Something seemed wrong, and then he realized what it was. "All its flippers are gone, its head too."

"Use the knife and try to get some meat from inside the shell."

Maria recoiled. "I'm not eating that!"

"Bait, Maria." Juan smiled through the smell.

Manuel tried to lift the edge of the shell, but it was too heavy. Juan reached inside the hole where the head had been. The meat was cold and slimy, and the smell burned his eyes.

"Oh, man." With his arm in up to its elbow, Juan twisted the knife around trying to loosen some meat, and then grabbed a handful of the dangling shreds. *Disgusting.*

After he pulled a wad free, Juan splashed his hands in the water to try to cleanse the slimy film and smell from his skin. He stuffed the putrid flesh into an empty bag and twisted it shut hoping the plastic could contain the stench. Their need to catch fish overrode his desire to throw the meat as far as he could. The little bird produced a small tuna earlier, but they'd had no other food since this afternoon, and Juan was afraid to fish at night—he didn't want to chance losing the remaining yo-yo to the darkness.

Fatigue got the better of them and they lay down for what Juan hoped was the night. Manuel started to search for his stars, but tonight the ritual was not necessary. The three survivors spooned each other and quickly succumbed to sleep. At the beginning of the trip Juan had fantasized about holding Maria, but doing it now, intimacy never entered his mind.

Please let us wake to land. It was his final thought before sleep overcame him.

35

AIRFORCE ONE SAT on the end of the runway at Homestead Air Reserve base. By the time the president and his entourage boarded, they felt as if they had run a gauntlet. From the moment their motorcade left the Royal Palm Resort they were barraged with demonstrators, honking horns, reporters, and last minute phone calls.

The pressure and anxiety combined with the humidity caused the president to perspire through his shirt before he ever settled onto Air Force One. Turner, Harvey Teitlebaum, and Steve Persico tried to keep the mood light, but the president wasn't buying it.

"I feel like Muhammad Ali after getting pummeled by George Foreman," he said.

The handful of print and television journalists he had allowed to fly aboard Air Force One were seated in the front of the plane. The president and his closest advisors had gathered in the back cabin.

"Can we cover the deal points?" Attorney General Persico asked.

"In a minute, I need some water—coffee—both," Winslow said.

Turner held his eyes then turned to the others. "Steve, Harvey, give us a couple minutes." When the door closed, she sat next to the president, who was rubbing his temples. "There's a clean shirt in the closet."

"Thank God. Castro will smell my nerves the minute we shake hands."

"Nobody besides you, me and Persico know the details behind the deal. If you have any second thoughts, or if Castro tries to pull anything, you can bail out."

"Second thoughts? Are you kidding? More like hundredth thoughts."

"Think of the context when you went public. You made the announcement in the middle of the refugee camp, with an antagonistic Governor and a bunch of political opponents sharing the dais, one of whom who had just launched a special investigation on you."

Winslow remembered the anger on Dunleavy's face.

"Then we spent the night near the worst riots in Miami's history and stewed all night listening to the news media pick you apart. If you'd made the announcement in Denver, or Cincinnati, nobody would have batted an eyelash." She paused. "Your father would be proud of you, George. I know I am."

He suddenly felt choked up at the mention of his father.

"Everything will be fine."

Winslow changed his shirt while Turner tried to change his state of mind. The holding area where the refugees were packed together like prisoners of war was visible out the window. A sea of protestor's placards waved outside the base beyond them.

"Maybe I'm a fool," Winslow said. "What if it's impossible to brush aside 42 years of mistakes? Maybe there's no room for honor, and maybe our system's too fat and self-satisfied to embrace change."

"We haven't had the chance to take thorough polls because we've been operating under the radar," Turner said. "You'll have plenty of supporters, I'm sure of it. If you believe what you're doing is right, then stick to your guns. We've already convinced Fidel to retire, nobody else has ever gotten that far."

"None of my predecessors have ever given up on this many prerequisites before."

"We didn't give up on everything, and we can't absorb political refugees indefinitely."

The sound of the jets roaring at full thrust silenced their conversation as the plane lumbered down the runway and banked south.

"We've set the wheels in motion, Terri, and you know what? It's pretty damn exciting. But it's also ironic that by doing the exact opposite of what the hard-line anti-Castro elements support, we'll be bringing an end to the hemisphere's longest reigning dictator."

"It may be months before the public knows that."

"Meanwhile, I'll be sucked into a maelstrom of criticism and second-guessing by every armchair political analyst and opposing party member, not to mention some of our own party hacks whose tits will be caught in a ringer. But when the other shoe drops—if we can survive that long—we'll be heroes."

"Shall I get Steve and Harvey?"

"You better, we're going to be sitting in Fidel's office in an hour. We need to go over the plan one more time."

CONTRARY TO THE streets around Miami, the road from José Martí International Airport into Havana was filled with throngs of cheering people. Cadillac One, the president's limo, was in line with three matching Mercedes limousines for the American delegates. Everyone else rode in a hodgepodge of obscure makes and models, together providing a classic car-show atmosphere. An official escort of police motorcycles led the column, with sirens blaring and lights flashing.

Terri Turner and Attorney General Persico were in the car with the president, and although the adrenalin was running high and nerves were frayed, they soaked up the scenery. The energy on the streets galvanized Winslow's conviction. Poverty was visibly endemic by American standards, while generous splashes of destitution filled in the gaps.

"Welcome to the Third World," Persico said.

Castro's decision to abandon urban improvement and focus on upgrading the infrastructure in the countryside was not America's fault, but the president knew that the tableau of crumbled concrete, pot-holed streets, layered rainbows of chipped paint, rusted metal, and overwhelming deterioration was partially the result of America's embargo. He also knew that once Cuba was reintegrated into the hemisphere the United States would wind up footing a significant amount of the bill to restore Havana.

"We're approaching the Plaza de la Revolución," the driver said over the intercom.

"Look at all the people," Winslow said.

People were six-deep on both sides of the street, all waving their arms, or flags, or jumping up and down. Without exception, everyone was smiling. American flags were everywhere, mixed in with the Cuban flag—which was vaguely reminiscent of the Texas flag. Gray-shirted Policia National Revolución ario were scattered along the route for crowd control, but there were far too many people to control. If the Cubans wanted to riot, or to mob the presidential motorcade, there wasn't much anyone could do, but they seemed content to cheer and show support.

"That's the Palacio de la Revolución." The driver pointed to the corner of the six-story building peeking through the trees atop a short hill. As the car climbed upward the Palacio disappeared into thick foliage, but the road opened up to a sea of humanity.

"Wow," Winslow said.

The motorcade inched forward. Motorcycles at the front of the procession were forced to stop so their drivers could disembark and wave the crowd back.

A towering pristine white sculpture of José Martí was the first thing Winslow saw. It reminded him of Rodin's *Thinker*. Behind it, the José Martí tower climbed high into the Havana sky. It was a ghastly gray edifice shaped like a giant X.

"That's where the wreath goes." Turner pointed at the monument.

As the car continued forward, a foot at a time, the president took in the entire scene. The people were barely contained in the Plaza, and beyond them he saw a giant face looming above the masses like the Wizard of Oz.

"What's that building there, that face and those words?"

"That's the Ministry of Interior, home to the secret police, or MININT," the driver said. "And that's Che Guevara."

"What's the slogan underneath it say?"

"*Hasta Victoria la Siempre*. Always Toward Victory."

A tingle passed down Winslow's spine. *That works for me.*

The scene was overwhelming, with only Winslow's inauguration providing a comparable memory as the limousine passed through a police line, and then the press line. Pedestrian barricades were slid across the road after they passed by. They pulled up to a long staircase to the José Martí monument, where a grandstand was erected at the statue's base.

"Like him or not, you've got to admit that Fidel's a master show-man," Turner said.

"This should be a nice reunion for you two."

Turner rolled her eyes.

Several prime-time network anchor people were here in the crowd at the Plaza. The president imagined standing at the podium that overlooked what seemed the entire two million population of Havana, but he knew that would only happen if the next few hours went well.

When the Secret Service was in position around the car, the president emerged, followed by the others. Camera flashes exploded, and an ear-splitting roar filled the Plaza. The president was overcome by their applause, cheers and whistles. He suddenly wanted to go shake hands with those just behind the barricades and turned in their direction, but Turner took his elbow and shook her head.

He saw her lips move, but the sound of the crowd drowned out her words.

They turned back to the tower and looked up the long stairway just in time to see Fidel Castro emerge alone from behind the immense white figure of José Martí. After he gave a sweeping wave to the masses, the crowd went berserk. Winslow couldn't help but smile.

The climb up the stairs felt like an out of body experience. At the top, the two men came face to face. Castro wore a business suit and looked every bit the elder statesman. The decibel level went off the scale when the two leaders shook hands, then turned to wave toward the Plaza.

Turner arrived at the top of the steps with a Secret Service agent who had lugged along a large wreath, and when the crowd saw them, the noise got even louder. She had insisted that they follow Cuban protocol for foreign dignitaries to place a wreath of good wishes at the base of the tower. The Americans honoring that tradition sent a positive message to the crowd, and they roared.

With a final wave, presidents Winslow and Castro and their respective entourages disappeared down the walk behind the tower, past uniformed guards that stood at attention, down through Flag Square and into the Palacio.

"Welcome to Havana, Mr. President," Castro said.

"It's a pleasure to be here."

Castro glanced back over his shoulder, caught Turner's eye and winked. Winslow spotted the gesture and pursed his lips to hold back a smile.

216

The delegation was led into a large, ornate conference area deep in the bowels of the building. Coffered ceilings rose up two stories with large crystal chandeliers and long expanses of mirrors between carved wooden pillars on the plaster walls. An erratic symphony of shoe heels sounded off the terrazzo floor, but when the doors closed it was as if the air had been sucked from the room.

Already present were Raúl Castro, the Vice President and Second Secretary of the Communist Party, Ricardo Allasandre, the Foreign Minister, and Jaime Ibarra who was the equivalent to the American Attorney General. Introductions were made and everyone took a seat, the Americans on one side of the table and the Cubans on the other.

"Good to see you again, Mr. Foreign Minister," Winslow said.

"I wasn't sure you would remember."

"Of course. We met at a governor's conference in New York, what, five years ago?"

"Your memory is good, Mr. President."

"Congratulations on your appointment as Foreign Minister. I hope we'll see more of you in the future."

Ricardo Allasandre bowed his head, suppressing a smile.

"Working within the time frame we discussed, our agenda is as follows," Castro said. "The legal teams can work out the final language on the Agreement, and if we're successful, we have a press conference planned for 1:00, two hours from now. You wanted to leave for the airport by 1:30, so that's the best we can do. If we do not come to an agreement, we'll have a much shorter press conference and you can still keep your schedule." His tone was neither conciliatory nor rude, he just stated the facts.

"That sounds right," Winslow said.

"While Raúl, Ricardo, and Jaime discuss the language with your people, why don't you and I meet privately?" Castro said.

"Perfect."

The butterflies the president had felt upon arriving were gone, now replaced with a sense of confidence. The two leaders disappeared into the corridor and Turner watched with apprehension as her old friend ventured alone, deeper into the lion's lair.

36

THE LIGHTS IN the television studio made the room feel like a sauna, and Senator Spinelli had sweated through the armpits of his shirt. His dark suit hid the perspiration, but his glistening forehead and scalp proved a challenge to the makeup artist.

"Two minutes," the director said.

Larry King was in his private dressing room and had not yet come out to speak with Spinelli. They delayed taping as long as possible to await word from Havana, but the press conference was an hour late and there was no time left to stall. The show was prerecorded for each night's broadcast, and the subject tonight was the president's controversial trip to Cuba.

Spinelli felt like royalty, with everyone running around catering to his needs. This would be his finest hour, his moment to shine. Winslow would regret ever thinking about Cuba when Spinelli's interview aired tonight. But, even so, the heat lamps made the job of the makeup artist look like a relief worker trying to dam up a midwestern flood.

"There, that should do it," the makeup artist said after applying another coating of pancake makeup. Her work looked like a bad putty job from a low budget body shop. But with a minute to go, it was as good as it was going to get.

"You're finished," she said.

Spinelli thought he looked ghoulish. "Is this supposed to look natural?"

"Take your places," the director said.

Larry King appeared from behind the screen of colored lights that made up the backdrop. "Senator Spinelli, thanks for coming."

"Of course."

Larry's makeup looked more natural than Spinelli's did.

"30 seconds."

"Any updates?"

"Nothing," Spinelli said. "The press conference is running late, so I expect Castro must be turning the screws on them." He pulled at the collar of his shirt.

"You're not nervous are you?" Larry said. "You've been on the show, what, a half dozen times?"

Spinelli shook his head and dabbed his handkerchief on his brow.

Larry looked at the director and winked. When guests were nervous there had to be a reason.

"10, 9, 8, 7, 6," the director finished the countdown with his fingers. Larry King positioned himself and greeted the audience.

"Good evening ladies and gentlemen. Tonight I have Republican Senator Robert Spinelli from New Jersey here to discuss the president's trip to Cuba. Senator Spinelli is on the record opposing the trip, and tonight we'll discuss his views and those of one of his largest supporters, the Cuban American National Council."

Larry then played the tape of his and Dunleavy's broadcast on Cuban television that led to the diplomatic breakdown and the subsequent Exodus.

"You know, Senator, many Americans blame you and Bob Dunleavy for the Exodus because of your aggressive position and sudden reverse during the meetings with Castro."

The comment surprised Spinelli. "Taking aggressive positions always attracts attention, and there are often critics," he said. "But doing the right thing is what matters."

"What about Cubagate? It would seem that based on the reports Winslow Oil has released—and the discovery of Warren Haslett, the former Executive Director of Southern Oil's Cuban operations—the wind has come out of the would-be scandal."

"That's true, Larry. I suspect the Democrats will withdraw their allegations at this point." Spinelli sneered at the camera. "Unfortunately, it was another groundless partisan attack."

"The unified support of the president during the war on terrorism has been on the wane, the international coalition is bickering, and now Congress is at each other's throats, divided over the Exodus. Is the international coalition doomed because of the Cuban situation?"

"No, this is entirely different."

"But Congress originally scheduled the emergency session to force the president's hand on the plight of the Exodus Cubans, then you cancelled that session when he announced his trip to Miami. Did Congress drop the issue because he released federal funds to Florida?"

"I wouldn't say we dropped the issue, but I had called for the emergency session because of the president's previous paralysis—"

"And then he went to Florida and released funds."

"Right."

"And he also surprised everyone by announcing his trip to meet Fidel Castro."

Spinelli hesitated. He hated to admit anything was a surprise, but there was no choice.

"Correct."

Larry went on to establish that Spinelli and the CANC opposed the president's trip, then spoke briefly on how the Helms-Burton Act was a unique piece of legislation that tied the president's hands against making unilateral foreign policy decisions in regard to Cuba. Helms-Burton was the only such constraint on the president and Cuba the only nation targeted in this manner.

"During his administration, President Clinton sought to ease the embargo by increasing people-to-people contacts, and Congress also approved limited sales of food and pharmaceuticals to Cuba, but conservatives such as yourself opposed those moves, continuing instead to support the embargo."

So, you want to fuck with me, is that it?

"That's right, Larry. Several members of Congress and I have stood firm against communism and the human rights offenses perpetuated by the Castro regime, and we'll continue to do so." He arched an eyebrow and looked directly into the camera assuming a pose reminiscent of the late J. Edger Hoover.

Larry glanced at his notes then looked up. "Polls taken after the Elian Gonzalez incident showed a broad ignorance among the American people on why we're even blocking trade against Cuba. Today, our CNN polls show strong support for the president's initiative to normalize relations with Cuba as a part of his overall goal of reducing international hostilities and reducing terrorism, yet you disagree."

"I absolutely disagree with supporting a ruthless dictator like Fidel Castro. I was just in Havana and what I saw made me sick. Poverty, crumbling infrastructure, a substandard living environment, and a government that controls every facet of its people's lives."

Between the heat, the make-up melting on his face, and Larry's line of questioning, Spinelli's nerves were frayed. He felt a tic begin to flutter in his right eyelid and feared that it would be evident on camera.

Spinelli was incredulous that a pencil-necked goon like Larry King would have the nerve to challenge him on American policy toward one of the last communist regimes. But when he bent his forehead, the levee broke on his makeup.

As the sweat trickled down the Senator's brow, the director looked at the makeup person, who shrugged and held up her hands.

"That's exactly what Fidel Castro uses as his excuse to the Cuban people on why they're so poor. It's always somebody else's fault. But that's not true, Larry. Well, it is and it isn't."

"It is and it isn't?"

"The embargo does cause some discomfort to the Cuban populous, but—"

"That's the 'is', what about the 'isn't'?"

Spinelli cleared his throat and teetered on his stool. "The goal of the embargo has always been to put pressure on them to release political prisoners, improve human rights, and hold democratic elections. And that's exactly why so many of my colleagues and I are against the president's trip. In fact, if he's not careful, we may invoke the Trading with the Enemy Act against him."

"Those are harsh words, Senator, can you back them up?"

"If he doesn't honor the letter of the law with respect to Helms-Burton we can."

"Why is your approach more appropriate?"

"Castro's desperate to cut a deal, but we don't need to be hasty. The U.S. dollar is now widely used in their economy, the influence of American culture is on the incline, and the growth of what he refers to as the 'guerilla internet' is increasing awareness of what Cubans are missing. After the Exodus, the pressure was increased to an unprecedented level, and now that we have him on the ropes, we need to go for the knock-out punch."

"So your position is to let the Cuban people continue to suffer, refusing them food, medical supplies, and restricted family visitations by Cuban-Americans in the hope that Castro will...what? Die? Give up? Be overthrown?"

"No, I don't support making the Cuban people suffer, but—"

"What else would you call it? What other purpose could there be? Fomenting an uprising, or another revolution?"

The director gave a signal from the wings.

"We'll continue discussing Senator Spinelli's position on these issues after a word from our sponsors," Larry said. The camera lights blinked off.

Spinelli's slow burn was now uninhibited by television cameras. The makeup artist rushed up to him with a brush in one hand and a bucket of Bondo in the other. As she tried to fix the decomposing mess on his forehead, Spinelli pushed her arm aside.

"What the hell are you trying to do, Larry? I haven't been able to get a word in edgewise. You're trying to make me look foolish!"

King's smug smile only angered him further. "This is big news, and your contrarian position is noteworthy in its uniqueness."

"That's bullshit! I have plenty of company in Congress."

"I'd love to know who, because we tried to get others to join us tonight, but nobody else would come."

"Bob Dunleavy, of course."

"Unavailable, and his press agent said in light of Mr. Haslett's revelation he now supports the president's trip."

Alarm bells sounded in Spinelli's brain. He suddenly felt like the loneliest man in the world.

"I can only do one more segment. I've got things I need to do," Spinelli said.

He desperately wanted to walk off the set and demand that they destroy the tape, but he knew that would only make things worse.

Larry King stared at Spinelli for a long moment, then nodded his head. As bad as the first segment had been, the editor would make it seem even worse by the time it hit the airwaves.

Nobody walks out on Larry King, and paybacks are hell.

37

FIDEL CASTRO'S OFFICE on the third floor of the Palacio de la Revolución revealed little of the man's personality. Devoid of personal photographs, mementos or anything that would give visitors insight into his interests, it was instead decorated with original Cuban paintings of rural scenes and one impressionist painting that looked like a parade in the Plaza de la Revolución.

"It's hard to believe that in the 42 years since the revolution, no acting American president has ever visited here," Castro said.

Winslow shook his head but kept quiet. Castro had made himself a pariah, and only since the fall of the Soviet Union had there really been a reason to open a dialogue.

"Times change, Mr. President."

"Fidel."

"The world is evolving faster today than it ever has. That's why we need to look to the horizon in front of us rather than behind."

"Context may have merit, but it's too simplistic to explain the history of our relationship. But as you say, times change, perhaps time will change again now."

Visions of the demonstrations in Miami and the argument with Spinelli flashed through Winslow's mind.

"Perhaps."

"Sometimes, even when we want to make change, history, perception, or the legacies of those before us make it difficult," Castro said.

"My constraint is less esoteric," Winslow said. "The Helms-Burton Act restricts my changing American policy toward Cuba. Without certain things happening, I can't do a thing, and even if I tried, Congress would overturn it."

"Miss Turner said your Attorney General devised a plan to circumvent that."

"Right, provided you schedule an election and release your political prisoners."

"Helms-Burton states that a transition government is sufficient."

"One that will lead to open, democratic elections in the near future."

Castro pulled on the end of his beard. "I will agree to nothing that has the appearance of the United States dictating the political process in Cuba."

A sinking feeling fluttered in Winslow's gut.

"However, because she convinced me of your sincerity, I shared with Miss Turner that I've been considering retirement later this year. She felt the timing would be close enough for you to claim it was a step toward elections."

"Our Agreement hinges upon the timing of your retirement—and the process of how your successor is selected."

It was hot in the office and Winslow was again perspiring through his shirt. Was Castro trying to change the terms? Would he back out all together?

"If we are successful today," he said, "I've already selected my successor."

Not Raúl.

"Ricardo Allasandre," Castro said. "But if we do not conclude an Agreement, then I will not retire, and my brother will succeed me upon my death."

Winslow held back a smile. "Allasandre seems like a good man. He is a logical choice to lead the transition government." He hesitated. "Attorney General Persico's memorandum of understanding spelled out the deal points as we see them. Aside from the drafting issues they're working on down the hall, are you saying that you have other thoughts?"

Castro stood and walked to an ornate wood cabinet in the corner of the room. He opened a panel and removed a bottle of chilled water. He raised an eyebrow to Winslow, who nodded.

"I have a question for you, Jorge," Castro said. "Our sources in Florida reported a significant amount of negative coverage about your trip here, and about this so called 'Cubagate'. You're not worried what will happen if you fly home and announce that the embargo is over?"

"It won't be over."

Castro nearly spilled the water he was pouring.

"Congress still needs to vote to end it, that's why the language and the timing of the events are so critical. They have to *believe* that real change has occurred."

"That's a problem," Castro said. "How am I supposed to trust you?"

"With all due respect, Fidel, how am I supposed to trust you? I'll be in a much more precarious position. If you sign the Agreement stating that within 180 days you'll retire and a transition government will be established, which will be followed by elections within two years, Congress may want to wait until all that happens before they agree to end the embargo. If you don't follow that course, I'll look a fool."

"And if I do, the world will think I capitulated to America's meddling."

The president took his jacket off and draped it over his chair. *Don't back out on me you son-of-a-bitch.*

"When were you planning to announce your retirement?" Winslow asked.

"Six months. Maybe."

"That wouldn't be soon enough. With no indication of a transition, I've got nothing to base my recommendation to end the embargo on."

Both men became silent. *What do you have up your sleeve? I can't imagine you let me come down here and got your people all hopped-up just to pull the plug.*

"Perhaps I have a solution," his host said. "Suppose that *I* initiated these discussions because of my intention to retire now, and that *I* proposed the deal terms, and you accepted."

"After all I've—" Winslow started, then stopped as the idea sank in. "That idea has merit. Let's discuss the details with the others, but it could work, provided everything else falls into place."

"Of course, everything else must also fall into place." Castro drank some water, and the smile reappeared on his face. "How rude of me, I haven't even thanked you yet."

"For what?"

"Winslow Oil's announcement this morning recognizing that Southern Oil Company's former assets here belonged to the Cuban people."

"Oh, yeah, well, we never considered them ours anyway." Winslow shrugged. "Too bad they're worthless."

The expression on Castro's face was unexpected.

"Yes, quite."

THE TEMPERATURE IN THE CONFERENCE ROOM made Castro's office seem chilly. Everyone had their jackets off and Attorney General Persico, who had 240 pounds packed onto a six-foot frame, had to loosen his tie to get some air into his shirt.

Winslow sat next to Castro and they watched intently as Terri Turner prepared to read down the salient points of the Agreement. She looked up and the room became quiet.

"This is what we've agreed to, so far. Normalize relations and open trade—"

"No special deals." Castro raised his arm as he spoke. "The U.S. can expect to get the same treatment as everyone else. Joint ventures with the Cuban government and no land ownership. We will not repeat the mistakes of the past."

"Yes, Mr. President," Turner said. "Why don't I finish the list, and then we can discuss each component separately."

Castro nodded and rested his hands on the table in front of him. Winslow looked at Castro's long fingers, still stained from years of cigars. His hands and knuckles were covered in liver spots.

"Next is to allow an increase of family remittances from abroad." Turner looked at Castro, who cocked his head sideways in an approving nod. "We will both immediately open our borders to allow tourism," she continued. "Extended visits to either country will require standard visas for fixed periods. In addition, both countries will seek to improve communications by opening embassies, installing additional telephone or fiber optic lines and allowing Internet traffic."

As Turner spoke, Winslow remembered what Castro had said about Ricardo Allasandre. He turned to study the former diplomat. As if sensing the stare, Allasandre glanced back and the two men locked eyes. Winslow raised an eyebrow, and the corner of his lip lifted in a subtle smile. Although he tried to suppress it, Allasandre smiled back and diverted his eyes like a shy debutante.

I'll be a son-of-a-bitch, Castro was telling the truth.

"Various foreign aid projects will open up to Cuba, but will be subject to financial constraints until all political prisoners are released and regular elections commence."

Raúl Castro shifted his expressionless stare toward his brother. Fidel looked back at him, but there was no expression either way. Yet somehow it seemed to Winslow that a silent communication had been exchanged between them.

"The United States government will not participate in any lawsuits involving former land or business owners seeking reparation from the nationalization of their property," Turner continued. "In return, Cuba will drop all lawsuits or claims for reparation stemming from what is commonly known as the Bay of Pigs, or from anything related to the embargo."

"Mind you," Attorney General Persico said, "we can't control what private individuals or companies do in the international courts, but we'll not get involved, nor will we support them in any way."

Jorge Ibarra, Persico's counterpart, nodded vigorously.

"Finally…" Turner gazed around the table. "The Cuban government needs to make an announcement that president Castro is retiring within six months, appointing an interim government, with elections scheduled within two years, or none of this will work. That's everything, isn't it, Senor Ibarra?"

"Yes—"

"Not quite." Castro said.

Every head turned toward him. The room was dead silent.

Winslow held his breath.

"That last point is impossible," Castro said. "I did *not* initiate these discussions, and invite you here for you to dictate our political destiny." His arms lifted from the table and began a mesmerizing swirl. "Nothing is worth giving up our self-determination." He rose from the chair to stand above them. "Nothing is worth the rest of the world perceiving that Cuba has succumbed to foreign intervention and imperialist will."

Turner turned to Winslow with a shocked face.

Castro's eyes looked fevered, and he manipulated his voice as if it were a violin, one moment speaking in soft, captivating tones, the next moment belting out a furious note that all but pushed the visitors back in their chairs.

"Our people have stood united through the endless period of isolation and hardship. They are heroes no different than the persecuted Russians or Jews from the Second World War. We have not suffered the atrocities of starvation, shortages of the basic necessities for survival, trading partners and international stigma to collapse at your feet!"

Silence followed, but only for a minute or two. Winslow recovered and sat forward. Then, in a quiet, controlled, almost reverent tone, he spoke up.

"We're on the brink of a monumental change for our countries. We're all nervous about what the future holds, we're all nervous about what our countries and for that matter the world will say about whatever comes from these meetings. But can we consider the big picture and not get bogged down in perceptions?"

Castro shot a quick glance at the president as if he had just insulted him, and then he panned the room. His steely eyes met every other before coming back to rest on Winslow's.

"We won't give up one iota of honor in return for our freedom," Castro said. "That is my position, and it is non-negotiable."

The air in the room suddenly felt as thick as wallpaper paste. Everyone looked at Winslow, but words were stuck in his throat. The room was so quiet he could hear his own heart beating.

Then Castro sat down, and the president suddenly stood.

Winslow looked around the table as he walked, starting with Steve Persico, then Terri Turner. Their expressions were dark, and he even saw hurt in Turner's eyes—not for herself but probably because she had convinced him that Castro would honor the deal. Her anguish lit a fire in Winslow's gut, and in a flash, his surprise synthesized into resolve.

He finished surveying the room. Ibarra, Allasandre, even Raúl Castro all looked shocked, disappointed, and resigned, but Fidel's eyes burned with the confident fury of a captain expecting to run his ship straight through an iceberg.

"You invited us here to discuss your interest in retiring," Winslow said. "Provided that we change our policies against Cuba."

Every eyebrow lifted around the table, except for Fidel's. He mysteriously began to smile instead.

"You've gathered hundreds of thousands of people across the street, and the entire planet is waiting to hear our press conference. For decades pundits have claimed that you clung to the embargo because it was the scapegoat for your economy's short comings."

He stopped directly across from Castro.

"So I ask you, President Castro, is that what you want your people to think? Is that what you want the world to think? Because I'm sure you would not have made this proposal if that were the case."

Castro chuckled, but his grin quickly faded. He stood up unsteadily and began to circle in the opposite direction from Winslow, who continued his walk around the table.

"I invited you here to propose that the termination of your blockade coincide with my plans to retire," Castro said. "And, most of what Ms. Turner just recited is in line with my proposal."

Castro abruptly stopped and pivoted on his heel to face Winslow.

"But, although you have agreed to many of my prerequisites, there is one other thing that I require. If you cannot provide us with this goodwill gesture, then I will cancel my plans to retire, and we will continue on, united as a people, proud of our sovereignty, and steadfast to our commitment toward the Revolution." His arms raised up like Moses ready to throw stone tablets at the infidels.

Winslow squared up to Castro as he approached him and held his breath like everyone else in the room. His smile was an attempt to mask his anticipation as to what this final stipulation would be.

39

THE WATER GRADUALLY changed from a deep purple to an ever-lightening emerald green. No land was visible, but when Juan spotted some large boats in the distance earlier, the threesome had become ecstatic. Between the constant beating from the sun, the dehydration, and the lack of food, the group was weak and spent most of their time asleep, but they were now more optimistic than they had been in days.

"I used to love to watch movies," Juan said. "I'd dream about being a rich American with a big house, big car, and lots of women. That's what I thought coming to America would be, but hell, I don't even speak English."

"I speak a little," Maria said. "I'll help you."

Her response surprised Juan, and he gave her a big smile.

"What about your brother," Manuel asked. "How come he didn't come with you?"

"As far as I know he's dead. We never heard from him again after Grenada."

Maria winced. Juan knew her acquaintance with death was much more current.

"What about your mother?" she asked.

"She moved to Santa Clara for work when I was thirteen. I lived with my grandmother after that." He felt a rush of emotion and covered his eyes with his forearm.

Another day had drawn to a close without landfall. Juan worried that last night's storm blew them too far east. And that they could be headed for the Bahamas. His entire body felt bloated from sea salt and dehydration. He teetered on whether or not to signal the next ship they saw. If intercepted at sea by the U.S. Coast Guard they would be sent back to Cuba, and all of their sacrifices would have been for nothing. But if they had been blown off course and were skirting the Florida Keys or even the Bahamas, they could miss land entirely and wind up in the Atlantic with no hope whatsoever.

We've got to make it to America. If we can just touch land, we'll be free.

As he drifted back to sleep, Juan decided that if there were no signs by morning, then he would hail the next ship and hope for the best. Even Cuba was better than death.

Sleep was anything but restful, and Juan tossed and turned on the platform. He bumped into Maria on one side then rolled close to the edge on the other. His arm slipped into the water, which slowly pulled his body closer to the edge. The cool water soothed him, and it provided a welcome relief from the heat. Juan's head was so close to the edge that the lap of waves hypnotized his weary mind.

Suddenly something sharp poked Juan's hand, which woke him up. Confused, he wasn't sure where he was, or if he was really awake. Then he felt it again, a sharp tug on his hand. Nearly immersed in the water, reality hit him and he lurched up in a fright.

"Heh!"

Maria opened her eyes. "What's wrong?"

"Something brushed my hand."

Manuel was still asleep and snored quietly. The sun had faded to orange as it began its descent toward the water's edge. Juan noticed red scrapes on his hand where he'd felt the tug.

What the hell?

He looked over the edge and saw the water move and writhe beneath the surface. The water was alive. Gold, blue, and green—the colors changed like a wheel of fortune.

Maria peered over the edge. "What is it?"

Juan's eyes opened wide as he finally understood what they were seeing.

"Fish! Tons of them! Dorado!" He wearily searched for the remaining yo-yo and found it in one of the plastic bags tied to the deck. "Get the turtle meat."

Maria untied the bag, her face twisting when the putrid smell hit her.

"Where's the knife?" Juan searched his pockets then he grabbed the other bag. He took a quick glance to see if the fish were still below. They were. He dumped the contents of the bag onto the deck: Vilma's bible and her dollar bill, and the letter Juan had brough with him.

"What is happening?" Manuel had been awakened by the ruckus.

"There's a shit-load of fish below us and I can't find the knife to cut bait!"

"I've got it." Manuel reached into his pocket.

Juan rolled his eyes and checked over the side. He baited the hook with a piece of slimy meat, tossed it in, and spun out line. As soon as the bait hit the water a small dorado struck—Juan pulled up hard to set the hook—the fish jumped.

"Yeah!"

"Don't lose him!" Manuel said. Without a bite of food in twenty-four hours, Manuel had threatened to eat the rotten turtle meat.

With strong, steady strokes Juan pulled the line onto the deck. He had not bothered to wind the line back onto the spool. He jerked the last few feet of line all at once and a dorado popped on board. Juan pounced on it and stabbed it with the knife. Blood spewed everywhere, but nobody cared.

"Catch another one!" Manuel said.

"Let me try," Maria said. Her eyes were brighter than they had been in days.

Juan hesitated, it was their only yo-yo. *How can I deny that look?* He handed it to her.

"All right now, take it easy. Just drop it over the side and one should hit it pretty fast."

She held the line with her index finger and thumb, just above where the meat hung on the hook, then dropped it over the side. Within seconds the line went taut.

"Hey! I've got one!"

Her smile was infectious, and the men laughed.

"Let him run, don't hold the line or it'll snap," Juan said.

She fought the fish for fifteen minutes. In the end, Juan hoisted the dorado onto the raft. It was twice as big as the one he had caught.

"All *right*, Maria!"

"I did it! I did it!"

Although there were no limes, and the brown meat was oily and fishy tasting, nobody complained. It was food. Careful not to eat too much, they used the plastic bag to store the rest. Their possessions still sat on deck from when Juan had searched for the knife. Maria removed the dollar bill from Vilma's bible. She looked at the picture on the front.

"George Washington, who is he?"

"The American Fidel Castro," Manuel said. "He led their revolution against England. You keep it, Maria. Vilma would have wanted you to have it."

She looked at Juan as if to gauge his approval.

"Take it, but you should use it like Vilma had planned to."

"How's that?"

"Remember? She was going to buy a bolita ticket?"

"You should take her bible," Maria said to Manuel.

He picked it up and opened it. "It's been a long time...."

Once Juan realized his letter still sat on the deck, he scooped it up and tried to stuff it into his pocket, but a picture fell out and landed face up. It was an old photo of a man in uniform, a woman, an older boy and a small boy.

"Is that your family?"

Juan's hand trembled when he picked it up. "When I was a boy."

"Who's the letter from?"

At Maria's innocent question, Juan covered his eyes with his palms for a moment but couldn't hide the rush of emotion.

"My mother..."

Juan hesitated, then removed the letter from his pocket and handed it to Maria. She looked him in the eye. He nodded to her.

The paper was old and yellowed. Maria read it aloud.

"Dearest Juanito,

I miss you my little pumpkin, but I'll be home next week. I found this picture of you, brother, your father and me that we took before he left for Africa, and I thought you would enjoy having it until I got back. My work here is nearly over and I look forward to coming home to you. The experience has been good, but not worth being away from my Juanito. Be a good boy to Nana, I'll see you in a couple weeks.

All my love, Mama."

His mother had drawn a small heart on the bottom by her name. When Maria finished, she looked up at him.

"She never made it home." His jaw quivered as he spoke.

"Oh, Juan…" Maria put a hand on his shoulder.

"She was walking down a narrow road on her way back from work—a bus passed her—its mirror hit her head. She was dead before she hit the ground—" His voice cracked.

Maria took Juan into her arms, and the two of them cried as one. Manuel silently closed his eyes as if to steel himself against their tears. His pain may have been buried beneath twice as many years as Juan's, and a lifetime more than Maria's, but it was no less sorrowful. He had just learned to hide it better.

A gradual hum turned into a growing roar, and the sound caught Juan's attention. He checked the sky.

"Look! A jet!"

The roar of its engines overtook them—no surprise now that they saw the huge white body of a 747 against the crystalline blue sky. The plane was remarkably low compared to the many distant lights they had watched pass overhead during the blackness of night.

"Where the hell is it landing?"

The horizon revealed nothing. Overcome with curiosity, Maria stood on shaky legs and checked in the distance.

"There! I see land over there!" She jumped up and down, the raft shook beneath her.

In awe of the plane, Juan suddenly noticed something incredible. His smile turned into a chuckle, and then an uncontrollable belly laugh.

"What's so funny?"

"The plane." He pointed up. "Look at the tail."

They stared open-mouthed as the plane drifted past, and its wheels slowly lowered from the fuselage. The Stars and Stripes of an American flag covered the tail section.

"America." Manuel struggled to his knees. "America!"

40

AIR FORCE ONE FLOATED through clear skies over the Florida Straits, and the president enjoyed a glass of champagne with Terri Turner and Steve Persico. They had done it. The end of the embargo against Cuba that had existed for nearly half a century had been agreed upon in principal between the two leaders.

Now they just needed to convince Congress.

The press aboard the plane was ecstatic to be here for such a momentous journey, and the atmosphere was festive even though everyone realized the work was not over yet. After he spent the first fifteen minutes in the front cabin with the reporters answering questions and basking in his success, the president left Harvey Teitlebaum there and retired to his cabin for a private celebration with the two people who helped him succeed.

"The Secretary of State will be disappointed," Turner said.

"He'll get over it. He's got enough going on in the Middle East."

"Don't expect pure celebration when we land in Key West. There'll be a lot of upset Cuban-Americans and politicians with egg on their faces who won't give up that easily," Persico said.

"That's what I love about you, Steve. You keep me grounded."

"Yeah, right."

"Have you faxed the letter yet?"

"Yep, while you were bullshitting with the press corps," Turner said. "Signed, sealed and submitted. The official presidential determination that Cuba has formed a transitional government with the intent to hold elections went to the majority leader of the Congress, along with your suspension of the embargo pursuant to Section 302 of the Helms-Burton Act. Done deal."

"I wonder how the news is playing at home," Winslow said.

"Spinelli's going to fight you, George, don't think he won't," Persico said.

"If the response around the country is what I expect, and once the Cuban-Americans realize that they can visit their homeland, it could be bedlam. Spinelli's not stupid. He'll pivot. Every issue has its time, and this one has run its course."

"Unsuccessfully," Turner said.

"Part of it was successful," Winslow said. "Our predecessors really had no choice. Based on the nationalizations, and then with Castro embracing the Soviets, what else could they have done? Unfortunately, in '59 they lacked the vision to see how the chain of events would lead to the embargo, but hindsight's 20/20. Cuba's paid a huge price for the land and industry they took, and even though the proceeds didn't go to the former owners, it's been a hell of a long amortization period."

"42 years."

The plane started its descent toward Key West Naval Air Station, just north of Key West on Boca Chica. Winslow had his feet up and savored the champagne. He glanced at Turner and knew none of it would have happened without her. The image of that night in front of her Houston condo popped back into his mind, and he enjoyed the memory for an instant before mentally shifting to the press conference and the joint announcement that happened at the foot of the José Marti monument.

The Cuban citizens that had jammed into the Plaza had gone wild. It gave him chills up his spine, down his arms, and to the tips of his fingers. The press had behaved poorly at the news conference, pushing and shoving each other for better camera angles or the chance to ask a question. They hung on every word of Castro's speech.

"That was a nice touch when the Cubans handed out pictures of the remains of the El Pilar refinery," Turner said. "It looked like a bomb had gone off there."

Winslow wouldn't be surprised if that wasn't exactly what had happened the day before.

"I liked the white doves fluttering up from Castro's feet," Persico said. "And those hands—he shook them like a maestro leading an orchestra to a crescendo."

"The real masterstroke was how Castro spun the idea to be his, so he could retire immediately and give Cuba the push forward it so desperately needs. It made the whole Agreement a win-win."

"That, and Castro's surprise final demand for us to vacate Guantanamo," Turner said.

"How will Congress feel about that?" Persico asked.

"They won't be happy about it, but we've got twelve months to demobilize. That was some serious brinksmanship on Castro's part, but a worthwhile trade for stability in the hemisphere."

"There's always the naval presence in Key West," Turner said.

A buzzer sounded and Winslow picked up a phone.

"Yes, Jim?"

"Sorry to disturb you, Mr. President, but Vice President Pulaski is on the sat-phone."

Winslow reached into a wood cabinet and removed a compact military telephone.

"Harold?"

"Congratulations, George. Great job down there."

"Thanks, I'm pretty satisfied. How's the press coverage?"

"Very positive for the most part. The networks are calling it a huge foreign policy coup. From the video it looked like a free-for-all at the press conference. Cameras were jiggling and the anchormen were out of breath they were so excited."

"Any news on the opposition?"

"It's been quiet. There's been very little mention about Cubagate, but Spinelli's been crying foul about Guantanamo. He's on Larry King tonight. A few conservatives have been flip-flopping, but I tell you, that was brilliant letting Castro take credit in return for retiring immediately. At least, I assume that's what happened."

"It was actually his idea."

"I hope you're ready for what's happening at Boca Chica. It's a zoo down here. The Navy erected a stage, and they've got some bleachers set up, but it's the crowd that'll blow you away. The highway's packed from Miami south, and people are pouring in faster than the military can figure out where to put them. You could walk across car tops as if they were stepping stones—"

"Can you repeat that?" Winslow stuck the phone up to Turner's ear.

The vice president repeated the comparison not realizing it was the same example Winslow had used to describe what could happen in the next boatlift—with the stepping-stones being not car tops but dead bodies from Havana to Florida. Turner's smile reflected the afternoon sunlight.

"The press has been flying onto the base in private jets and helicopters, the shore's covered with small boats, and Key West High School is sending the Conch Marching Band over to top off the festivities. The mayor of Key West changed their unofficial nickname from Margaritaville to Mojitoville for a couple days, so I hope you're ready for a party."

"I wasn't sure what to expect, but what your describing sounds better than what I'd feared. I wish you could have seen Terri and Steve in Havana, they were great."

Turner smiled at the compliment as the president hung up. He then leaned closer to Terri, and in a low voice said, "When I run for reelection, I'd like you to be my vice presidential running mate."

Her eyes grew wide and her cheeks flushed. She didn't say a word—couldn't by the look of her—but she nodded.

Steve Persico, who had been staring out the window, suddenly turned to face the them.

"Jesus Christ! You're not going to believe this."

"What is it?" Winslow slid over to look outside.

"Look at the water, can you see that?"

"What? I don't..." He froze, squinted, then looked up in amazement.

"What is it?" Turner got up out of her seat.

"A raft," Persico said.

"Seriously?"

Winslow nodded. His eyes welled up.

"You've got to be kidding." Turner looked down at the tiny raft. "There are three people on there pointing up at us!"

"They've got to be Cubans," Persico said. "They say only half the people who try to cross survive, but at least the Coast Guard's repatriating them again."

"That's probably what'll happen to those three," Turner said.

"No!" the president said. "Not that raft. Not today." His voice cracked. "Our borders are open today, I want to make sure that raft makes it to land, and that those people are allowed to stay. God only knows what they've been through."

Persico's eyes opened wide, but Turner smiled. The president grabbed the headset.

"Hey, Jim, do me a favor. Mark this spot on the GPS and call the Key West Coast Guard station. Have them send a boat out to collect a raft of what I assume are Cuban refugees."

"Roger, sir,"

"Make the following instructions very clear: bring them to shore, and do not, I repeat do NOT repatriate them. Have them delivered to the INS and keep tabs on them. Food and medical care if they need it, okay?"

When Winslow looked back out the window, the raft was gone.

"That, my friends, will be the *last* raft."

41

THE 270' MEDIUM-ENDURANCE CUTTER Mohawk sliced through the choppy December water with effortless grace, while captain Scott Hawkes scanned the water through high-powered binoculars.

"Distance?"

"Nine miles," Lieutenant Hildebrand replied from the Combat Information Center.

Hawkes stepped back from the rail-mounted binoculars. "Course one-nine-zero, speed fifteen knots."

"Aye, Captain."

During the Mohawk's six-year tenure in Key West, the crew had kept a tally on the illegal immigrants they intercepted and returned to Cuba. A month ago the number was 1,842 for the year, but during the Exodus they collected ten times that amount alive, and nearly as many dead. But based on the speech President Winslow had just made at Boca Chica, the count was over.

At fifteen knots cruising speed, the Mohawk quickly closed the distance on the coordinates radioed in from the base. The captain stepped up to the binoculars and scanned the horizon in ten-degree segments. He studied each area thoroughly before moving to the next. On his third segment to the southwest he spotted an object. He adjusted the focus and the image cleared.

"There you are."

He marked their location and turned to the first lieutenant.

"Course one-eight-seven, maintain speed, contact in sight."

"Aye, Captain." The lieutenant smiled.

The horn sounded and the intercept team began rushed preparations on the rear deck.

"Chief Jaegle, this is the captain. Be ready to launch the RHIB in ten minutes."

"Yes sir, captain."

When the government established the Migration Accords with Cuba in 1995, the Coast Guard's mandate had become clear. Captain Hawkes liked to have a clear mandate. It made his job more efficient and focused.

The rules had again changed today, but Hawkes focused on intercepting this contact, and to getting the people on board without harm to his crew, the illegals or his ship. The raft would be scuttled.

THE HEAT OF the sun felt more searing today than any day previous. The wind had died down to nothing, and the heat was insufferable as the raft bobbed ever-slowly toward land. The thin sliver of earth on the horizon was barely evident, but they hadn't taken their eyes off of it as they speculated on time and distance.

Maria sat up and stretched her arms. The sparkle of amber that was once in her eyes was now gone, and her beauty had withered under the sun. She noticed a speck on the horizon.

"Hey! Is that a ship?" she pointed.

"Where?"

Manuel stared at the same silhouette on the horizon. "What if that's a government boat?" he said.

"What would happen if it was?" Maria asked.

"If it's a government boat and they catch us, they'll take us back to Cuba," Juan said.

Maria just stared at the distant ship then laid back down and curled into a ball.

"What kind of ship is it?" Manuel whispered.

"A big one."

A sense of defeat washed over them like the indomitable waves from the storms they had endured.

"I can't fucking believe it," Juan whispered.

"My God, it's giant," Manuel said.

Maria's stomach had tied into a knot. She lowered her eyes to the scarred wood planks of the raft. Images played her mind like silent pictures: Ernesto's laugh, him as he fixed the leaky drum, and his scent as he slept in her arms. She remembered the joy of feeling the slight movement in her womb, and Vilma's courageous determination to leave her beloved homeland in order to fight for her life.

She looked at Juan, then Manuel, and remembered the stories of their lives, the pain, the suffering and the hope of starting anew.

Everything's gone, our lives are failures.

She shuddered and turned back toward the ship. It was even bigger now. Then she squinted at the sight of something strange about its bow—it was moving. It was…

Dolphins.

One, two, three dolphins jumped in front of the ship and played in the spray that shot up from its sides. The sight sent a shiver through her, and for reasons she could not understand the dolphins brought hot tears to her eyes. She convulsed in sobs as she watched them jump again and again. Maria succumbed to her trembling and lay down. She took hold of the ropes that held the platform together and wrapped them tightly around her hands.

She lay motionless and stared at the big ship become the horizon until it slowed at a safe distance. A horn sounded and something was lowered over the side. It was another boat that looked like a toy compared with the giant ship. Hollow, numb and speechless, she watched everything happen as if it were a film.

MANUEL'S DISAPPOINTMENT WAS TEMPERED by his expectations. Aside from the stars, failed dreams were his only companions, and even though he had risked his life and watched others lose theirs, Manuel was at peace with himself.

It's just not meant to be.

He looked at Juan, and then at Maria. *You're still young, it's not your fault. Tomorrow you'll be back in Cuba, but your dreams will not.*

A noise blared over a loudspeaker and even in the distance he understood the words spoken in Spanish. "Remain calm, he says? Remain on board? Where do they think we'd go?"

Neither Juan nor Maria responded. Maria was curled into a tight ball with her eyes pinched shut and the familiar tracks of tears down her cheeks. Juan wore a defiant expression and coiled himself up as he watched the RHIB approach through narrow eyes.

A faded image of Manuel's father as he had argued with Ramon del Torres flickered in the hollows of his mind. Manuel's throat became thick. As the small boat pulled up to the raft, Juan met the boat captain's eyes.

"*Hola, Amigos,*" one of the three men in orange vests said. "Welcome to America. We're going to bring you on board. There's nothing to be afraid of, don't worry."

Manuel stared at their orange helmets. He turned and touched Maria's arm, and then looked sharply at Juan.

"Be proud," he said. He tried to stand up but collapsed, too stiff and weak to balance his weight.

Juan helped him up, and together they stepped toward the launch. Manuel dragged his legs and leaned heavily on his young friend. Once Manuel sat down on the rubber pontoon, he pointed to Maria.

"Come on, Maria, we'll be all right," Juan said.

A sailor with the name "Mooney" sewn on his jacket pointed to the dried blood on Maria's dress and turned to Juan.

"Blood?"

"She lost her baby."

"Sorry, man." Then, to Maria, "Ma'am, we need to get you to a doctor."

Everyone could see Maria's body quiver. Although her back was turned to him, Manuel knew she was crying. He and Juan kept calling her name, but she didn't answer, wouldn't budge.

Mooney stepped onto the raft and bent down next to her.

"Can you move, ma'am?"

A wail sounded in return. The ropes were wrapped so tightly around her hands they had turned white.

"Please come with us, we can help you."

"I can't...leave...I can't leave them...here alone..." she said between sobs.

Mooney looked up at Juan, then stepped back onto the launch. Manuel remembered the rural police who had dragged his father from their home.

JUAN STOOD UP and climbed over the pontoon on wobbly legs. The raft seemed so small now after just a moment on the boat. He knelt next to her and put his hand on her shoulder.

Ernesto, if you have any clout up there, let me help her.

She glanced up into Juan's eyes and she cried harder. His heart screamed for her.

Okay, God, please let me ease her pain.

Juan bent down to whisper in her ear, surprised when tears fell off his own cheek to land on hers. "It's all right, Maria, we're safe now."

"I don't want to be safe. Why should I be safe when everyone else has died?"

Her pain twisted his heart, his tears poured freely now. She saw this and there was an understanding between them. He had been there, he knew.

"Ernesto wouldn't want you left alone." Juan fought to bring his own quivering jaw under control, but couldn't. "I promised him that I'd watch out for you, that I'd take care of you."

Once his words sank in her eyelids fluttered.

I won't tell you that I made that promise to Ernesto's ghost.

He reached down and took her in his arms, repeating her name in a whisper: "Maria... Maria, it's all right... Maria."

"*Hush! For they are sleeping,*" Manuel sang. His voice cracked, and tears filled his eyes as he croaked out the lyrics:

> "*The spikenards and lilies,*
> *I don't want them to know about my sorrows*
> *Because if they see me weeping*
> *They will die.*"

It was the last verse of Vilma's song. Juan's memory of his mother when she had sung the same tune at his father's funeral finally came clear. He shook, but the feel of Maria quivering in his arms brought calm to his heart. Strength filled him and the tears subsided.

"Let's go, Maria. These men will take us home."

The sailors, along with Manuel, watched from the boat. Juan could hear the old man whimper, and as he wiped his own tears away, Juan's heart longed for Maria to respond.

She did.

She released her grip on the ropes and sat up. Juan got onto his knees and lifted Maria in his arms like a baby. Mooney helped them both onto the launch.

One of the sailors took out an axe and lifted it to strike the raft, but when Juan saw the horror in Maria's eyes, he grabbed the man's arm. The American looked to the sailor at the helm, who paused, then shook his head and restarted the engines.

Manuel gave the raft a final glance.

"Wait!" He struggled to his feet and pointed toward the raft.

The boat stopped and idled back. Manuel grabbed the plastic bag tied to the deck, then reached inside and pulled out Vilma's bible with the dollar bill and the letter from Juan's mother. He handed the dollar bill to Maria. She clutched it to her chest.

Relief spread through Juan's heart when he saw the letter. He turned to thank Manuel—and saw that the old man's eyes were shut tight, and that he was holding firmly to the bible.

Whatever would happen next didn't matter. The group had survived the journey, and though the cost was beyond anything they could have imagined, their individual strength had prevailed.

When you have nothing else, strength is a necessity.

EPILOGUE

ONCE THE NEWS of the embargo's suspension spread through the country, a massive reverse boatlift spontaneously commenced. Cuban-Americans from all over the United States traveled to the Florida Keys. They trailered boats, rented them, or hired charters to ferry them across to Cuba. Many carried whatever possessions they could hold, and some said they were returning home for good.

Confusion reigned for weeks throughout the Florida Straits, and both the American and Cuban governments practiced newfound restraint in allowing their citizens to travel back and forth freely. Commercial flights into Havana from Miami and New York started a month to the day from the carnival-like ceremony at Key West Naval Air Base, and every flight was filled with tearful men and women excited to travel one way or the other to be reunited with long lost family members.

One such visitor was José Mas Fina, who, even though he feared for his life, had abandoned his hard-line stance to visit his ailing mother.

True to the president's prediction, the American people quickly became the most effective diplomats in changing the course of politics when the Cuban people welcomed their former countrymen and an incredible number of curious Americans with open arms.

President Winslow was given broad acclaim at home and abroad for ending the long and painful embargo, and little time was wasted in seeking to heal the wounds between the countries.

Manuel Vidal located his wife and sons in the phone book and surprised them with a phone call that found them preparing to take their yacht to Cuba to hunt for him. Vidal & Sons Enterprises' private helicopter met Manuel in Miami, where he, along with Juan and Maria, flew to Naples to be reunited with his family.

Juan took a job with Vidal & Sons, and Maria has been resting at the home of Manuel's wife until she decides what to do next.

Juan is trying hard to persuade her to stay.

Vilma's last dollar was used as she had wished, but Maria did not win the lottery.

The End

ACKNOWLEDGEMENTS

I began to write this book in the late 1990s. Having lived in the Florida Keys on and off since the late 1970s I have had many friends of Cuban origin, have witnessed the constant influx of Cuban émigrés that have arrived in Florida on rafts boats or any means possible, and have seen the pain and anguish of Cuban Americans whose families lost everything to the Revolution in 1959, or soon after. As a child of the 1960s, I vaguely recall the Cuban Missile Crisis, and the rhetoric surrounding the Soviets in Cuba. As a student of International Relations in the early 1980s, I had lived through the Cold War and Vietnam in my formative years—and recall the nuclear attack drills in elementary school where we were instructed to hide under our desks. Bottom line is I have always been interested in the world around me, and Cuba was actually the closest foreign country to me for much of my life.

Although not widely discussed, the argument can be made that Eisenhower / Nixon and then Kennedy pushed Fidel Castro into the arms of the Soviet Union by playing a high stakes game of manipulating our sugar subsidy and oil production to reign Castro into American hegemony soon after he became prime minister of Cuba. The strategy to control Castro backfired and resulted in the nationalization of American assets in Cuba and the Soviets replacing America as Cuba's largest trading partner.

It began with the American embargo on the sale of arms to the Batista regime in March 1958, which was kept in place as leverage after Castro's revolution succeeded. Citing the American embargo on the sale of arms, Castro began to buy weapons from the Soviets in October 1960. Eisenhower responded by strengthening the embargo to prohibit the sale on all goods except food and medicine. In response, Cuba nationalized American oil refineries and agricultural assets. Subsequently, the United States severed diplomatic relations with Cuba in January 1961, and in April, the ill-fated Bay of Pigs occurred where an American-backed coup was thwarted. It was then, in December 1961, that Castro stated that he was a Marxist-Leninist for the first time.

In February 1962, Kennedy strengthened the embargo to include almost all exports. Once again, in retaliation, Castro invited the Soviets to place strategic nuclear weapons in Cuba, which led to the Cuban Missile Crisis in October 1962. By then it was all too clear that Castro would never succumb to what he claimed was the continuation of hundreds of years of exploitation of Cuba by foreign nations, and he would counter-punch any attempt the United States made to control Cuban policy. Even their relationship with the Soviets proved difficult as Castro charged them over ten times the world price on Cuban sugar and constantly demanded increased aid, which included billions of dollars in infrastructure and military assistance, and comprised 70% of Cuba's trade.

In 1991, when the Soviet Union was dissolved, the financial umbilical cord to Cuba was cut, and the island nation became destitute in what Castro called the "Special Period," which lasted for nearly ten years, until Hugo Chavez, Venezuela's president, became their next benefactor.

Perhaps it was the history of the Monroe Doctrine, which had been America's policy of preventing European intervention in Latin America since 1823, combined with the fact that foreigners owned the majority of Cuba's infrastructure, including 70% of arable land, 90% of telephone and electrical services, 50% of public railways and 40% of raw sugar production at the time of Castro's revolution, and the Eisenhower administration's rebuffing of Castro during the Cuban Prime Minister's visit to the United Nations in September 1960, which led to Castro meeting then Soviet leader Nikita Khrushchez for the first time, that was the cause and effect that led to the last sixty-plus years of American embargo on Cuba. As a result, the eleven million Cuban people have continued to suffer.

Soon after the Revolution, wealthy Cuban families and those who feared life under the violent Castro regime, fled their homes and businesses, many of who relocated to Florida with no recompense for their properties taken by the Cuban government. Today, the United States still holds $6 billion worth of claims against the Cuban government for nationalized assets. In the stalemate that ensued, Fidel, and then his brother Raul, have ruled Cuba with an iron fist. Along with all of this, human rights violations, the incarceration of political prisoners and the demand for free and open elections have been the rationale behind the United States' continued embargo. Meanwhile, eleven American presidents have come and gone.

At some point, as is postulated in this book, democracy must overtake tyranny in Cuba, and after sixty-plus years of pursuing a strategy that has not produced the desired results, perhaps it is time to let the American people help bring change through person-to-person contact, open borders, open business and diplomatic relations. Many believe that this approach would lead to a tsunami of freedom that would wash over the island nation and strip bare the oppression its citizens have endured for generations.

The Last Raft is a work of fiction, one that is apolitical since no elected official, either democrat or republican, have done anything to successfully improve the situation and bring end to the longest embargo in our country's history. Hopefully, change will come during our lifetime.

I would like to thank several people who have assisted me with the development of this story over the years, starting with my friends Lou Cardenas and Gloria Garcia who joined me for my initial research trip there. We were pleasantly surprised to find the Cuban people as warm, friendly, engaging, and interested in Americans, even under the shadow of machine gun toting police who were highly visible throughout Havana. I would also like to thank Wayne Smith, former Chief of Mission of the US Interests Section in Havana for having read an earlier version of the manuscript and providing insights.

Thank you to Renni Browne, Julie Miller and Ross Browne of The Editorial Department; Tim Harkness for creating the book cover and

Ann-Marie Nieves of Get Red PR for her advice and for being my longtime publicist.

Thank you to the fans of the Buck Reilly series—this was a detour—but Buck will soon land back in Key West, I promise.

Special thanks to my brothers Jim and Jay, and their wives Mary and Beth, Ron and Linda Weiner, Holly, Bailey, Cortney and Will Prendergast for their love and support.

ABOUT THE AUTHOR

John H. Cunningham is the author of the best selling, eight book, Buck Reilly adventure series, which includes Red Right Return, Green to Go, Crystal Blue, Second Chance Gold, Maroon Rising, Free Fall to Black, Silver Goodbye and White Knight.

The Last Raft is John's first historical fiction novel. John has either lived in or visited the many locations that populate his novels, and he mixes fact with fiction and often includes real people in the cast of characters. Adhering to the old maxim, "write what you know," John's books have an authenticity and immediacy that have earned loyal followers and strong reviews. With a degree in International Relations from the University of Maryland, John writes stories that concern themselves with the same tensions and issues that affect all of our lives, and his choices for the places and plots that populate his stories include many settings that he loves, including Key West, Cuba, Jamaica, and multiple Caribbean locations. John splits his time between New York, Virginia and Key West.

BOOK LINKS:

RED RIGHT RETURN (Buck Reilly book 1):
http://www.amazon.com/Right-Return-Reilly-Adventure-Series-ebook/dp/B00D8HOSN2/

GREEN TO GO (Buck Reilly book 2):
http://www.amazon.com/Green-Buck-Reilly-Adventure-Series-ebook/dp/B00D6Q0WOE/

CRYSTAL BLUE (Buck Reilly book 3):
http://www.amazon.com/Crystal-Blue-Reilly-Adventure-Series-ebook/dp/B00EWSAZ92/

SECOND CHANCE GOLD (Buck Reilly book 4):
http://www.amazon.com/Second-Chance-Reilly-Adventure-Series/dp/0985442271/

MAROON RISING (Buck Reilly book 5):
https://www.amazon.com/Maroon-Rising-Buck-Reilly-Adventure-ebook/dp/B016QUC76C

FREE FALL TO BLACK (Buck Reilly book 6):
https://www.amazon.com/Free-Fall-Black-Reilly-Adventure/dp/0998796506

SILVER GOODBYE (Buck Reilly book 7):
https://www.amazon.com/gp/product/B07G6BRQWX/

WHITE KNIGHT (Buck Reilly book 8)
https://www.amazon.com/dp/B07WZKQ715/

MUSIC LINKS:

"THE BALLAD OF BUCK REILLY" (Download the song or all of Workaholic in Recovery from iTunes at):
https://itunes.apple.com/us/album/workaholic-in-recovery/id908713680

"RUM PUNCH" by Thom Shepherd, and co-written by John H. Cunningham, is available on iTunes at:
https://itunes.apple.com/us/album/rum-punch-single/id1051324975

"LONG VIEW OFF A SHORT PIER" by Dave McKenney and co-written by John H. Cunningham, is available on iTunes at:
https://itunes.apple.com/us/album/back-in-time/id1161935367?ign-mpt=uo%3D4#

"HANGING OUT AT LE SELECT" by Keith Sykes and co-written by John H. Cunningham, is available on iTunes at:
https://music.apple.com/us/album/hanging-out-at-le-select-single/1439181610

"SILVER GOODBYE" by Donald James and co-written by John H. Cunningham, available on CD Baby and iTunes

9 780998 796567